Journey to the
MOUNTAIN
of GOD

Also by David D. Ireland, PhD

Activating the Gifts of the Holy Spirit

Failure Is Written in Pencil

Perfecting Your Purpose

Secrets of a Satisfying Life

What Color Is Your God?

Why Drown When You Can Walk on Water?

Journey to the
MOUNTAIN
of GOD

A 40-Day Approach to

Pursuing Intimacy

with Your Creator

David D. Ireland, PhD

New York Boston Nashville

Unless otherwise noted, Scriptures are taken from the HOLY BIBLE: NEW INTER-
NATIONAL VERSION®. Copyright © 1973, 1978, 1984 by International Bible Soci-
ety. Used by permission of Zondervan Publishing House. All rights reserved.
Scriptures noted KJV are taken from the King James Version of the Bible.
Scriptures noted *The Message* are taken from *The Message: The New Testament in
Contemporary English*. Copyright © 1993 by Eugene H. Peterson.
Scriptures noted NCV are taken from *The Holy Bible, New Century Version*®, copy-
right © 1987, 1988, 1991 by Word Publishing, a division of Thomas Nelson,
Inc. Used by permission.

Warner Faith
Hachette Book Group USA
1271 Avenue of the Americas, New York, NY 10020

Visit our Web site at www.warnerfaith.com
The Warner Faith name and the "W" logo are trademarks of Time Warner Inc.
or an affiliated company. Used under license by Hachette Book Group USA,
which is not affiliated with Time Warner Inc.

Printed in the United States of America
First Edition: August 2006
10 9 8 7 6 5 4 3 2 1

Library of Congress Cataloging-in-Publication Data

Ireland, David
  Journey to the mountain of God : pursuing intimacy with your creator /
David D. Ireland.
      p. cm.
  ISBN-13: 978-0-446-57851-6
  ISBN-10: 0-446-57851-7
  1. Christian life—Biblical teaching. 2. Christian life—Meditations. I. Title.
BS680.C47I73 2006
248.4—dc22

                                                    2005035640

*This book is dedicated to all the people who
have struggled to discover spiritual intimacy with
their Creator. If you are wondering,*
How do I connect with God
in a most meaningful way?
*I wrote this book for you. May you discover
and experience real intimacy with God.*

Contents

Step 4: A Heart of Holiness

Step 5: Disciplines for Mountaintop Living

Step 6: Ingredients for Spiritual Health

Step 7: Unleashing God's Blessings

Step 8: A New Beginning

The Sweet Spot

Where is life's *sweet spot*? I mean that place where everything finally comes together and you find yourself experiencing the best quality of life possible. In baseball, the sweet spot is a small area of the bat that causes a powerful blow to the ball upon contact. In the world of tennis, a player experiences the sweet spot when the ball hits the string bed of the racquet and produces the best combination of feel and power.

This cliché is also used in business. Salespeople claim that they have found the sweet spot when their product practically sells itself without the need for any persuasion, strict adherence to a well-polished sales technique, or schmoozing of the customer. There seems to be a sweet spot in every area of life.

But when it comes to your relationship with God, which forms the foundation of every area of life—where is the sweet spot? Living outside of the spiritual sweet spot is boring. In fact, it's only the mediocre ballplayers and mediocre businesspeople who live outside the sweet spot. Your life is far too precious for you to settle for a mediocre and dull existence. You can live in the sweet spot and regularly experience exhilarating moments of closeness with your Maker. *Journey to the Mountain of God* is about finding the spiritual sweet spot of life—the place of deep intimacy with God.

The Book's Goal

Repeatedly the Bible uses the phrase "the mountain of God" or "the mountain of the LORD" to represent the place where one experiences a dramatic revelation of God. This revelation kindles or rekindles a passion in your heart for unbroken intimacy with Him. Over the course of 40 days, I will take you on an eight-station journey; each is designed to equip you with the necessary tools to bring you to the mountain of God. At each station, I will spend five days (or five chapters) equipping you with the necessary ingredients to achieve personal renewal. Thus, at the end of the journey, your heart will become like kindling—dry wood—that can catch ablaze for God at the slightest touch of the Holy Spirit.

The invitation to journey to the mountain of God comes directly from God. The Bible says:

> *In the last days*
> > *the mountain of the LORD's temple will be established*
> > *as chief among the mountains;*
> *it will be raised above the hills,*
> > *and all nations will stream to it.*
> *Many peoples will come and say,*
> > *"Come, let us go up to the mountain of the LORD,*
> > *to the house of the God of Jacob.*
> *He will teach us his ways,*
> > *so that we may walk in his paths."*
> *The law will go out from Zion,*
> > *the word of the LORD from Jerusalem.*
> *He will judge between the nations*
> > *and will settle disputes for many peoples.*
> *They will beat their swords into plowshares*
> > *and their spears into pruning hooks.*
> *Nation will not take up sword against nation,*
> > *nor will they train for war anymore.*
>
> (Isaiah 2:2–4)

As Isaiah indicated, the purpose of the trek is for you to be taught about the ways of God by God Himself. The process of being taught by God will not only prove to be transformational, it will deepen your relationship with God exponentially.

The singular goal of *Journey to the Mountain of God* is to facilitate your experiencing a personal renewal in your relationship with the Lord. Deciding to go is the first step in the process. Only you know the temperature of your heart toward the things of God. A low temperature signals a lukewarm heart. A person exhibits this through indifference toward ongoing spiritual development and growth. A high temperature translates into a heart that is akin to a blazing inferno—one that is intentionally disposed to the service of God and the expansion of His kingdom on earth.

Anywhere in the middle is unacceptable. If you are in a neutral position, the possibility of your slipping farther toward indifference and ultimately into a cold state is very real. If you're not on fire for God and you want to be, this book is a Godsend. You can't afford to put it down until you have completed the 40-day journey and gained the personal benefit of a renewed relationship with the Lord. If you're already on fire for God, reading this book will only make the fire more intense.

Throughout the Bible, the number 40 symbolizes a new beginning, a firm foundation, a transformed life, and even a lasting deliverance. Consequently, your commitment to take the next 40 days to read this book and subsequently experience its intention—a revitalized walk with the Lord—is an achievable feat that captures biblical precedence of how lasting change occurs through 40-day experiences.

Go ahead! Pack your bags! Seal the decision! It's time to journey to the mountain of God and become refreshed and revived. God has too much for you to do for Him. Your work can be accomplished only through a fiery heart kept ablaze by spiritual intimacy.

God has too many unfulfilled promises for your life. You cannot afford to live beneath or apart from these promises any longer. The place of intimacy with God is the place of power—power to live . . . power to do . . . and power to be—to be the best husband, wife, father, mother, son, daughter, leader, or supporter for God you can be. Go for it! Start the journey!

How to Read This Book

Each chapter should take approximately thirty minutes to complete, including the reflection activity at the end. Don't skip over this activity—it is essential in promoting introspection, which leads to experiencing a deeper intimacy with God. In fact, the process of reading this book is so important that I encourage you to sign your name and that of an accountability partner on page xvii (titled "My Promise"). This is a way for you to affirm before the Lord your sincere desire to complete an intentional process that leads you into deeper spiritual intimacy.

Because spiritual journeys are often undertaken by individuals who have a passion to draw closer to God, along the way their passion drives them to invite others to join them on this spiritual pilgrimage. This is precisely what happened to King David after he repented of adultery with the beautiful Bathsheba. In his repentance, David renewed his desire to pursue intimacy with God. Psalm 51 captures David's change from spiritual apathy to spiritual hunger. He cried: "Restore to me the joy of your salvation / and grant me a willing spirit, to sustain me. / Then I will teach transgressors your ways, / and sinners will turn back to you" (vv. 12–13). In short, David became interested in the spiritual passion of others only after he began to pursue intimacy with God. The conclusion can be easily drawn: one of the signs that you're journeying to a place of spiritual passion is that you acknowledge the need for others also to draw near to God. Consequently, this book is designed for group study as well.

To form a study group of people who are interested in taking a 40-day journey to the mountain of God, invite some friends, family members, or members of your congregation who share the desire for achieving a deeper walk with God. Pick a group leader who will organize a weekly meeting where he or she can present a lesson from this book in a discussion format. To draw on the unique personalities of the different members within the group, rotate discussion leaders each week until the journey is complete.

Whether you choose to journey individually or with a group, you will find yourself becoming more in tune with the heart of God over the course of 40 days. Everyone has a mental picture as to what ultimate satisfaction or the sweet spot looks like. Professional athletes envision being the most valuable player in the most significant game of the century. Singers fantasize about singing the song that will immediately go platinum, while actors dream of having the lead part in a blockbuster film that will attain similar or better status as the historic classic *Gone with the Wind*. As a Christian, you should desire to know and experience the sweet spot in serving God with your whole life. So, let's journey to the mountain of God!

My Promise

Through God's grace and strength, I promise to take the next 40 days to learn how I may pursue a more intimate relationship with the Lord Jesus Christ.

Your Name

Accountability Partner's Name

David D. Ireland

David D. Ireland, PhD

As the deer pants for streams of water,
So my soul pants for you, O God.
My soul thirsts for God, for the living God.
When can I go and meet with God?
(Psalm 42:1–2)

Step 1

Invitation to God's Mountain

*In the last days
the mountain of the LORD's temple will be established
as chief among the mountains;
it will be raised above the hills,
and peoples will stream to it.
Many nations will come and say,
"Come, let us go up to the mountain of the LORD."*
(Micah 4:1–2)

Day 1

The Search for Spiritual Intimacy

One of the greatest needs human beings have is the need for intimacy. God has wired us in such a way that feelings of acceptance, affection, and companionship are vital to our sense of personal fulfillment. Without satisfaction in this area, we spend money, time, and other vital resources attempting to fill the void. In fact, many resort to immoral practices as a way to fill the vacuum that the lack of intimacy creates.

Although we cannot force people to love us the way we need to be loved or create perfect environments or circumstances that yield the emotional satisfaction we crave, we can create a relationship with God that satisfies our need for deep intimacy. *Journey to the Mountain of God* is intended to help you discover and experience this level of spiritual closeness with God.

Spiritual intimacy is so satisfying that it makes you depend less on human relationships to fill your need for relational fulfillment. I am not suggesting that you become lax in your desire to bond with your spouse, family members, and friends. Rather, I am simply pointing out that the Scriptures declare the "joy of the LORD is your strength" (Neh. 8:10). Strength to work through relational difficulties, strength to find your niche within your spiritual and natural communities, and strength to learn how to achieve intimacy on a human level are all easier once you have secured your strength *in the Lord*.

The Picture of Intimacy

Intimacy is such a confusing word that solid definitions and metaphors are always needed to clarify it. *The Random House College Dictionary* defines *intimacy* as: (1) a close, familiar, and usually affectionate or loving, personal relationship; (2) a sexually familiar act; a sexual liberty.[1] Although people frequently use the word *intimacy* in connection with sex and sexuality, the word more commonly conveys a deeper sense of relational bonding.

Intimacy occurs when a parent consoles a crying child. Imagine a little girl who falls off her bike and scrapes her knee. Her dad sees the fall, runs over to her, helps her up, uses tender words to comfort her, and gives her a reassuring embrace. Although he's not directly addressing her wounded knee, his fatherly touch is medicine to his daughter's entire body and soul.

If you were a passerby who witnessed the entire event, this snapshot of intimacy would be indelibly printed on your heart and mind. If such a beautiful picture can be seen on a human level of intimacy, what would a picture of spiritual intimacy look like? Let me try to paint the latter impression.

Spiritual intimacy looks like a psalmist writing a new worship song to God. I have seen my wife, Marlinda, on countless occasions weeping before God as she seeks Him for a new song that our church can use to worship Him. Marlinda is a gifted musician who also serves as the performing arts pastor at Christ Church. Even as I write this paragraph, I am at a loss for words to fully describe the picture of intimacy I've seen so often when I've peeked into her study and found her lying on the floor, weeping before God.

I am fascinated to see her emotions for God on display. But I am also struck with an awkward feeling of spiritual jealousy. I am envious of the level of intimacy she has with God. Although we have been married since 1984 and have enjoyed a deep friendship, the depth of her intimacy with God lets me know that I cannot intrude on this area of her life. It's hers and God's alone.

I have also seen spiritual intimacy displayed through the surrendering of someone's heart to the will and purpose of God. One such occasion was on a Saturday morning at my church following a breakfast meeting we call *Meet the Pastors*. This event affords new members of our congregation a chance to meet our pastoral team in a relational setting. John, a man in his thirties, was not attending the breakfast but had been in another part of our cathedral, attending the membership classes, before he decided to seek me out. When he introduced himself and asked for a moment of my time, he was almost at the point of tears. As we walked into my office for a private chat, the floodgates burst open as he sought the words to describe what he was feeling.

John shared that he was a new Christian and had migrated from Jamaica, West Indies, about one year before. Several weeks prior to our conversation, while he was at work, he was overcome with the need to pray and cry out to God.

This kind of spiritual urgency was foreign to him. Further, John's preconverted religious background had been very stoic and devoid of passion. In obedience to his feelings (we seasoned Christians would say, "in obedience to the Holy Spirit's promptings"), he took his lunch break and sought out a private area where he could engage in a period of uninterrupted prayer. During his prayer time, John felt an overwhelming burden to return to Jamaica and plant a new church there. The urge to do this increased each minute he stayed in prayer.

Because John had never experienced anything like that before and didn't want to do something rash or spiritually unsound, he went to his car in the hopes of finding guidance from a Christian radio station.

My radio program, *IMPACT,* was on the air and I was telling the story of how Christ Church was planted. John said he hung on every one of my words, spellbound by the timing of my story and the dealings of God with his heart. He scribbled down the church address and had been attending Christ Church for several weeks before the day he approached me with this humble confession: "I don't know how to do what God is asking me to do, but I will obey nonetheless."

As John shared his heart with me, I, too, became teary-eyed because I was fascinated by the way God pursues those He wants to invite into a deeper relationship. In response to John's question about church planting, I explained the importance of obeying God by preparing for such a calling. I told him that he would qualify for the role of a church-planting pastor by exhibiting the appropriate qualities in his character, family life, biblical knowledge, and spiritual pursuit of God—which would take several years to develop. I promised to help him prepare for such a noble undertaking.

John was elated, and I was surprised at how God allowed me to witness a new convert surrendering his will to God's plans. That episode is spiritual intimacy in motion. John's true friendship with God had begun!

The Importance of Spiritual Intimacy

At the core of spiritual intimacy is the pursuit of deep friendship with God. We often don't use the word *friendship* to describe our devotion to Jesus Christ since it conveys a familiarity that can be misinterpreted as disrespect. Yet, the usage of the word *friend* was the choice Jesus made as He described to His disciples the kind of relationship their obedience to His divine commands would yield. Jesus said, "You are my *friends* if you do what I command. I no longer call you servants, because a servant does not know his master's business. Instead, I have called you *friends,* for everything that I learned from my Father I have made known to you" (John 15:14–15, italics mine).

Jesus still extends this invitation into friendship today to those who do what He commands. The fact that Jesus chooses to disclose private plans and activities not usually revealed to servants suggests that He sees us in a relational role and not simply as menial workers in His kingdom. This role of friendship intimates that regular communication of one another's intentions and whereabouts freely occurs. He is describing a friendship.

We've learned that spiritual intimacy is expressed through

words and actions that display genuine friendship with and devotion to God. While usage of the word *friendship* captures the companionship aspect associated with the pursuit of God, *devotion* describes our homage and worship of God. The psalmist described his desire to worship God with this word picture: "As the deer pants for streams of water, / so my soul pants for you, O God. / My soul thirsts for God, for the living God. / When can I go and meet with God?" (Ps. 42:1–2).

This song was written by one of the sons of Korah—a priest and worship leader during David's reign—and it expressed the longing of his heart for communion with God. Deer run to water when they are thirsty or attempting to escape a pursuing enemy. The psalmist is describing a similar desperation for intimacy with God. The word picture he paints is that of a parched, panting deer seeking the cool, satisfying relief that only water from a running stream can provide.

Equally important to the rejuvenation and safety of our souls is the living water that flows from the living God. This passage tells us that spiritual intimacy is important because it leads us to the only place where real peace can occur: in the presence of God.

If you're looking for peace of mind and soul, look no farther. You've found your rest—the place of intimacy with God. If you're looking for solace from your wearisome situation, be it financial pressure, a backstabbing coworker, or a wayward family member, you've turned to the right source. The pursuit of God is medicinal to earthly conflicts. In the presence of God we find wisdom to combat difficult problems, and we find healing to combat the troubled soul. You're at home when you are in the presence of God! This is what your soul has been thirsting for.

Intimacy at Christ Church

Imagine helping five thousand-plus people discover and experience spiritual intimacy. That's what happened with my congregation one year before I penned this book. Our congregation had been through quite a two-year spiritual ordeal trying to secure a one-hundred-acre property for a future church campus. Hardly a week went by that we were not the topic of articles in publications ranging from local community papers to the illustrious *New York Times*. Our struggle to secure the property also drew attention from the major news networks, including ABC, NBC, and even the nationally broadcast *CBS Evening News*.

Dealing with my pastoral responsibilities while reporters were camped out in the sanctuary, waiting for a juicy angle for a new story, had taken its toll. During my devotional reading one morning, I found myself captivated by Exodus 19—the story where God invited Moses to bring the children of Israel to the mountain of God: the place that represented refreshing and spiritual intimacy with God.

I didn't connect the passage with my situation until a few moments later. As I meditated and prayed about what I had just read, I was kneeling in my study and became enraptured with a thought that the Holy Spirit placed in my heart. I felt the Lord telling me, "David, bring your congregation to My mountain for spiritual refreshing." At that thought, my mind swirled with all kinds of word pictures as to what "refreshing" meant.

Now, don't get me wrong. Worshiping with thousands of people is an exciting and dynamic experience, but I knew that the congregation was in desperate need of a sustained touch of God. We needed to journey to the mountain of God for renewal and personal breakthrough.

Armed with that personal command, I reread Exodus 19 and discovered that Moses took eight intentional steps to enable the million-plus Israelites to journey to the mountain of God. These steps were internal movements that had to occur in each person's heart to move him or her closer to the heart of God. God's heart would be displayed as the Israelites stood at the foot of Mount Sinai:

Step 1:   Invitation to the Mountain of God

Step 2:   Preparing My Heart for the Climb

Step 3:   Valuing the Fear of the Lord

Step 4:   A Heart of Holiness

Step 5:   Disciplines for Mountaintop Living

Step 6:   Ingredients for Spiritual Health

Step 7:   Unleashing God's Blessings

Step 8:   A New Beginning

When I took Christ Church through these steps, I had a new congregation at the end of 40 days. The church was teeming with a revived zeal for God despite the ongoing battle we still faced in securing our future home.

The one thing that became real to each of us at the end of the 40-day journey was this: it doesn't matter what life, the devil, evil people, or even the doubts that creep into my mind may say, I am anchored in an intimate relationship with God. This is the same conviction that I hope to see magnified in your life through this journey.

Preparation, Preparation, Preparation!

Work is involved in journeying to the mountain of God. The journey requires a commitment to read through each chapter on a daily basis with your study group or by yourself. As I mentioned in the introduction, you should complete the brief reflective assignment at the end of each chapter in order to reinforce and rehearse that step on the journey to the mountain of the Lord. This will prove crucial to attaining true intimacy with God.

These assignments pale in comparison to the greater reward of achieving a precious state of intimacy with God. During the first five days of our journey, the lessons focus on preparing you to take the journey. To the uninitiated, the preparation phase of any journey may seem unnecessary, but when the journey is meaningful or complex, preparation is invaluable.

One of the midlife accomplishments I'm especially proud of is successfully completing the 2005 New York City Marathon. Just imagine running 26.2 grueling miles voluntarily! The effectiveness of the race is not based on the runner's mental drive or strength of will, but rather on the five or so months of preparation *before* the day of the race. If I am not able to successfully run long distances, plow uphill like a mad man, or do wind sprints during the five months of preparation, completing the marathon with dignity will not be possible. The key to the successful completion of a goal is the quality of preparation invested. Similarly, the key to achieving intimacy with God is found in your willingness to prepare to meet God.

Read on! You have 39 days to go!

Day 1: Steps to Rehearse

In order to journey to the mountain of God with a deep sense of excitement, you have to formulate an attractive picture of spiritual intimacy. Spiritual intimacy must encompass these dimensions:

1. Intimacy is a close, familiar, and usually affectionate or loving personal relationship.

2. Spiritual intimacy must be sought intentionally.

3. Achieving spiritual intimacy is not instantaneous—it is a process.

The Mountain of God

We live in a society that deems righteousness as unfashionable. In fact, good people are afraid to be good. They are afraid to be powerful disciples of Christ, afraid to abandon themselves to the service of God, and afraid to love people unselfishly. As a result, many believers in Jesus decide that living on the borderline of intimacy with God is acceptable because it allows them to fit comfortably within our fallen society.

Although they do not consciously seek this lukewarm behavior, few Christians discover the power and adventure inherent in a life that is passionately on fire for God. That's what I want to help you attain, and that's what I believe God wants for you, too. He desired it for the children of Israel, and I believe He's calling you and me to that place of newfound intimacy with Him.

Invitation to God's Mountain

Immediately after the young nation of Israel escaped the clutches of Egypt—the place of their 430 years of servitude—God took them on an unforgettable journey that He intended to keep them hungry for more of His presence. Moses, the leader of this ragtag bunch, was lying around one day after the Israelites had won the victory against the Egyptian soldiers, when he was called to the mountain of God. That calling came from none other than the Deliverer of Israel—the Lord Almighty. Imagine how Moses must have felt at the moment he heard the voice of the Lord ringing with both a clarion call of might and a sweet longing to speak face-to-face with him, His friend. Moses quickly responded and climbed Mount Sinai—the mountain of God—to hear what was on his Friend's heart.

On the mountain of God, Moses learned that God's desire was to meet with the people—the Israelites whom He had helped escape Pharaoh's sword. They needed to know with *whom* they were going to meet and how they should prepare for such an encounter.

Whenever you meet a president of a country or a dignitary, a key representative of that official will instruct you about how to speak with the honored personage, the length of time you are afforded, and the types of questions that are acceptable for the meeting. If you do not heed the representative's instructions to the letter, the distinguished person will stand up in the middle of the meeting, thus signifying that the meeting is over—whether you have exhausted your time or questions or not.

God was no different when He instructed Moses about how to prepare the people to meet with Him. The Lord told Moses: "Go to the people and consecrate them today and tomorrow. Have them wash their clothes and be ready by the third day, because on that day the LORD will come down on Mount Sinai in the sight of all the people" (Exod. 19:10–11).

The Reason

Why did God want to meet with the people of Israel? I believe that God wanted to create a passionate nation of worshipers who were not afraid to put their emotions for Him on display. God did not want a bunch of lukewarm, halfhearted people who had been beaten down by life's experiences to be His representatives on earth. He needed people who were devoted to pursuing Him and zealous about having a dynamic relationship with Him.

To build such a people, God had to call them to His mountain. They had to personally eyewitness God communicating with them. No secondhand experience was going to work. No relaying of God's desires would suffice. No heavenly liaison would carry this message. It was too important. The zeal of the Lord had to captivate this group so it could move to the highest level of

spiritual intimacy. God wanted pov   d the Israelites needed a firsthand experien   ome such
followers.

When I was in seminary, my cla   shocked
when our professor of American R   that we
needed to stop reading about New   d instead
take a trip to a local New Age center   merging
preachers piled into the school van w   nd rode
off to learn in a new way. Firsthand e   g to dispel our ignorance about this destructi   merican
society.

The trip accomplished our professor   ere able
to ask the director of the center all sorts   the trip
gave new meaning to the textbook concepts we studied in class: it
permitted us to mix a personal encounter with the intellectual
thoughts captured by the textbook's author.

This is what God wanted to do for His people: give them an
in-person experience of who He was. God wanted to put a fire in
their bosoms that would make it easy to serve Him, to live for
Him, to love Him, and to walk in a way that honored Him. They
needed an encounter that would awaken them to the understanding that He was real and that spiritual growth was essential to
godly living.

Time Is of the Essence

What would you do if, after a routine visit to your doctor, you
learned that you had only 40 days left to live? After the whirlwind
of emotions and thoughts settled to some degree of sanity, you
would most likely establish a plan that included spending quality
time with your loved ones and visiting places you had always
wanted to. And, since death is the doorway to meeting God, you
would spend a sizable part of the 40-day plan preparing to meet
your Maker. *Journey to the Mountain of God* is about the latter part
of your preparation—becoming intentional about drawing closer
to God.

Oftentimes crisis is the greatest motivator. It takes a medical crisis to cause some people to get their financial houses in order. It takes an employment crisis before you dust off the old résumé and update it in the hopes of landing a better job. It sometimes takes a life crisis to bring someone to faith in Christ. And it most often takes a spiritual crisis to move someone from the doldrums of being spiritually lukewarm to being on fire for God. A spiritual crisis can occur when a person's local church loses its pastor due to an illness, retirement, or moral failure. All of a sudden, the notion of not having a spiritual giant to turn to during personal challenges awakens this person to their need to really draw closer to the Lord.

Since it is impractical and, as most people would agree, insane for you to create a crisis in order to become motivated, you may have to imagine one to get the desired result.

So let's go back to imagining the threat of having just 40 days to prepare to meet God. With that looming over your mind day and night, I guarantee that you would toss all excuses concerning drawing closer to God, reading the Bible, walking in obedience to His laws, and all the other ways spiritual growth occurs, out of the window. If you're like me, you never want to be caught unprepared, even in matters that are seemingly inconsequential.

My parents drummed that personal policy into me from childhood. I can still hear their words of urban wisdom: "David, whenever you leave this house, always be prepared for an emergency. Don't leave home without a few dollars in your pocket." And, since I grew up in the Big Apple, their street-smart advice went a bit farther: "David, make sure that you put half of your money in one pocket and the other half in another pocket. This way, if you get mugged, you can give the robber just the money from the one pocket and you'll still have money to catch the subway home."

I've carried such advice along my spiritual journey. Similarly, I don't want to die and stand before God without a deep sense of personal intimacy with Him, and I am certain you feel the same. My assumption is that you already have the ticket that grants you access into heaven: acceptance of God's gift of personal salvation, Jesus Christ. The matter at hand is your level of personal intimacy with God.

The heart of God is where you experience sweet communion and personal experiences with the Holy One, encounters that are transformational and intensely addictive. In other words, your migration from spiritual lethargy to spiritual passion carries the bonus prize of giving you an insatiable hunger for the presence of God. The more you experience His presence, the more satisfying your life becomes. The more you are away from it, the greater the craving becomes for another fix.

So time is of the essence. You need to experience spiritual renewal. An awakened appetite comes only when the craving for intimacy intensifies. Your heart should be softening toward the things of God as you read each word. This is part of the preparation process of drawing near to God.

Day 2: Steps to Rehearse

My journey toward the mountain of God happens when I prepare my heart for intimacy with God. The natural steps to experiencing a renewed heart include considering these issues:

1. How spiritually lethargic have I become?

2. What crises have stirred me to pursue God?

3. Why it is so important for me to journey to the mountain of the Lord?

Learning to Trust

When my daughter Jessica was in middle school, she nonchalantly told me about a program her school made available to the entire eighth-grade class to host twenty exchange students from Mexico. To make the responsibility easier on participating families, the exchange student would stay just two weeks.

I excitedly told Jessica that this would be a great opportunity—especially since she wanted to improve her Spanish. But even after all my encouragement and outlining how the pros outweighed the cons, she wanted no part of the experience.

After the first week that the exchange students were at her school, Jessica heard reports of how the Mexican girls had made life so exciting for their American hosts—her friends. And she became envious. As I drove her home from school one afternoon, she said, "Dad, I wish you would have forced me to become a host to one of the Mexican exchange students. It seems so cool. All of my friends are having a great time being hosts. Why didn't you force me?"

Jessica taught me that afternoon that there are times when we must trust the judgment of the person who is looking out for our best interests, despite the lack of clarity or excitement we may have on the matter. This is why the cliché makes perfect sense: hindsight *is* twenty-twenty vision. At first, my daughter couldn't see how inviting a total stranger into her home and life would be profitable, even if it were just for a two-week stint. Jessica wanted her life to flow the same way it usually did. She wasn't interested in change—none whatsoever.

Many people reflect Jessica's mind set: they repeatedly pass up wonderful opportunities because they seem inconvenient and un-timely. We all want a desirable outcome without the undesirable work. In Jessica's case, she wanted to improve her Spanish, have an international pen pal, and enjoy lots of fun with her Mexican guest without having to do any work. But she was unwilling to trust my judgment.

In the same way, trusting God's judgment is critical to your preparation to journey to His mountain. What would your life be like if you did not accept God's invitation? What reason would you give for not adjusting your schedule in order to take the trip? Amidst the possible excuses for not journeying to the mountain of God, distrust of God Himself would be at the foundation.

Do You Trust God?

As a pastor of a very large congregation representing over twenty-five different nationalities, I have learned to spot the signs of people's distrust in God. No matter how they craft their excuses or justify their unwillingness to exercise faith in God, these are the real issues: people don't trust God when they are afraid; disappointment with God turns off their receptivity to trusting Him; or they are confused as to why God allowed something negative to happen. For you to journey to the mountain of the Lord, you must overcome these obstacles to trusting God.

1. Are You Afraid?

Fear is crippling! It shouts that your situation is impossible to navigate, and you feel as if trying is simply futile. Yet, when all is said and done, fear is not a reason to distrust God. Those people who hide behind fear as an excuse not to journey to the mountain of the Lord maintain this rationale: *I don't know what I'll be like after achieving the place of intense passion for God. Will I be like that kooky person in my church who says, "Praise God, alleluia!" every time something happens? Even if an usher just hands him an offering envelope, he yells, "Praise God!" If the church bookstore opens ten minutes earlier than normal, he proclaims, "Alleluia!"*

My response to your fearful concern: that person was kooky *before* he became passionate for God. The two are unrelated. You have absolutely nothing to worry about. Drawing closer to God does not change your personality or social behavior—it will simply make you more devout in your faith and more apt to honor God in all you do.

2. Are You Disappointed in God?

Disappointment can strike any one of us at any time. It has nothing to do with our moral position. Bad people experience pain just as good people do. How we process our pain and disappointment is the main concern. When you lay fault at the feet of the Lord for your predicament or your problem, what you are really saying is, "God, You willfully [or accidentally] allowed this problem to occur in my life."

Think about it for a moment. You are accusing God of intentionally taking the time to pick you out of some six billion people just to create pain in your life. After giving it some thought, you'd have to laugh at yourself, because this accusation is simply ludicrous.

Now, this fact does not dismiss your genuine disappointment or pain. But to find healing and peace, and to regain trust in God, which is vital for achieving spiritual intimacy, you must redirect your emotional anguish into a new question: "God, how do I remedy my disappointment?" This rephrasing of the problem invites God to provide a solution to your legitimate state of disappointment. The difference is that now you view Him as an ally and no longer as an adversary or architect of your pain.

3. Are You Confused About God's Plans?

Disappointment with God and confusion about His plans are two different problems. The first accuses God of willfully or accidentally disappointing you. The second lays the problem of confusion at your feet. The latter issue deals with the question of why unexpected, and often painful, events occur in your life. In essence you may be asking, *Why did God let this happen? Where is God when I'm hurting?*

I am thoroughly convinced that every generation must address these philosophical questions in order to experience the peace of God. Since God tells us, "As the heavens are higher than the earth, / so are my ways higher than your ways / and my thoughts than your thoughts" (Isa. 55:9), we should automatically surrender to the reality that we will not understand everything that happens to us in this life. Nor will we be able to comprehend the wisdom in which God operates. Isaiah put it clearly: God's ways and thoughts are beyond our full understanding. David settled his confusion about life with these words: "Such knowledge [referring to life's paradoxes] is too wonderful for me, / too lofty for me to attain" (Ps. 139:6).

Another answer to the problem of confusion is the one Augustine—one of the great thinkers in church history—gave. He concluded that pain precedes joy.[1] In other words, we are able to experience pleasures *because of* the existence of pain and confusion. We couldn't distinguish joy unless unhappiness also existed. You cannot have one without the other.

This may sound like a pat answer to a complex problem, but you have to admit that it is an intellectually honest answer. I tackle these soul-searching questions in a more comprehensive manner in my book *Secrets to a Satisfying Life* (Baker Publishing Group, 2006).

Whether you are confronting fear, disappointment in God, or confusion, you will have to escape the tentacles of this vicious threesome in order to discover the benefits that trusting the Lord yields.

The Value of Trust

When the call came for the children of Israel to journey to the mountain of God, they had a choice either to obey or disobey. Similarly, as God is calling you to His mountain, you can obey or disobey. Since disobedience seems so unpleasant, the politically correct thing to do is to come up with a number of excuses to legitimize your negative response to God's invitation.

The call to the mountain of God never comes at an opportune time. You are probably incredibly busy right now: busy with family plans, job demands, and the pressures of keeping your life's goals on track. However, achieving intimacy with God is so important, you can't afford not to obey. Hearing the call is one thing, but answering it is an entirely different matter.

Fortunately, the children of Israel did not come up with any excuses. They recognized the importance of accepting God's invitation to journey to His mountain. The Israelites did not extend this trust because they had great personal experience with the Lord. To the contrary: their experience had been limited. God had revealed Himself personally to the people of Israel only a few months prior (Exod. 19:1–2). They knew Him as their Deliverer, the one who freed them from the cruelty of Egyptian slavery. Now they were going to learn to trust Him relationally.

God acted first by voicing His desire to meet with them. Israel accepted. The date was made.

Right now you're experiencing much of the same opportunity. God is calling you aside and you must heed the call simply because you trust His judgment. Even though you may not fully comprehend what intimacy with God looks like, you should obey because it is *God* who is calling you to His mountain. In order to heed the call, you must trust God's judgment that something special is awaiting you in His presence. We can immediately acknowledge that God knows what's best for us, yet there lies a great gulf between acknowledging His wisdom and heeding His wisdom. Solomon instructed us in the Book of Proverbs about the value of trusting God: "Trust in the LORD with all your heart / and lean not on your own understanding; / in all your ways acknowledge him, / and he will make your paths straight" (Prov. 3:5–6).

This word translated "trust" is the Hebrew word *batah,* which, according to the renowned Hebrew scholar Allen P. Ross, "carries the force of relying on someone for security; the confidence is to be in the Lord and not in human understanding."[2] Solomon advised that we trust in the Lord and not in ourselves, our feelings, or solely in the counsel of another human being. This is to be a complete trust, with *all* our hearts, in the Lord. Having this kind of a confidence in God conveys the picture of our leaning on an immovable wall that will always sustain us, despite the pressures or the problems we may be facing.

The other aspect of Solomon's exhortation is for us to acknowledge God in *all* of our ways. Since we have limited knowledge, it is important that we never try to sustain our decisions on our own knowledge base. It will mislead us every time. This is why we're urged to acknowledge God in every single way at every single time. This kind of dogged allegiance to God's wisdom and knowledge will lead us into experiencing wonderful things at His hand.

This point brings me back to my daughter's reluctance to host a foreign exchange student. Marlinda and I tried to get Jessica not to lean on her understanding, but the picture she created of what life would be like with a foreign person in our home outweighed the one we as parents were painting for her. She couldn't see God in it.

What about you? Can you trust God to initiate a call for you to come to His mountain? Although you don't see all the glorious things that will happen to you, you must build a foundation of trust in the fact that God knows what's best for you. And that reality is good enough for you to prepare your heart to seek the Lord over the next 37 days.

Day 3: Steps to Rehearse

In preparing to journey to the mountain of God, you must work out your issues of trust in God. En route to trusting God, remember these points:

1. Trust means to rely on God's judgment despite your level of discomfort or lack of comprehension.

2. People who don't trust God typically use one of three excuses: they are afraid; disappointment with God turns off their receptivity to trusting Him; or they are confused as to why God allowed something negative to happen in their lives.

3. The Bible urges us not to lean on our own understanding but to acknowledge God in all of our ways.

Day 4

Day 4

The Treasured Possession

In planning to visit a friend, you would like to know that the person you're to see enjoys your company. I am quite reluctant about taking a journey if the person at the destination is not excited about my coming. But when I know I bring delight to the host, the visit is all the more enjoyable and inviting. The packing and preparation, though sometimes arduous, seem more pleasurable when I'm confident my visit is positively anticipated. The welcoming embrace and reception of a dear friend makes the minor inconvenience of preparation less stressful.

As you prepare for the journey to the mountain of God, you should feel a genuine exuberance in your heart because of how God feels about your visit with Him. It was an easy sell for Moses when he told the children of Israel that God wanted to see them at His mountain. God's choice of words to Moses, which he shared with the Israelites, made all the difference:

Then Moses went up to God, and the LORD called to him from the mountain and said, "This is what you are to say to the house of Jacob and what you are to tell the people of Israel: 'You yourselves have seen what I did to Egypt, and how I carried you on eagles' wings and brought you to myself. Now if you obey me fully and keep my covenant, then out of all nations you will be my treasured possession. Although the whole earth is mine, you will be for me a kingdom of priests and a holy nation.' These are the words you are to speak to the Israelites."

So Moses went back and summoned the elders of the people and set before them all the words the LORD had commanded him to speak. The people all responded together, "We will do everything the LORD has said." So Moses brought their answer back to the LORD.

(Exodus 19:3–8)

God's invitation was loaded with kind language that conveyed to the Israelites His affection for them. To hear how the God of the universe feels about you, particularly when those feelings are positive, is a life-giving experience. I am certain that the children of Israel were excited about the prospect of having a personal encounter with the God who loved them, despite their inability to offer Him anything beyond their simple lives.

This is what God is looking for from you. He wants you—all of you. Preparing to take this journey is about readying yourself to be given to God as a gift—a sacrifice, free and unrestrained.

How Does God Feel About Your Visit?

I want you to picture the scene where Moses' exhortation occurred. The children of Israel had escaped the despotic rule of Pharoah and his army three months prior. This difficult feat involved being delivered from 430 years of brutality and slavery in Egypt. Their freedom culminated as they passed through the Red Sea and came into the desert of Sinai. The ex-slaves had nowhere to call home, nowhere to lay their heads at night. And they did not fully understand where they were going or what they would encounter along the way. Anxiety filled the air. Uncertainty prevailed in each family's tent.

As they camped in the desert in front of Mount Sinai, Moses was invited to meet with God atop the mountain. The people, on the other hand, had a chance to rest from their journey. This time also gave them the opportunity to speculate about what would happen next.

You can imagine the barrage of questions occurring in each tent: "What's going to happen to us?" "Where is God going to take us?" "Does Moses have the leadership abilities to facilitate our stability and bring us into the promised land?" These questions are the natural response that thinking people would have. On the other hand, they would not be thinking: *Are we prepared emotionally, psychologically, or spiritually to attain God's promises for our lives?* Most people, especially those who have been demoralized by slavery and brutality, don't have this perspective.

Once, while I was lecturing in Soweto, South Africa, on the topic of leaders and their visions, a South African leader asked a very poignant question. Although apartheid had been lifted for a few years by that time, the minds of the oppressed still carried the scars of their battle. When I insisted that leaders must dream great dreams, the man asked, "Can the mind of an oppressed person dream?" His response revealed that he was like a deer caught in the headlights of an oncoming vehicle—he could not imagine anything but danger and avoiding it. Apartheid had damaged his creativity and his visionary faculties. In response to his question, I blurted out, "Certainly you can dream! You can dream of your freedom, if nothing else!"

A brutal regime had also damaged the Israelites. Physical damage is one thing, but emotional scarring is another thing altogether. To prepare the children of Israel to embrace their destinies, God had to work on their self-esteem.

When Moses returned from speaking with God, he followed God's instruction: "This is what you are to say to the house of Jacob and what you are to tell the people of Israel: '. . . Out of all nations you will be my treasured possession'" (Exod. 19:3, 5). Wow! God called those ex-slaves His "treasured possession."

To be described in such a rich metaphor by Almighty God is beyond imagination. A treasured possession is something priceless. The eminent Hebrew scholars, C. F. Keil and F. Delitzsch, comment: "[That the Israelites] should be a costly possession to Him out of all nations . . . does not signify property in general, but valuable property, that which is laid by, or put aside . . . , hence a treasure of silver and gold."[1] God viewed those people as such a distinct and valued treasure that He set value on them in a special way for a special relationship.

This designation becomes even more significant because God

pointed out that "out of all nations" He had set aside Israel as His treasured possession. This verse supports the point that the Bible portrays God as the only God. He is God of "the whole earth" (Exod. 19:5), not simply a national deity. Although the whole earth is His because He is our Creator and Preserver, God still verbalizes His pleasurable thoughts concerning Israel.

If you're not theologically careful, you can get sidetracked by intently focusing on present-day Israel rather than interpreting the Scriptures from the belief that those who accept Christ as Lord and Savior are the true Israel of God. This is the view that the apostle Paul taught to the Galatian Christians (Gal. 3:6–9) and the one we New Testament believers use when interpreting the applicable Old Testament promises.

You Are God's Treasured Possession!

In other words, we New Testament believers can legitimately interpret the term "treasured possession" as an appropriate metaphor God uses to refer to us today. Apart from Saint Paul's perspective as to how Christians are to view themselves in light of Old Testament promises, the book of Deuteronomy even confirmed this point when Moses again used the term "treasured possession" to describe the people of God. That time around he gave an historic and a futuristic view as to why the term was appropriate, and why it would remain appropriate for those who experienced salvation in Christ. Moses declared:

> For you are a people holy to the LORD your God. The LORD your God has chosen you out of all the peoples on the face of the earth to be his people, his treasured possession.
> The LORD did not set his affection on you and choose you because you were more numerous than other peoples, for you were the fewest of all peoples. But it was because the LORD loved you and kept the oath he swore to your forefathers that he brought you out with a mighty hand and redeemed you from the land of slavery, from the power of Pharaoh king of Egypt. Know therefore that the LORD your God is

*God; he is the faithful God, keeping his covenant of love to a thou-
sand generations of those who love him and keep his commands.*

(7:6–9)

The term "treasured possession" was steeped in the historic
fact that God had made an oath to the Israelites' ancestors,
namely Abraham, that He was going to create a nation out of
Abraham's seed. This promise conveyed that Abraham and his
descendants were God's treasured possession. According to
Deuteronomy 7:9, the futuristic development of this same promise extended to "a thousand generations." Therefore, it is right
and appropriate for you to consider yourself God's treasured
possession.

Not only is this term inviting to all those desirous to journey to
God's mountain, the significance of the one making this assertion
makes the phrase more meaningful and powerful. Imagine how
the Israelites must have felt, particularly being ex-slaves. This ac-
colade would certainly prove a self-esteem builder—especially to
a group of people whom the Egyptians had despised and mis-
treated for their entire lives.

You must dust off your self-image and get your heart in the
right place because God is expecting you to journey to His
mountain. Since God feels so great about you, preparing for the
journey should be a delight. You are His supremely valued one.

In the 1979 Clint Eastwood movie *Escape from Alcatraz,* Doc,
an inmate who had been imprisoned since his youth, was still
serving out his life sentence as an old man in the most brutal
prison in America of its time. The movie tugs on the viewers'
heartstrings as it depicts how Doc kept his sanity by using his
treasured possession—painting—as a mental escape from the de-
moralizing treatment the warden gave prisoners.

One day when the warden was doing his rounds he saw one of
Doc's incomplete paintings, which featured him as the subject. Although the painting was not a caricature, the warden became angry
because Doc had dared to paint an image of him. In anger, he had
Doc's painting privileges removed immediately. Doc was crushed

and insisted, "But painting's all I have!" In a fit of rage, to protest this unreasonable and improper exercise of authority, Doc cut off his own hand with an electric saw in the prison's machine shop.

When that scene in the movie occurred, it conveyed how precious and priceless a treasured possession is to the holder. What is more mind-boggling is to know that God sees you and me as His treasured possessions.

Please take a moment right now and pray this prayer:

Heavenly Father, please forgive me for not appreciating You the way I should. Help me to prepare my heart so that I can capture a greater realization of Your love for me. Give me a fresh perspective about what it means to prepare myself to seek Your face because I now know that I'm Your treasured possession. And, just as I desire a deeper walk with You, I know You desire a deeper relationship with me. I ask You these things in the name of Your Son, Jesus Christ. Amen.

Day 4: Steps to Rehearse

Preparation is the key to success! The more you prepare your heart to seek God, the more you'll receive from God. Consider taking these preparatory steps as you anticipate journeying to the mountain of God.

1. Fast one entire day this week, drinking only water. If you prefer to take a smaller step, consider missing one of your normal meals and turn that time period into a partial fast. As you fast, ask God to let you see how He feels about you.

2. Jot down five things that demonstrate how God sees you as His treasured possession.

3. What are three treasured possessions you have?

A Glimpse of the Future

Even in spiritual things, the cliché is quite accurate: a picture *is* worth a thousand words. What image comes to mind when you think of spiritual intimacy with God? The way we visualize our spiritual future is often shaped by our past religious experiences, our present spiritual environments, and our biblical perspectives. Thus, misconceptions can easily enter our minds when we visualize what intimacy with God will be like.

As part of your mental and spiritual preparation to journey to the mountain of God, you must test your concept of what the future will be like for complete accuracy.

What Does Your Future Look Like?

While on a mission trip to Kenya, I saw people with almost no worldly possessions demonstrate a richness of relationship with God that is unparalleled in the lives of many American Christians. As an American, I felt poor when I saw this. When I walked the marketplace, a number of the vendors who recognized me as the conference speaker at the large church in their village offered me gifts. I felt awkward accepting these gifts when I knew how little they earned from selling wooden artifacts to tourists. I felt as if I were stealing a meal from a person who had very little.

Yet, material poverty did not prevent the Kenyans' ability to express their love and passion for the Lord by offering me presents. They raised no philosophical assertions that blamed God for the state of their national economy or personal battles with life's difficulties. Rather, they pondered how to draw closer to God and how to lead their loved ones to accept God's salvation made possible through Jesus Christ.

I wept as I saw how the Kenyans valued their relationship with God. Yet, so many Christians around the world value *things* instead—meaningless things that could be taken away or lost at the slightest dip in the economy. And it seems that we, Western Christians, think that it is our inalienable right to worship God *if* He makes us happy. Never mind the fact that God deserves our praise regardless of life's circumstances or our emotional and physical states. We hold worship over God's head by making the subconscious statement: "My worship is payment for *Your* blessings. No blessings, no worship. So it's up to You, Lord, if You want to be worshiped today."

God wanted to keep this thinking from entering the minds of the Hebrews. He announced to them that He viewed them as the "house of Jacob" and the "people of Israel"—changed people who knew their God. What do you want your future to look like? Do you want to become prey to materialism or someone who embraces the fire of spiritual companionship with God? While the former has no room for God, the latter has capacity for God and His many blessings.

Your Background Doesn't Determine Your Future

God wanted the children of Israel to decide what future they wanted. Moses' exhortation prepared them for the future that a journey to the mountain of God can bring: one filled with rich relationship with God amidst material blessings. Let's look again at what God said:

> *Then Moses went up to God, and the LORD called to him from the mountain and said, "This is what you are to say to the house of Jacob and what you are to tell the people of Israel: 'You yourselves have seen what I did to Egypt, and how I carried you on eagles' wings and brought you to myself. Now if you obey me fully and keep my covenant, then out of all nations you will be my treasured possession. Although the whole*

earth is mine, you will be for me a kingdom of priests and a holy nation.'
These are the words you are to speak to the Israelites."

(Exod. 19:3–6)

God touched on a number of significant areas that shaped the Israelites' perspectives on their future. With a few words, however, God also addressed a real sore spot. It became clear to the people of Israel that God did not look at their background to determine their future.

Picture this: at this juncture in history, Israel had just been delivered three months prior from centuries of Egyptian bondage. Undoubtedly, this ragtag group of men and women resting in the desert of Sinai still looked and thought like slaves. Their self-image probably ebbed between low and none. The whippings and cutting words of their Egyptian slave masters had damaged their psyches. The thought of accepting God's invitation into intimacy must have been frightening to them.

To think that *anybody* would want to have a personal relationship with them—much less the God of the universe—must have been quite a stretch for the Israelites. Furthermore, to consider visiting with God through intimate worship, passionate prayer, and the opportunity of petitioning for the fulfillment of historic promises given to their predecessors would certainly have sounded like a daunting task.

Yet, God did not allow their wounded self-images to lead them farther down the path of self-destruction and self-pity. Christian psychologist Gary R. Collins says, "We help [people with low self-esteem] by assisting them to consider who they are and what they want through exploring *what they are listening to, looking at, feeling for, and acting out.*"[1] This is precisely what God was preparing to do for the Israelites when He mentioned two key terms: "house of Jacob" and "people of Israel."

1. "House of Jacob"

The phrase "house of Jacob" appears some twenty-one times in the New International Version of the Scriptures. Its first appearance is in Exodus 19:3—the very discourse Moses had with the Israelites was to convey God's invitation to meet Him at His mountain. The term reflects their lineage—they were descendants of Jacob, who was the grandson of Abraham. We always read of the "house of Jacob" in association with Jacob's being a patriarchal foundation of the Hebrew people. In the biblical narrative, we often overlook the significance of the term "house of Jacob." It's interesting to note that based on the placement of the phrase throughout the Bible, various meanings are derived that connect to different aspects of Jacob's nature and tendencies.

In the Exodus 19 passage, the phrase reflects a connection with Jacob's rise from poverty and abuse to prosperity and wholeness. When Jacob was delivered from Paddan Aram—the home of his deceitful father-in-law, Laban—God brought him into Canaan, the land He had earlier promised to Abraham and Isaac (Gen. 31–33). Jacob's deliverance from an ungrateful and oppressive relative into his own prosperous land was equivalent to the Israelites' deliverance from Egypt. And as Jacob left Paddan Aram with livestock and prosperity that he'd shrewdly taken back from Laban with God's help (Gen. 31), so the children of Israel left Egypt with the spoils of the Egyptians with God's help (Exod. 12:35–36).

What God was emphasizing through using the term "house of Jacob" was the deliverance from struggle, bondage, and victimization that the Israelites received in Egypt. In our modern day, a mere mention of the term "house of Jacob" does not solicit any feelings of freedom, victory, or breakthrough. But when we see anything that shows three simple numbers—9/11—all kinds of emotions and patriotic feelings rush through us.

Because of the terrorists' bombings against the United States on September 11, 2001, the mere mention of those numbers in that sequence brings our entire nation to emotional attention. This is just what happened when Moses said "house of Jacob" to the Israelites. They understood that God cared for them deeply and equated what He did for Jacob hundreds of years prior to what He had done for them three months earlier, as He powerfully delivered them from the clutches of Egypt. This reference gave them a future perspective. They could see that God was up to something wonderful, and they had no hesitation to journey to the mountain of God.

2. "People of Israel"

God's usage of this second phrase had a different meaning altogether from "house of Jacob." Although Jacob and Israel are names that refer to the same person, the first phrase symbolizes deliverance from struggle. The second, however, highlights a new spiritual image that Jacob received from God. When Jacob left Laban, he had an experience with God that would transform his spiritual life forever (Gen. 32:22–32). After Jacob wrestled with God all night, he who had dealt deceitfully with his brother, Esau, and who had been abused and victimized by his scheming father-in-law, changed. Jacob prayed and wrestled with God that night and this was the outcome: "Your name will no longer be Jacob, but Israel, because you have struggled with God and with men and have overcome" (Gen. 32:28).

God doesn't use words capriciously. There's meaning behind every word, every phrase, every name. The mention of the name "Israel" sparked the idea in the minds of the Israelites that it was now showtime. God was about to demonstrate how He can change people who seemingly are so far away from Him emotionally, spiritually, and devotionally. The ex-slaves were tuning into God's transforming powers. They were getting a glimpse of their future. Just as Jacob was changed from being a selfish, opportunistic hustler, who was victimized by another hustler, into a devoted follower of God, the Israelites were about to get the same spiritual makeover.

Change Is Possible

The power of spiritual intimacy with God is more revolutionary than chemical warfare or atomic bombs. While the latter can wipe out nations and kill millions of people at one blast, it cannot heal or correct broken lives. The former agent does just the opposite. When God woos someone to His mountain of change, He gives an imperfect person a bright future by transforming his or her self-esteem and overall outlook in life. The invitation He extends to journey to His mountain reveals His love, His desire for deep friendship, and His longing for a person's commitment to trust Him as He does a profound work of grace in his or her life. Throughout the Bible, we see how God used imperfect, broken people who later shaped their societies because of the meaningful relationships they formed with Him.

Do you remember Moses? He had a speech impediment. Do you remember Elijah the prophet? He was suicidal. What about Rahab? She arose from a lifestyle of prostitution to serve the living God. How about Samson? He was codependent. He just loved the ladies too much. Remember Gideon? He was a coward before he drew near to God. Do you recall Jonah's issue? He was a self-righteous prophet who hated to see God pardon guilty people.

When you turn to the New Testament, the characters change, but the same brokenness exists in the lives of the people depicted there. God continued to show His awesome grace by drawing them into passionate relationship with Himself. Peter was a bigmouth. Thomas was a doubter. John and James—the two brothers—were called the "sons of thunder" (Mark 3:17) because of their desire to see fire burn up stubborn people. The list goes on. What about Paul? Remember this self-righteous Pharisee who thought he was the sheriff in the kingdom of God? It was he who traveled from city to city, incarcerating Christians. This continued until he met the Savior en route to the city of Damascus. Do you recall Martha? She was a worrywart.

I can continue naming powerful Bible heroes who started off as flaky people with a lot of issues. Such small-minded people would hesitate when asked, "Can God do something powerful with you?" Wherever you find yourself in the process of drawing near to God, I want you to be encouraged. God *can* change you into a radical, fully devoted follower of Christ. You *can* become a passionate, society-changing Christian. The answer is found in journeying to the mountain of God.

Day 5: Steps to Rehearse

Preparation can be frightening if you don't have an accurate picture of what you will look like when you get to your destination. Fortunately, God prepares us by telling us how He feels about us and the process of change that is up ahead. Rehearse these steps for a successful journey.

1. What in your past may hinder you from journeying to the mountain of God? Is it greater than Jacob's betrayal of his brother, Esau? Even if it is, think of how God freed Jacob and drew him close to His heart. God wants to do the same with you.

2. If God works through your past indiscretions, what do you hope your future will look like? Write down two things that reflect a glimpse of this future should the Lord fulfill the desires of your heart.

3. Cite two Bible characters I did not name who had major character flaws, yet were able to have a close relationship with God. Then consider: *If God can do it for them, He can do it for me.*

Step 2

Preparing My Heart
for the Climb

Create in me a pure heart, O God,
and renew a steadfast spirit with me.
(Psalm 51:10)

Day 6

Spiritual Cardio

We have reached the second step in our eight-step process to the mountain of God: the preparation of the heart. In the first step of the journey, we explored preparing your perspective for developing intimacy with God. The second step, which we will cover in chapters 6 through 10, will address the readiness of your heart to engage in activities that promote spiritual intimacy.

Throughout the Bible, the word "heart" refers to the center of our spiritual activity, the foundation of our motivation, the seat of passion, and the fountainhead of our desires and emotions. *Easton's Bible Dictionary* defines *heart* as "the home of the personal life."[1] Based on the words that flow from a person's heart—the home of the personal life—he or she is characterized as good, wise, bad, or foolish. In other words, you know a person by his or her heart.

For this reason Solomon wrote, "Above all else, guard your heart, / for it is the wellspring of life" (Prov. 4:23). This tidbit of wisdom points to the fact that your heart—the home of the personal life—is so critical to the overall quality and success of your life that you must "guard" it. The word *guard* means to protect, maintain, watch, preserve, and inspect. It is quite clear that achieving personal intimacy with God can occur only if your heart has been inspected and found in good health.

Since the heart is the wellspring of life, a healthy heart will promote a healthy perspective toward God and His creation. Conversely, an unhealthy heart will draw the wrong conclusions about God's plans and formulate a diminished view of life.

Further, a heart in poor condition may not have the stamina to go the distance toward personal intimacy with God.

The Parallel Between the Natural and Spiritual Hearts

To understand the metaphorical meaning of the heart more clearly, let's compare it to the physical heart.

Generally, the manufacturer of a fitness product or personal trainer provides a cautionary warning: "Before beginning any exercise program, get approval from your physician." The personal trainer or manufacturer is protecting himself against liability should you become injured, fall ill, or die as a result of the physical exertion of your new exercise regimen. The manufacturer or personal trainer also wants to ensure that you have the basic health foundation to undergo the rigor of exercise. If you do, great! You can set the start date of the workout program immediately. If not, you'll have to undergo a rehabilitation plan prior to engaging in any strenuous activity. In the latter case, rehabilitation is a prerequisite to starting an exercise plan.

Similarly, when you take a spiritual journey to the mountain of the Lord, the fitness of your heart—the home of your personal life—must be intact before you begin. If you have extreme bitterness or unforgiveness in your heart, you will not be able to journey to the mountain of the Lord. This spiritual sickness will cause you to keel over on the side of the road. Bitterness and unforgiveness are as damaging to the heart as cancer, and they spread quickly.

In preparing my congregation to take a 40-day journey to the mountain of God, I recall how, after three weeks of preaching sermons tailored to produce repentance, forgiveness, and similar heart-purifying effects, one lady verified my conclusions about the need for a pure heart. I had preached: "If your heart is hardened toward God or others, you will not be able to benefit from this spiritual journey. You must solve the problem of your heart first."

The lady sent a note that read:

Pastor, thank you for pointing out how vital a clean heart is in pro-moting spiritual intimacy with God. I had not realized that my un-willingness to forgive my sister for a childhood offense had become such a stumbling block to my passionate pursuit of God. Thankfully, I have repented and now I feel free to journey with you and the congregation to the mountain of God.

After reading that note, I was grateful for her honesty. I also knew, however, that she represented thousands, if not millions, of Christians who deeply love God but are unable to connect with Him in a meaningful way. Their unconfessed sins blind them to the glorious relationship they could be enjoying with God.

What is the position of your heart toward God? In the same way that some people need to take a physical exam before they can begin a jogging program, you need God's blessings upon your spiritual exam to verify the healthy state of your heart.

Is Your Heart Healthy?

Typically, a cardiologist will conduct five tests during a heart checkup: 1) a complete medical history, 2) a general physical exam that includes a blood test and checking the heart rate and blood pressure, 3) an electrocardiogram (EKG) test, 4) a choles-terol level check, and 5) a stress test to see how your heart be-haves during exercise. While tests #1, 2, and 5 are easily understandable for us nonmedical people, tests #3 and 4 need some clarification.

An electrocardiogram is an electrical recording of the heart, which is often displayed on a monitor as a series of pikes and peaks. Cholesterol, as you may know, is a waxy, fatlike substance found in the body that helps us digest fats and strengthens cell membranes. Eighty percent of the body's cholesterol is produced by the liver, and the other 20 percent comes from a person's diet. When we have poor diets, our cholesterol levels go into un-healthy ranges.

Drawing from this five-pronged approach to examining the

wellness of the heart, I've established a spiritual checkup to help you determine the state of your heart—the home of your personal life. I have developed five major questions to correspond with the five tests cardiologists perform. Do your best to answer them honestly and accurately.

1. Have you had frequent (four or more) problems with forgiving someone within the past twenty-four months?

2. How quickly do you repent of your sins—immediately or a long time thereafter? How angry do you become when you see hypocrisy in your heart/life?

3. Do you regularly practice this biblical truth: "Confess your sins to each other . . . so that you may be healed" (James 5:16)? In other words, how transparent are you with heart issues?

4. How do you view the Bible? Do you feel that its teachings simply block you from doing what you want to do, or do they serve as an easy, do-it-yourself guide to effective living?

5. Do you consistently seek out and apply biblical principles in the ongoing activities of marriage, parenting, or business? In other words, when you deal with stress, what role do the Bible and its principles play?

How well did you do? If you found yourself becoming defensive, you're like a patient who argues with the doctor because he did not like the way the heart tests were administered. The problem, however, was not how the test was conducted, but the results that appeared. The result is the result. If you're not pleased with the outcome of this spiritual heart exam, it is a clear indicator that something is wrong with your heart. The good thing is that you caught the problem at this stage—before it has progressed further.

On the other hand, I'd like to congratulate you if you scored well on all five questions. This result shows that you have a healthy spiritual heart and that you're on your way to achieving a deeper level of intimacy with God.

If you're someone who did well on one or two of the test questions but scored low on the other three, you are likely someone who is hard on yourself, who actually passed the test. Your three negative responses could also mean that you are someone who needs rehabilitative work—and you know it. If you're too hard on yourself, a journey to the mountain of God will mellow you to the grace of God. If you're in need of rehabilitative work, the remainder of this chapter will serve you well.

Heart Rehabilitation

To rehabilitate the physical heart, you may think you're supposed to live in a cocoon, far away from any activity. But physicians recommend just the opposite. Dr. Kenneth H. Cooper, founder of the world-acclaimed Cooper Aerobics Center in Dallas, Texas, wrote: "Regular, medically supervised exercise is an integral part of most cardiac rehabilitation programs. The safety of exercising as part of a monitored rehabilitation program may be greater than exercise in the general population!"[2] Drawing again from the world of medicine to establish a parallel with spiritual heart rehabilitation, I affirm that you must perform exercise if your heart is to function properly as the home of your personal life.

If you did not fare well with the five questions, you may want to undergo some heart rehabilitation. The rehabilitative exercises that will help get you moving in the right direction are supervision and exercise.

The Role of Supervision

Dr. Cooper said that medically supervised exercise is a key component in rehabilitating the heart. Just as you cannot personally administer the five-pronged heart checkup in the physical sense, so you cannot evaluate your heart's motives in the spiritual sense. Although I've given you a spiritual heart test to help you determine where you are, that test is more accurate when someone other than yourself administers it.

You need feedback from family and friends, the people who have a good sense of the reasons for your behavior and actions. While I recognize that only God knows your heart fully, it is safe to say that the people closest to you are usually the ones who call your actions into question. Although they may not be 100 percent correct in their assessment of why you do some of the things you do, I suspect that they are not wrong 100 percent of the time either. I am sure that some of the time their suspicions, and perhaps outright accusations, about your actions—the ones stemming from a wounded or hardened heart—are absolutely correct. And this correction may have been brought to your attention before you even took the time to evaluate your own motives and intentions of your heart.

This is why I believe we need friends and relatives who can question our intent and the heart motivation driving our actions and judgments. If you really want to get perspective regarding the health of your heart, ask one of your friends what he or she thinks is behind your actions. Just come right out and ask: "What do you think my heart attitude is? Do you think my actions indicate bitterness? Do you think the condition of my heart shows a readiness to seek God?"

I am sure you will get an assortment of answers. Some answers will be out in left field, while others will be extremely accurate and insightful. Use the appropriate answers as a launching pad to exercise your heart. In order to avoid receiving a number of inaccurate answers, ask friends who have good judgment in understanding human behavior.

The Role of Exercise

The heart is a powerful muscle. Cardiovascular activity such as jogging, biking, and swimming exercises the heart. In the spiritual realm, activities such as submitting to the will of God, accepting responsibility for your mistakes, and committing to doing things God's way even when it hurts are various ways you exercise your heart.

Remember, your heart is the home of your personal life.

When God is in charge of your home, your life, and everything that you possess, you live another level of existence altogether. You are no longer a person driven and governed by the appetites of your flesh. Rather, you are a person who knows how to voluntarily bring your passions and appetites under the lordship of Jesus Christ. This ability demonstrates that you are governed by God's laws—morally, financially, and spiritually.

Someone who regularly and voluntarily chooses to obey God is someone who has a spiritually healthy heart. The ability to deny yourself for the purpose of bringing pleasure to God can occur only if you have regularly exercised your heart in the benefits of submission. David the psalmist understood this need for surrender to God when he wrote: "The sacrifices of God are a broken spirit; / a broken and contrite heart, O God, / you will not despise" (Ps. 51:17).

At this point in our daily reading, ask yourself: *Is my heart right with God? Have I exercised submission to God's Word, God's will, and God's way?* If not, don't try to justify your actions or lack thereof. Your response should be prayerful:

Lord, You are right in all of Your ways; I am wrong in trying to make the home of my personal life resistant to Your will. Please forgive me. Renew my heart that it may be tender toward You. I want a healthy heart, one that is eager to seek after You. I ask You these things in the name of Jesus. Amen.

Day 6: Steps to Rehearse

The condition of your heart is critical to the process of seeking God. A hardened heart is not inclined to draw near to the Lord because it is slow to repent of sins and to obey God. Test the state of your heart by rehearsing your answers to the critical questions I posed earlier. Let's examine the questions again.

1. How quickly do I repent of sins? Is it long after I commit the sin or quickly thereafter?

2. Do I allow others to see my heart by confessing some of my sins to them? The Bible says I can be healed by this practice (James 5:16).

3. Do I seek out and apply biblical principles in the ongoing activity of marriage, parenting, or business? When I deal with stress, what role do the principles of the Bible play?

Day 7

The Heart's Soil

Never before in the history of humanity had such a horde of people been on the threshold of encountering God collectively. Moses knew that if the children of Israel were to be changed due to this encounter with God, their hardened hearts needed to be tenderized. God knew it, too. This is precisely why His instructions to Moses specifically communicated that Moses was to take two days "and sanctify them" (Exod. 19:10 KJV). "Sanctify" means "to set apart an object from ordinary usage for special or religious purposes."[1] Without preparing the hearts of the Hebrews, Moses would not have been able to present them to the Lord, and they would not have been ready to receive from God when they met with Him.

Almost anyone can pray, read the Bible, and sing worship songs. Almost anyone can go to church and interact with the congregation. But not everyone can receive spiritual truth or insight about the nature of God or get a response from God that endears the heart and transforms the life. In order to receive from the Lord, your heart must first be prepared.

The prophet Jeremiah instructed his generation with these words:

This is what the LORD says to the men of Judah and to Jerusalem:
  "Break up your unplowed ground
    and do not sow among thorns.
  Circumcise yourselves to the LORD,
    circumcise your hearts,
  you men of Judah and people of Jerusalem,
    or my wrath will break out and burn like fire

> *because of the evil you have done—*
> *burn with no one to quench it."*

(Jeremiah 4:3–4)

Just as the people in that infant nation needed to prepare their hearts to seek God, so the established nation of Israelites had to go through the same process of breaking up the unplowed fields of their hardened hearts in order to seek God.

Hearts Can Get Hardened Really Fast

It doesn't take much to get a hard heart. Just live for a few weeks or months without pursuing God doggedly, and you'll wake up one day feeling estranged from God. It can happen to any one of us. You might think that living a life of sin is the way to get a hardened heart toward the Lord. You're right. But simply living without pursuing intimacy with God will get you a hardened heart also.

Godly people can grow cold toward the Lord if they become prone to distractions. In other words, when your faith is merely a routine or a cultural practice, you're on your way to becoming hardened. This is how much of Europe turned into a spiritually cold continent: Christianity simply became a cultural, nonrelational faith that the people pursued daily. The United States, too, is becoming immune to God, to the point where many Christians are adopting a nostalgic and cultural view of the Bible. We must fight against this trend by embracing biblical practices on a daily basis.

The world we live in has distractions at every turn. It's easy to veer off course in natural and spiritual pursuits. Let me show you how easy it is to wind up off course spiritually—answer this question: When was the last time you worshiped God with all your heart, soul, mind, and strength? This question is like an x-ray machine that reveals the essence of your spiritual life. Avoiding a hardened heart requires a conscious watchfulness of your inclinations. Now imagine how much easier it becomes to get a hardened heart once you add life's pressures to the mix.

One danger of a hardened heart is that it prevents you from receiving from the Lord. Jeremiah delivered his prophetic word to herdsmen and farmers. They understood the necessity of cultivating the land prior to sowing seeds. If the land was not properly tilled, the farmer's seeds would not be effectively planted. Hence, there would be no germination of seeds and no harvest. The farmer's work would have been in vain and his expectation of a harvest would have been futile. As the tilling and preparing of soil is critical to a forthcoming harvest, likewise, the cultivation of your heart is critical to achieving the desired result of intimacy with God.

The children of Israel would not have benefited from journeying to the mountain of God if their hearts weren't first cultivated to seek Him. What's the antidote to a hardened heart? Jesus answered this question through the parable of the sower.

Cultivating the Heart

A parable is more than just a story—it is an argument. In her book *Parables of Jesus: Introduction and Exposition,* Eta Linneman wrote, "A parable is an urgent endeavour on the part of the speaker towards the listener. The man who tells a parable wants to do more than utter something or make a communication. He wants to affect the other, to win his agreement, to influence his judgment in a particular direction, to force him to a decision, to convince him or prevail upon him."[2]

Imagine the great crowd that gathered to listen to Jesus. He knew that unless the people's hearts were in the right place, His words would be meaningless to them—even if He was God in flesh. To cultivate their hearts for receptivity of spiritual things, Jesus shared this argument.

> *Then he told them many things in parables, saying: "A farmer went out to sow his seed. As he was scattering the seed, some fell along the path, and the birds came and ate it up. Some fell on rocky places, where it did not have much soil. It sprang up quickly, because the soil*

was shallow. But when the sun came up, the plants were scorched, and they withered because they had no root. Other seed fell among thorns, which grew up and choked the plants. Still other seed fell on good soil, where it produced a crop—a hundred, sixty or thirty times what was sown. He who has ears, let him hear."

(Matthew 13:3–9)

In most of Jesus' parables we readers have to dissect the message and formulate an interpretation. This one, however, is different. Jesus gave the step-by-step analysis and explanation to His disciples. But before I unpack the meaning of the parable of the sower, I want to first point out that there are four different types of soils— each representing the human heart—in this poetic argument. Similarly, there are four types of readers reading this book. As you learn about these different perspectives, ask yourself: *Which one represents my heart?* More importantly, ask yourself: *Which one of the soils do I want to reflect my heart?*

Here is the meaning of the parable. Jesus said to His disciples,

Listen then to what the parable of the sower means: When anyone hears the message about the kingdom and does not understand it, the evil one comes and snatches away what was sown in his heart. This is the seed sown along the path. The one who received the seed that fell on rocky places is the man who hears the word and at once receives it with joy. But since he has no root, he lasts only a short time. When trouble or persecution comes because of the word, he quickly falls away. The one who received the seed that fell among the thorns is the man who hears the word, but the worries of this life and the deceitfulness of wealth choke it, making it unfruitful. But the one who received the seed that fell on good soil is the man who hears the word and understands it. He produces a crop, yielding a hundred, sixty or thirty times what was sown.

(Matthew 13:18–23)

This parable demonstrates how life's complications can so easily distract people's hearts from spiritual things. Notice that while describing the four different types of soil, Jesus never labeled the heart of the person as evil or bad. People fall prey to distracted hearts by merely giving more allegiance to their lives' priorities than to the pursuit of God. Again I ask you, which type of soil do you want to represent your heart?

Never mind the type of soil that your heart looks like currently. The more important matter is determining the type of soil that you want to start cultivating. This was precisely why God instructed Moses to sanctify the children of Israel. God knew the propensity of the human heart to stray from spiritual pursuits and get hardened through entanglement of daily living. Since He loved the Hebrew people, God was going to get them ready to seek Him by helping them cultivate their hearts toward spiritual pursuits.

Cultivating the Heart Is Your Job!

Jesus shared that the person who received the Word of God, or the one with the cultivated heart, produced a harvest yielding a crop that was thirty, sixty, or a hundred times what was sown. Note that in all four cases, the responsibility to receive the seed—the Word of God—was the soil's and not that of the one delivering the message. Let me make myself perfectly clear: *you* must take full responsibility for the state of your heart. Regardless of what is going on in your life right now, you must take charge of your heart's preparedness for spiritual things.

Cultivating the heart must start right this minute. If it doesn't, you will keep putting it off to another day and, as you know, that day will never come. Deciding to break up the hardness of your heart is like deciding to start a new diet. If the pain of being out of shape and overweight is not greater than the joy in eating the wrong foods, you will never start the diet and exercise program.

I know, because I recently lost sixty pounds over a ten-month period. I instituted a lifestyle change by exercising six days per week and eating healthily. I remember sharing this testimony with a registered dietician while on a national radio program. She asked me, "What was your epiphany?" I said, "Nothing happened that was a catalyst to my initiating this change. I just got tired of being out of shape and overweight." In the same way, if you're tired of having a hardened heart, make the decision right now that you're going to change.

Just as you can seldom tell how out of shape you are unless you glance at a photograph, diagnosing a hardened heart also calls for reflection. Looking at a personal photo causes you to recall the moments and the other meaningful dynamics of the scene, such as your mood, how you felt about your appearance, and so on. Similarly, when you reflect upon your perspective, behavior, or verbal responses in a personal encounter with another person, or a worship encounter with the Lord, you get a chance to measure your effectiveness. If it takes you a long time to offer an apology after you've wronged a number of people, you may be guilty of having a hardened heart. If you worship and praise God only in response to His blessings and not His Person, you may have a hardened heart. A hardened heart is evident when you have a slow or no response to living the way Jesus calls you to live.

If you're guilty of a hardened heart, find a quiet place in order to get alone with God. Repentance is needed. You have allowed yourself to get distracted by life's activities and busyness. If your heart looks like the hardened soil—where birds swooped down and ate the seeds—Jesus is available to help your heart become soft and fertile again. Your soil may be the result of an incorrect perspective you formed against God's Word. For example, if you frequently debate whether or not you're going to obey the Bible, your perspective calls for an adjustment. The Bible must become the guidebook by which you live. Fortunately, you can quickly change your perspective by acknowledging that God's Word is now your life's playbook because it works. It has the potency to bring fruitfulness to your life.

If your heart is like the rocky places—the type of soil that makes you unstable—decide today that you will embrace a relentless conviction about godly living. Conviction is not simply the ability to believe something, but the courage to die for something. God wants more than mere belief on your part. He wants to see within you a deep-rooted conviction that you're willing to lay down your life for the cause of Christ. God also wants to know that you want intimacy with Him more than you want your next salary increase or anything else.

If your heart is like the seed that fell among thorns—worries of this life—God wants to help you govern your life by biblical principles and not by schemes that promise quick results. Get-rich-quick schemes don't work. They are similar to fad diets: they seldom bring lasting results. The way to fruitfulness begins when you get in a quiet place and ask God to do a work of grace in your heart. Pray this prayer:

> *Heavenly Father, it has been a while since I really cried out to You. Today I'm asking for nothing except to have a heart that is cultivated and receptive to Your purposes. Please break up the clods in my heart. Pour out Your Spirit upon me that I may enjoy seeking Your face as I used to. Remove the rocks and thorns from my life that I may eagerly await Your blessings. May my hardened heart become soft and prepared to receive Your Word, daily. I ask You these things in the name of Your dear Son, Jesus. Amen.*

Day 7: Steps to Rehearse

Our hearts can easily become hardened toward God and spiritual things. Christianity can easily become a part of our culture rather than a daily source of power. To avoid getting a hardened heart, consider these practices:

1. The danger of a hardened heart is that it prevents you from receiving from the Lord. What steps have you implemented to avoid this trap?

2. What are two practices in your life that would slowly make Christianity a routine if you do not avoid them?

3. What action can you take right now to begin the cultivation of your heart?

Day 8

A Pure Heart

Over fifteen years ago, I had my first speaking engagement in Africa. I was invited to the nations of Nigeria and South Africa. Since apartheid had only been recently lifted, many African countries were still not allowing travel directly to South Africa. I had to fly from Nigeria to Cairo, Egypt, and then continue on to Johannesburg, South Africa. The flight schedules, however, meant I had to spend one whole day in Egypt before I could go on to Johannesburg.

Before I left the United States, a number of veteran missionaries counseled me to write "teacher" on the customs document when traveling to strongly Muslim countries. The missionaries' experiences indicated that many Muslim countries and other nations that were antagonistic to the gospel of Jesus Christ were extremely difficult to enter when one listed his profession as "pastor." The label "teacher" was safe. I *am* a teacher. I teach the Bible every week to my congregation and via books just like the one you're reading.

The moment my feet hit the Egyptian shore, I was leery about what would happen. I wrote "teacher" on the customs document as I was encouraged to do. Nothing happened. I was given clear and easy passage through customs and immediately went to the baggage claim area to retrieve my luggage.

With luggage in hand, I was suddenly accosted by a young taxicab driver who spoke in broken English. Once we understood one another, my luggage was loaded onto his taxi. Before I got into the car, he asked me, "Sir, what kind of work do you do?" I remembered that my answer was to be "teacher." So that's what I said. He then asked, "What do you teach?" I said, "I teach people about Jesus Christ and His love." He looked at me with innocent eyes and then asked, "Teach me about Jesus, but don't charge me. Don't charge me anything."

His naiveté was shocking. He had no reference point for the gospel. He had never heard the message of Jesus Christ. His entire world was consumed with Islamic doctrine. His worldview knew nothing of mine. His question revealed the purity of his heart with the need for forgiveness and acceptance of the Savior. Suddenly I was confronted with the reality that my words about Jesus Christ were the first, and maybe the only ones, he would ever hear.

The Picture of a Pure Heart

That young man's plea revealed the picture of innocence and a pure heart. A pure heart in this context is one that does not assume anything, but one that is eager to learn. This level of receptivity is not tainted with preconceived notions or a bad experience with some other Bible teacher. And this kind of purity reflects the spiritual place where God wanted the children of Israel to be when they met with Him at His mountain. But first, they would have to take a couple of days to sanctify themselves (Exod. 19:10).

The process of sanctification—of purifying oneself for God—is shown in Exodus to require time. Quite obviously, sanctification is a spiritual action that can occur within a split second—especially when God is helping to facilitate repentance and forgiveness. For example, when Joshua led the Israelites, he said, "Sanctify yourselves: for to morrow the LORD will do wonders among you" (Josh. 3:5 KJV). We see in Joshua 3 that sanctification occurred that very day. It was not a protracted process but a quick action.

Yet, in the Exodus passage, God told Moses, "Go to the people and consecrate [sanctify] them today and tomorrow" (19:10). Why the need for multiple days when the process of sanctification technically occurs upon repentance? Although sanctification can occur in the instant it takes to repent, sanctification over a multiple-day period may reflect the time a worshiper would need to feel contrition and deep sorrow for his sin. These emotional feelings often precede repentance and the forsaking of one's sins.

When a protracted time of sanctification is occurring, the person is undergoing a deep cleansing of the heart. To journey to the mountain of God, a partially clean heart won't do. That kind of heart is divided. Part of it yearns for the courts of the Lord while there's also a tug for the courts of the world. Divided devotion is no devotion at all. God wants and deserves total devotion.

Steps to a Pure Heart

David illustrated in Psalm 51 how he purified his heart before the Lord. The occasion that precipitated this heart-revealing psalm was David's repenting of adultery and murder. David had had an affair with the beautiful, married Bathsheba. Upon learning of her pregnancy, David had her husband, Uriah, murdered.

In looking at the first two verses of the psalm of repentance, you will see that David wanted to repent and sanctify himself wholeheartedly, just as he had wanted to wholeheartedly commit his sin. Here is what David shared with the nation in song.

Have mercy on me, O God,
*   according to your unfailing love;*
according to your great compassion
*   blot out my transgressions.*
Wash away all my iniquity
*   and cleanse me from my sin.*
(vv.1–2)

In David's cry for a pure heart, he asked God to: blot out his transgressions, wash away his iniquity, and cleanse him of his sin. All of these processes drew language from the task of laundering clothes. David's heart was stained like that of a garment. A simple act of repentance was inadequate. He had learned to live in his sin, and only a deep cleansing would return him to having a pure heart before God.

Notice the three actions and how they correlate to the area of need. David used the terms "blot out," "wash away," and "cleanse" to correlate with "transgression," "iniquity," and "sin." Let's explore these meanings so that you can apply the same principles to your life—even if your heart is not as far gone as David's was.

"Blot Out My Transgressions"

In biblical days, when a launderer wanted to remove a stain from a garment, he first blotted it. The process of blotting consisted of wiping, rubbing, and stroking the stain to erase it.[1] David was serious about the stain in his heart. He had fallen away from God; his heart was hardened to the point where he was able to sin recklessly. Now, he was asking God to wipe and stroke his heart until the transgression of his soul was removed.

Transgression is "a premeditated crossing of the line of God's law, a rebellious act of rejecting God's authority."[2] It is the attitude that says, "I know that what I'm doing is wrong in the sight of God, but I don't care!" David had so fallen into waywardness in the interior of his life that he eventually became comfortable living in a state of transgression against God.

David's only recourse was to ask God to pick up his heart like a soiled garment and beat it against a rock. This is a radical approach. In fact, the Old Testament scholar Derek Kidner said, "David was comparing himself to a foul garment needing to be washed and washed" vigorously, because it was badly stained.[3] If you really mean business with God, and even though you have been living in a willful state of defiance against the Lord, you will not waver in performing this action—asking God for a thorough cleansing.

I have been there. It's not pretty when you stop caring what God thinks about your actions. But the road to intimacy requires the drastic action of saying to God, "Take my heart and beat it against Your rock until the transgression is gone."

"Wash Away All My Iniquity"

David did not stop there. His passion for a pure heart led him to a second step toward sanctification. He asked God to wash away *all* of his sin. The term "wash away" is also a launderer's term. It calls "treading with the feet, kneading, and beating clothes in cold water."[4] The Hebrew scholar J. J. Stewart Perowne comments that to wash away meant "the washing of dirty spotted garments."[5] David recognized that his heart had become spotted with iniquity.

Iniquity is a different form of sin from transgression. Someone engaged in iniquity is more prone to human trickery, craftiness, in fulfilling his or her carnal pleasures. David was finally being honest. He had been very deceitful about the way he seduced Bathsheba and how he schemed for Uriah to be murdered.

David knew that his heart required a deep soaking in order to have the deception washed from his soul. This kind of soaking is not a quick job of asking for forgiveness in a twenty-second prayer. This is a protracted action of soul-searching and inspecting each of one's deceptive actions with contrition and repentance. Although David had sinned greatly before God, he then repented greatly before God.

"Cleanse Me from My Sin"

You would think that all that repentance was enough, but not so. David added one other step in his desire to have a pure heart. He asked God—the heavenly Launderer—to cleanse him from his sin. "Cleanse" is another launderer's term that in a general sense means the removal of stain. This cleansing action brought the launderer very close to the stain in an attempt to wash it away. David described his stain as "sin." The word *sin* means "the divinely appointed goal that has been set for us has been completely missed."[6] The historical foundation of the word occurred when an archer shot his arrow toward the target. When he missed, it was said that he sinned.

David was asking God to take His mallet and beat the stain of sin out of his heart so that he would no longer miss the mark of righteousness. David was acknowledging that he had veered off course. Repentance meant that David no longer wanted to be off track but to walk and live the course God planned for him. This is where true repentance should lead us: back on track with God.

To journey to the mountain of God, you need a pure heart. This will keep you moving in the right direction—God's direction for your life. This is precisely why Jesus said, "Blessed are the pure in heart, / for they will see God" (Matt. 5:8). To experience intimacy with God is, in essence, seeing God. With a pure heart you are assured you will see God.

If your heart is pure, repentance is easy. Making changes that promote godliness is easy. Accepting godly correction, although painful, is easy. This is why sometimes a few days are required to repent and purify oneself. God wants pure vessels—people who can fellowship with Him in the beauty of His holiness.

Day 8: Steps to Rehearse

David knew how to sin with the best of them. Conversely, David knew how to repent with the best of them. He sought God for a pure heart. David became vulnerable with God by asking God to make the following things take place in his heart:

1. David asked God to blot out his transgression.

2. David invited the Lord to wash away all of his iniquity.

3. Finally, David prayed for God to cleanse him from his sin. Take a few moments alone with God and ask Him to perform these three sanctifying steps in your heart right now.

How to Handle Conviction

One of the most difficult things we deal with is the conviction of the Holy Spirit. I'm referring to the feelings that surface in your heart after the Holy Spirit points out something in your life that is unacceptable to God. What do you do at that point? You have a choice. You can accept God's correction regarding your sin by repenting and striving to change, or you can decide to do nothing about the problem. How do you handle conviction?

In readying the Israelites to journey to the mountain of God, as we've seen, Moses was to "go to the people and consecrate [sanctify] them today and tomorrow" (Exod. 19:10). God knew the ex-slaves needed time to wash their hearts before they received the spiritual experiences that would shape their destiny. Journeying to the mountain of God is a destiny-shaping time.

As a result of your communion with God, you will gain clearer insight into God and His purposes for your life. But before that can occur, the Holy Spirit will deal with your heart about wrong decisions, ungodly actions, improper motives, and other inclinations and behavior that ultimately pull you away from God. This evaluating of the heart and recognizing ungodly behavior is referred to as *coming under conviction*. How you respond to conviction is an indicator of your moral maturity and your moral flexibility to God's adjustments.

Confronted by Truth

Recently I counseled a young Christian woman in my congregation that living with her boyfriend is morally wrong. According to God's Word, fornication—sex outside of marriage—is a sin. Phyllis (pseudonym) looked at me as if I were speaking a foreign language. Apparently, she had never heard God's moral law banning premarital sex. I gently shared with her that if she really meant business with God, she had to make a choice in how she cherished her body. After I walked Phyllis through several Bible verses outlining God's moral high ground as it relates to human sexuality, she became convicted and agreed that there was a better way to live. To my surprise, Phyllis quickly decided that she would move in with her sister until she and her boyfriend were married.

Upon hearing her plans, I thought, *We'll see.* I was quite skeptical because I've seen people who did not handle conviction in a timely fashion. They simply learned to live with the knowledge that their actions were unacceptable to God. They applied philosophical justifications and other analytical rationalizations that kept them from changing their lifestyles.

To my surprise, my skepticism was proven wrong. The very next week Phyllis pulled me to the side and shared, "I have moved in with my sister. Thanks for telling me that fornication was not the Bible's way. I want to honor God with my body. My boyfriend wants to do the same. Since he couldn't afford the apartment on his salary alone, he moved back in with his parents. This will afford us the opportunity to pay off some bills and save up for our marriage."

I walked away with a big smile on my face, saying, "There goes a young lady who's going places in God."

Armed with a Piece of Truth

Truth is powerful! It arms you to know what course of action to take. Truth is freeing! Once you know the truth, Jesus said, it "will set you free" (John 8:32). Responding positively to conviction is a liberating exercise. Conviction of the Holy Spirit is counseling aimed at remedying your moral and ethical dilemmas. Why ignore it?

According to Jesus, one of the Holy Spirit's most significant job descriptions is to "convict the world of guilt in regard to sin and righteousness and judgment" (John 16:8). Conviction reveals you are guilty of violating one of God's laws. Becoming aware of your infraction but choosing to ignore it is a dangerous practice. Imagine that God is working to equip you to live successfully, but instead of accepting His help, you say, "No thanks." That would be insane. But many people, good people, have learned to ignore the conviction of the Holy Spirit.

Excuses are so easy to make. Certainly when I confronted Phyllis with the truth of God's Word, she could have reasoned away her conviction: "Well, Pastor, my boyfriend and I are getting married in twelve months. God understands." She also could have promised not to engage in sex until the marriage date—a year away—while she and her boyfriend lived together. She could have even used the excuse of all time among live-in lovers: "It's more economical to live together than it is to get two apartments." Phyllis chose none of these options because they would have shown that she was ignoring the conviction of the Holy Spirit.

Conviction of the Spirit is synonymous with the wisdom of God. When God convicts a person of sin, He is sharing His wisdom with the individual. Through conviction, God silently but clearly communicates that He offers a better road to travel, a better way to live, and a better course of action to take. How we respond to that advice is proof positive of our moral strength.

Oftentimes, however, people would rather live in the darkness—the absence of moral illumination—than the light of the Word of God. This is precisely why Jesus said,

This is the verdict: Light has come into the world, but men loved darkness instead of light because their deeds were evil. Everyone who does evil hates the light, and will not come into the light for fear that his deeds will be exposed. But whoever lives by the truth comes into the light, so that it may be seen plainly that what he has done has been done through God.

(John 3:19–21)

Don't Fear the Truth

Change can be frightening at times—especially when making righteous choices has financial implications and the money seems to be out of view. The conviction of the Holy Spirit can cost us. Yet, it is far cheaper to live the way God wants you to live. Keep in mind that God has an affordable solution for whatever He's convicting you about. The truth must not be feared. Remember the words of Jesus: "The truth will set you free."

Don't Ignore God's Conviction

Truth is never to be ignored. Regardless of your circumstances, you should never put truth on the back burner with the excuse: *I'm waiting for a better time to practice it.* When God confronts you about a sinful area of your life, respond to His desires by making the necessary changes. Although God is patient, gentle, and compassionate, we ought not to take advantage of such wonderful attributes. It shows a lack of appreciation on our part. We should follow conviction with action.

In counseling one of the men in my congregation, I saw that the Holy Spirit was clearly convicting him concerning his diet and weight. I cautioned him to not ignore the conviction: "Make changes in your diet and adopt an exercise program quickly," I told him. "If God has been dealing with your heart, don't delay—especially when you know God has repeatedly warned you." One of the worst things to do is to learn to live in conviction. You can become immune to the convictions of the Spirit when you begin to ignore them.

Although the Holy Spirit demonstrates a stubborn love, or put another way, a deep commitment, to helping us change, the Holy Spirit is not a pest. That is, the Holy Spirit's job is not to bother you continuously about your need for change. This cannot be the operational format of the Spirit of God. We are called to maturity in our relationship with God, and pestering will not facilitate that outcome. Instead, it may create animosity and emotional distance from God. Certainly the fault is ours when we refuse to change.

We can avoid dysfunctional outcomes to conviction if we learn to respond quickly to the Holy Spirit's nudges. To fail to heed these promptings will result in spiritual callousness to God's leadership.

About ten years ago, the Holy Spirit was convicting me regarding my diet. Since my weight wasn't an issue to me back then, I kept blowing off the conviction with the thought, *I'll start eating right next week.* The problem was that "next week" never came. I learned to ask God to bless my food quickly without reflecting for a split second upon the goodness of God.

I finally recognized that I was learning to live with conviction. I knew I was wrong, but I was too lazy to change. Every meal was a reminder that I was living outside of God's choice for my life, but I was not making the required adjustments to enjoy the pleasure that obedience brings.

It was not until my weight started becoming a problem, and I began noticing little health challenges, that I made an effort to change. Although I have finally got it right, I understand how scary it is to live with conviction. I felt alienated from God because I was ignoring His desires. To know that my unwillingness to obey was affecting my intimacy with God was frightening.

I hope that you never find yourself in that awkward spot. If you are there right now, the solution is twofold: First, ask God for His forgiveness. Second, make the necessary changes immediately. Do what the Lord wants you to do. Go where He wants you to go. Say what He wants you to say. Free your soul from the bondage of disobedience. Respond positively to the Lord's conviction and say to yourself, *I'm free at last!*

Day 9: Steps to Rehearse

Conviction is God's way of introducing positive change. How you respond to it is important. Equally important is *when* you respond to His conviction. A quick response and an appropriate adjustment enables you to accelerate your spiritual intimacy with God, which will result in a shorter journey to the mountain of the Lord.

1. Conviction occurs when the Lord makes you feel awkward about some area of your life in which He wants you to make changes.

2. The Holy Spirit's job is to convict you and the rest of the world of guilt in regard to sin and righteousness and judgment.

3. Don't delay in introducing positive change when the Holy Spirit convicts you. This is when real moral growth begins.

Getting Rid of the Excess Weight

After a recent teaching opportunity in Wellington, New Zealand, I flew to Brisbane, Australia, via one of New Zealand's discounted airlines—Freedom Air. Every time he spoke of the airline, the pastor of the church in New Zealand, who also was the one who arranged my flight, told me that I was in for a "treat." Since he said it sarcastically, I didn't know what in the world to expect. I thought maybe I'd be flying outside, on the wing of the plane.

When I arrived at the airport, the "treat" began. Immediately I learned that my bags had to be a certain weight, which is understandable and normal. However, the weight restriction on Freedom Air was lower than that of other airlines. I guess that having no bags at all is really flying with freedom. To my dismay, my computer bag was too heavy as a carry-on item, even when it was completely emptied. After I pleaded with the agent, I was able to carry on my computer bag and its normal contents, albeit for a slight fee. But I had to give all of my other property, including gifts, local newspapers, CDs, and other small items to my New Zealand friends. I had to get rid of all "excess" items to board the plane.

Similarly, taking the journey to the mountain of God requires getting rid of all of your excess baggage—namely, the things in your life that keep weighing you down, pulling you off course, and burdening your heart with moral confusion. Moses had to take two days to help the Israelites lighten their spiritual loads in order to encounter God. You must do the same thing.

This requires a close inspection of your heart by the Spirit of God to ensure that you're not sneaking things in. I had to literally lighten my load when I boarded Freedom Air. Even though I did not want to give away my valuable items, I had to in order to meet the airline's weight restrictions. On reflection, I realized that everything I left behind was unessential to my trip and the quality of my life. Yet, prior to my encounter with Freedom Air, I would have never believed it.

Lay Aside the Excess Weight

That's how life is. We think we need things, situations, activities, and even our vices in order to survive and enjoy life. But when the pressure is on, we learn that all those things were nonessential to healthy living. What is weighing you down? Have you made a full inspection of your life, your heart, and your emotions? If not, you could be hindering yourself from really soaring in your spiritual life because of excess baggage that you've become attached to or unwittingly accumulated in your life.

The writer of Hebrews encouraged us to lay aside our extra baggage with these words:

> *Therefore, since we are surrounded by such a great cloud of witnesses, let us throw off everything that hinders and the sin that so easily entangles, and let us run with perseverance the race marked out for us. Let us fix our eyes on Jesus, the author and perfecter of our faith, who for the joy set before him endured the cross, scorning its shame, and sat down at the right hand of the throne of God.*

(12:1–2)

The writer drew from the world of sports to make his point understandable and memorable. As a runner, you need to do four things if you want to complete the race marked out for you: acknowledge that spectators are watching, throw off the hindrances and entanglements of sin, run with perseverance, and fix your eyes on Jesus. All of these points are essential in readying you to journey to the mountain of God.

Be Conscious of the Spectators

You've heard the story: When the thief broke into the home, little did he know that he was going to be accosted by a talking parrot. The parrot said to him, "Look out . . . Moses is watching you." The thief laughed and said, "What's your name?" The parrot replied, "I'm Joshua. But look out . . . Moses is watching you." The thief cynically asked, "Who is Moses?" The parrot said, "Moses is the Rottweiler standing behind you."

Sometimes we forget that others are observing our spiritual walk. In Hebrews 12, the writer referred to a footrace where "a cloud of witnesses" or throngs of people were viewing the games from their seats and cheering on the runners. The runners were not looking at the spectators, because their eyes were fixed on the prize. And the guys who had already finished their legs of the relay race were viewing those to whom the batons had been passed.

People are watching you every day to see how you are progressing in your spiritual life. Are you growing? Have you settled into a stale, lukewarm relationship with God? Or have you thrown aside some baggage in order to lighten your load while moving to the next stage of spiritual maturity? I trust that your spectators will testify to the latter being the case.

Throw Off the Hindrances and Entanglements

Had I boarded Freedom Air with all those gifts and small items, they would have constantly demanded my attention, bogged me down, and kept me always juggling things from one hand to the other. The airline's restrictions really liberated me from the entanglements of nonessentials. Still, it was hard to part with those items. Sometimes we need someone detached from the affairs of our lives to spot the nonessentials we put up with daily. In the Hebrews passage, the hindrances and entanglements were connected with sin—actions that cause one to miss the mark of righteousness.

Sin is deceptive. You become more and more entangled with it the longer you are involved. It's like soap operas. Talk to people who are hooked on the plots and characters of soap operas: it is extremely hard to pry them away from these shows. It's sad to think about these people going to bed with the idea, *I can't wait until tomorrow afternoon comes. What is Jane going to do when she finds out that her father-in-law loves the gal at the newspaper stand?* This kind of addict lives for the drama the program creates. This person has become entangled.

The solution to any ungodly entanglement is repentance. Repentance is not an emotional response to the need to abandon a sin or an error. Neither is repentance connected with the idea of doing penance or making satisfactory actions in response to committing particular sins. The New Testament scholar William Douglas Chamberlain points out that true "repentance is the reorientation of a personality with reference to God and his purpose." Chamberlain adds, "A wrong attitude toward God and man leads to wrong actions toward God and man. A transformation of the mind transforms the man; a transformation of the man transforms his conduct."[1]

Throwing off your hindrances and becoming disentangled from sin calls for this kind of radical reorientation and transformation. You must see things from God's point of view. God is right and you are wrong—end of discussion. Anything more is going to be a plea on your part to justify the actions in your life that fall short of the standard of God. Sin must be destroyed by repentance. The mountain of God must be approached, and the journey requires a light load.

Run with Perseverance

In preparing to run my first marathon—26.2 grueling miles—I was told by seasoned marathoners that the race has two major components: the physical and the mental. To complete the race with dignity, I needed to do physical preparation for at least four to six months prior to the marathon. And I had to be prepared to know what I was going to fix my mind on when the actual race day came, I was on mile fifteen, and a mile-long hill was in front of me. Well, the advice is that I must persevere by thinking happy thoughts: the finish line, a tall glass of water, or whatever else would ease the pain. Rather than concocting something during the competition, the expert marathoners say, "You learn perseverance skills *before* race day. You learn these skills during the five months of training."

Armed with that advice, I started training myself on what to think about when the actual physical run gets tough. I just came back from running ten miles of hills. It was hard going, but I persevered by thinking how I could add a paragraph in this book about perseverance, drawing the example from my morning run. It worked.

In order to begin persevering in your life, which may feel like a marathon, lay aside unnecessary weights and complications by asking yourself: *Is my tiredness temporary? Can I hang in there a little longer? If I quit now, what will I lose out on?* You can increase your ability to persevere by remembering that blessings come to the one who endures temporary hardships because of the splendid prize that is forthcoming.

Fix Your Eyes on Jesus

A competitive runner must have a set reward that spurs him on to the finish line. The Bible motivates us in our spiritual lives to fix our eyes on Jesus. In journeying to the mountain of God, the fixed point is Jesus. You want to fellowship with Jesus, enjoy Jesus, understand Jesus, and grow in intimacy with Jesus.

Your eyes are not to turn to somewhere or someone else. The New Testament scholar Leon Morris comments on this Hebrews 12 passage: "It is he [Jesus] toward whom we run. There must be no divided attention."[2]

The main reason Jesus is the sole focal point is because He is the Author and Perfecter of our faith. He is the one who first walked the way of faith and brought it to full completion. The goal of pleasing Jesus is more than satisfactory motivation for us to finish our race.

Are You Ready?

At this point in our study, your heart should be squeaky clean and ready to take the journey to the mountain of God. You have repented of your sins, laid aside all of the excess weight, and now you're ready to draw closer to God. Remember, your eyes should be fixed on Jesus, not on what He can do for you, or what you can get from Him. The goal is to achieve a greater intimacy with the Lord. Everything else that you might receive on this spiritual journey is nonessential to the overall objective of drawing closer to God.

Congratulations! You have just finished the second step, or the end of the tenth day, in the journey to the mountain of God!

Day 10: Steps to Rehearse

Repentance is one of God's greatest gifts to the human race. It frees us from carrying the excess baggage that sin creates. Strive to get free and stay free!

1. Repentance is the reorientation of a personality with reference to God and His purpose. Therefore, repent as often as you feel the need for reorientation.

2. Those who run the spiritual race do so successfully because they: acknowledge that spectators are watching, throw off the hindrances and entanglements of sin, run with perseverance, and fix their eyes on Jesus.

3. Repentance is not necessarily emotional. It is making a 180-degree turn that leads toward full obedience to God's laws. If you have not repented of your hidden sins, please take a moment and find a quiet place to pray. Once there, ask the Lord to help you remove all of the excess baggage and cleanse your heart with His forgiveness and love.

Step 3

Valuing the Fear of the Lord

Better a little with the fear of the LORD
than great wealth with turmoil.
(Proverbs 15:16)

Day 11

The Fear of the Lord

I am a staunch advocate for honesty—especially in dealing with God and His house. My life before Christianity had few boundaries. I did what I wanted to do when I wanted to do it. But following my acceptance of Christ, I valued the joy associated with pleasing God. I also adopted a simple discipline very early in my discipleship: *David, don't fool around with God.* This was a way I reminded myself to fear the Lord. Even to this very day, after some twenty-five years of walking with the Lord, I still have a healthy fear of God.

As a pastor, I get the firsthand opportunity to instruct, coach, and guide others into adopting the value of fearing the Lord. While some people understand the need for fearing God and value it dearly, others merely look at God as a new toy. God has ways of correcting this perspective. Let me warn you: it's not pretty, but it works. God will be feared one way or another.

God told Moses to sanctify the children of Israel (Exod. 19:10). Then God gave Moses another set of instructions to pass on to them:

> *Put limits for the people around the mountain and tell them, "Be careful that you do not go up the mountain or touch the foot of it. Whoever touches the mountain shall surely be put to death. He shall surely be stoned or shot with arrows; not a hand is to be laid on him. Whether man or animal, he shall not be permitted to live." Only when the ram's horn sounds a long blast may they go up to the mountain.*
>
> (Exodus 19:12–13)

The boundaries God verbalized created a healthy sense of awe, respect, and understanding among the children of Israel. If they ignored those strong words, the result would be death. But these were not the only words God wanted relayed to them. If this were so, the "fear of the Lord" would mean only the terror and dread of God. The people would not have wanted anything to do with Him because, without additional words of affirmation, He would have appeared brutal. No, God did not want the Hebrews to view Him as a despotic deity. Not only because He wasn't, but especially because He was (and is) loving, kind, and slow to anger.

The other words God had already communicated to the Israelites: that they could be His treasured possession and He had carried them on eagles' wings and brought them to Himself (Exod. 19:4–5). Therefore, it is unmistakable that the boundaries God set had nothing to do with creating a sense of dread but rather with preventing the people from being harmed by the power of His holiness.

God wanted to fellowship with His people without their getting hurt. Real intimacy with God, however, could not occur unless they valued the fear of the Lord. The Bible uses the term "fear of the LORD" to mean reverence, honor, and respect. In Old Testament literature the phrase also meant someone who has "true religion." We saw this point illustrated in the days of King Jehoshaphat. In the appointment of judges, he commanded, "Now let the fear of the LORD be upon you. Judge carefully, for with the LORD our God there is no injustice or partiality or bribery" (2 Chron. 19:7).

In the New Testament, the term also signified Christians who held a reverence for God's awesomeness. The book of Acts cites: "Then the church throughout Judea, Galilee and Samaria enjoyed a time of peace. It was strengthened; and encouraged by the Holy Spirit, it grew in numbers, living in the fear of the Lord" (Acts. 9:31). We see that a whole community of believers lived in the awesomeness of God. The result of this choice was strength, encouragement from the Holy Spirit, and numerical growth of the church's membership.

Living in the Fear of the Lord

Living in the fear of the Lord is a choice. Not every Christian selects this option. Some, as I shared in the opening of this chapter, choose to play games. They put on a facade in public, but privately they see God as a casual friend—someone they don't go out of their way to see. If they bump into God, they are polite and respectful, but the visit is short and courteous.

Is that the way you relate to God? I trust not. That kind of person would not dare pick up a book like this one because he or she would view it as crossing the line. He or she would no longer consider God safe. It would be too uncomfortable because of the changes that God would promote. On the other hand, someone who is willing to transform his or her casual relationship with God into one of passionate intimacy will find great encouragement from this book, because it outlines specific steps to achieving that kind of relationship with the Lord.

The phrase "fear of the LORD" appears some thirty times in the King James Version of the Bible. In order to understand this phrase's meaning and how we can apply its benefits to our journey, let's take a closer look. Since God introduced the subject as He was preparing to meet with the children of Israel at His mountain, He must have seen that fear was a vital ingredient to spiritual intimacy. Respect, honor, regard, and awe are critical to new relationships that have a long-term goal.

Where Is the Relationship Going?

When Fred approached me about his troubled relationship with his girlfriend, Mary (both pseudonyms), I asked if he respected her. He said he had been going out with her for four years, but they rarely agreed on anything. I pointed out to Fred that he did not answer my question. I repeated, "Do you respect her?" He searched for words but responded only, "Apparently not."

My next question was: "Why are you trying to make something work that lacks the innate ingredients to endure the normal challenges most marriages face [i.e., money issues, in-laws and out-laws, parenting challenges, and so on]? Either you respect her, or you should end the relationship and save both of you from additional heartaches."

My directness surprised him. He did not expect a pastor to lay it all on the line like that. But I had witnessed enough troubled relationships to see that this one was headed for a rocky future.

This was what God was doing with the Israelites. He had just led them out of the misery of a slave relationship with the Egyptians, and now He wanted them to become acquainted with the values of respect, honor, and appreciation. These virtues are nowhere to be found in a slave-master relationship. But they are critical to a loving relationship between God and His creation.

We humans tend to project our feelings about a failed critical relationship onto another key relationship, even though one has absolutely nothing to do with the other. One day, a woman approached me at church as I was walking into the sanctuary. She said, "I'm mad at you." "Why?" I asked. (I had never had a conversation with this woman before, but she had been visiting Christ Church.) She said, "You look like my ex-husband."

I walked away thinking, *That's strange. She's going to attempt to deal with me the way she dealt with her ex-husband just because we resemble one another.* Although this response is immature, it demonstrates an unusual course of behavior; and while it is seldom verbalized this way, many people subconsciously subscribe to this same practice.

How many times do you see someone take a guarded posture with a total stranger because he or she was hurt in a previous relationship? I understand the need to protect oneself against future emotional pain, but suspicion and guardedness point to a weakness in our ability to build strong relationships. God does not want us to use these debilitating habits in the way we relate to Him. This is why we must explore the subject of the fear of the Lord—to learn what we need to correct in our thinking about God.

I once found myself constantly in conflict with a female church leader named Susan (pseudonym). After one of my discussions with Susan, I asked my wife to evaluate the words I had used, hoping that some tidbit of wisdom would surface to aid me in dealing with her. But to no avail. Marlinda thought I had handled things well.

I was hoping and praying that I was the culprit; that way, at least I could correct the matter. I even asked Susan: "Have I offended you in any way? Please tell me so that I can make things right." Every time she answered, "You didn't do anything, Pastor. Everything is fine." All along, I knew that everything wasn't fine.

About one year later, Susan and her husband moved out of state to be closer to their family. When they returned to New Jersey for a visit, Susan and her husband scheduled an appointment with me.

I wondered what they wanted to discuss. I obliged them and opened my schedule. After we greeted one another, Susan handed me a letter. She took the time to craft her thoughts rather than struggle in front of me to communicate her pent-up feelings. The letter shared how she had been extremely mean toward me while at the church and now she wanted to apologize and explain her behavior. Susan said that when she was growing up, her mother forced her to speak properly—no slang—and behave above the call of normalcy. She was even forced to eat in a certain formal way.

Susan finally rebelled against her mother and her style of doing things. And when she came to Christ Church, I reminded her of the very things she was not. I speak articulately and perform with a certain level of excellence. Even the way I eat reminds Susan of what she never achieved. So, unconsciously she took out her childhood frustrations on me.

I thanked Susan for sharing her heart with me and clearing up the pain in our relationship. The lesson taught me that unresolved conflicts will surface in new relationships unless we deal with them adequately. God did not want the past conflict between the Hebrews and their ex-slave masters to surface as disrespect and dishonor toward Him. So, He had Moses introduce and teach the fear of the Lord to the children of Israel. They were to hold God in awe and respect because of His love and commitment to them.

Day 11: Steps to Rehearse

The fear of the Lord is an invaluable trait to learn and employ in your daily life. Through the fear of the Lord you will learn:

1. That we are to honor, respect, and hold God in awe. We are not to view Him as a despotic ruler because that is not who He is.

2. Respect is a key foundation to a long-lasting relationship.

3. We should be careful not to project failed relationships onto God. He did not fail us—others did. God deserves to always be treated with respect and honor.

Learning the Fear of the Lord

The fear of the Lord is one of the principal ways God influences the behavior of human beings. I found this out during a missionary trip to Kenya. On the last day of the trip I read the local newspaper as I ate breakfast. That day, the headline read: "*Saba Saba.*" Since I didn't know Swahili, I asked the Kenyan waitress what these words meant. She laughed and walked away. I didn't know what to make of her response, but I figured that I would soon find out its meaning.

Fortunately, when my host picked me up in the hotel lobby, he explained the whole thing. *Saba Saba* means "seven seven." The date was July seventh—the seventh day of the seventh month of the year. But, he explained, the focus was not merely the date. *Saba Saba* was the anniversary of a political uprising that took place in Kenya some years ago.

My visit was during election time in Kenya, and a faction of the country was angry that there were not more voting options. Hence, an obscure party hired people to create trouble in the country in order to demonstrate that the ruling party did not have the nation under control. The trouble this renegade group created encompassed death threats, vandalism, robbery, arson, and only God knows what other type of mayhem.

As my host drove toward the airport on *Saba Saba,* we had to circumvent fires and downed telephone poles in the middle of the road. At one spot on the highway, a group of teenage boys ran out of the bushes toward our car. They all held rocks, preparing to stone our vehicle. I started rubbing my hands together as I envisioned some type of excitement. I thought we were going to have to physically fight our way through, and having grown up in New York City, I felt up to the challenge.

The host pastor reached into the glove compartment of the car. I hoped he was getting a gun, but to my surprise he pulled out a large, family-sized Bible. My heart sank. Then the pastor held up the Bible to the windshield, exposing the spine where the boldly printed title could be easily read. The gang of teenagers quickly waved us to pass on in peace. There I realized firsthand how the fear of the Lord affects people's behavior. Those boys, although unruly, had a knowledge and fear of God made clear by their respect for the Bible and the people who honor its teachings.

The Role of the Fear of the Lord

Solomon said, "Now all has been heard; / here is the conclusion of the matter: / Fear God and keep his commandments, / for this is the whole duty of man" (Eccl. 12:13). We are more apt to keep God's commandments when we fear Him—that is, when we have a healthy respect for God, we are more prone to live in obedience to His laws.

This is critical to establishing a strong, intimate relationship with God. Spiritual intimacy is steeped in spiritual maturity. You cannot have the former without the latter—although you can be spiritually mature without being spiritually intimate. To readily grasp this point, just think about an old married couple who have a solid commitment toward one another though the fire of intimacy long ago burned out. This same thing can occur in our relationship with God. That is why we must pursue and maintain spiritual intimacy.

Spiritual intimacy is not simply emotional excitement about God. It is emotional excitement coupled with a true commitment to obedience to the laws of God. Emotional excitement without true commitment will make your relationship with God one based on feelings. Likewise, true commitment without emotional excitement will render your relationship with God cold and unfeeling. It takes both ingredients to establish a passionate relationship with God that has obedience as a strong underpinning.

The Fear of the Lord Can Be Taught

Since the fear of the Lord is critical to guiding the behavior of Christians and non-Christians alike, it must be taught. David did a fantastic job in Psalm 34 in his teaching of the fear of the Lord. Here is what he wrote:

> *Come, my children, listen to me;*
> *I will teach you the fear of the LORD.*
> *Whoever of you loves life*
> *and desires to see many good days,*
> *keep your tongue from evil*
> *and your lips from speaking lies.*
> *Turn from evil and do good;*
> *seek peace and pursue it.*
> *The eyes of the LORD are on the righteous*
> *and his ears are attentive to their cry;*
> *the face of the LORD is against those who do evil,*
> *to cut off the memory of them from the earth.*
>
> (Psalm 34:11–16)

The first point of David's instruction was to urge us to express a childlike reverence in the way we walk before Him and in the respect we attribute to Him. The psalmist was instructing his listeners to allow the fear of the Lord to become a measuring rod for their behavior and the foundation of their worldview. Living in the fear of the Lord produces a mind set that says: *I am concerned about how I live because God is watching me. What God thinks about me is important to me.*

People guided by these instructions are more apt to make wise decisions about how they live their lives. And certainly children are the most impressionable. David, though a king and a warrior, did not find it insulting to train them in the art of successful living, teaching them how to be guided by the fear of the Lord.

Teaching the fear of the Lord is couched in the perspective of "whoever of you loves life / and desires to see many good days." Talk about an attention grabber. I don't know anyone who doesn't desire to see many good days. Even if one doesn't love life, he still desires to see *many* good days. David thought that this subject was worth learning. He did not say, "Come, let me teach you how to play the harp," although he was an expert harpist (1 Sam. 16:16–18). Neither did he say, "Come, let me teach you how to become a powerful warrior," although he was a brilliant soldier. David did not even say, "Come, let me teach you how to establish an influential kingdom," although he was a king. Rather, David thought it most vital to teach the children how to fear the Lord.

The fear of the Lord is foundational to all of life. It is a subject that will keep students properly focused over time. Interestingly enough, the fear of the Lord cannot be taught in one session. That is why I've spent five chapters exploring this crucial step toward achieving personal intimacy with God. David said, "I will teach you the fear of the LORD." In other words, you need a good teacher to teach this lesson and this lesson is an ongoing one. David was committed to offer his services to protégés in order to ensure that they really understood this critical life lesson.

The Fear of the Lord Is Comprehensive

Charles Haddon Spurgeon, the great English preacher, commented on verse 11 of Psalm 34:

The Master of Sentences dwells, from this verse, on the four kinds of fear: mundane, servile, initial, filial. Mundane, when we fear to commit sin, simply lest we should lose some worldly advantage or incur some worldly inconvenience. Servile, when we fear to commit sin, simply because of hell torments due to it. Initial, when we fear to commit it lest we should lose the happiness of heaven.

Filial, *when we fear, only and entirely because we dread to offend that God whom we love with all our hearts.*[1]

Spurgeon recognized David's attempt to be comprehensive with his lesson on the fear of the Lord. David covered all of life in his teaching: motive, behavior, and the temporal and future impact of one's actions. Because the fear of the Lord encompasses all of these areas, this is yet another reason to conclude that this subject cannot be taught in one sitting.

While knowledge in many disciplines can puff up and make you feel intellectually superior to others, knowledge in the fear of the Lord will humble you. The more you know about God and His ways, the more humble you become. The more you know about God, the more apt you are to submit to His ways.

The Wisdom of the Fear of the Lord

The intent behind any intentional teaching process is to pass on knowledge and wisdom. Wisdom provides a careful and insightful way of looking at life. David's life provided him with a lot of invaluable lessons that he gained both joyfully and painfully. He could pass these to another generation in hopes that the students would avoid the same mistakes and avoid painful outcomes.

The fear of the Lord is a guiding principle for all of life. It guides us in making decisions that factor God into every area of life. The fear of the Lord is a form of wisdom that God gives us through which we can filter our lives. Hence, we can ask questions such as, *Does this decision reflect a healthy fear of God?* The answer *no* will cause me to think through the matter again until I can create an outcome where the answer is *yes*.

Willem A. VanGemeren, a scholar in the wisdom literature of the Bible, commented on Psalm 34 by writing:

The fear of the Lord expresses itself in a submission to his way. . . .
The reward of wisdom is already enjoyed in this life (v. 12), because
God is good to those who seek him (vv. 8–10). He looks on them
with favor and is responsive to their needs (v. 15). He cares for them,

protects them, answers their prayers, and delivers them from trouble. But he hates evil and will completely rid the earth of all the wicked. His "face" has turned against them (cf. 80:19) so that they will be no more (v. 16).[2]

VanGemeren is absolutely correct. The fear of the Lord is a ruler by which you can measure all of life's questions, paradoxes, and possible actions. You will be guided in the best possible way because you are governed by a healthy fear of the Lord. This intentional filtering process shows maximum submission to the Lord.

Day 12: Steps to Rehearse

Living in the fear of the Lord demonstrates a true submission to God and His Word. The fear of the Lord can be taught to others. They will learn that:

1. The role of the fear of the Lord is to facilitate the establishing of an intimate relationship with God. Spiritual intimacy is steeped in spiritual maturity.

2. Embracing the fear of the Lord communicates, *I am concerned about how I live because God is watching me. And I want to please Him constantly.*

3. Walking in the fear of the Lord ensures that your desire to see *many* good days will be met.

Wisdom and the Fear of the Lord

Anyone can become unbalanced. If you don't regularly monitor your activities, heart motivation, perspective, and actions, you may wake up one day to discover that you've been living in error due to an imbalance in your life.

Imbalance occurs in many different ways and stems from many different sources. One such cause is *error by emphasis.* This catchy little phrase simply means that you regularly emphasize one truth, and in so doing, you ignore other valuable truths. This unconscious action leads to error. We ought to live in the fear of the Lord. That principle is a wonderful truth to guide your life. But this cannot mean that you throw away the value of wisdom, which is another important truth.

Fortunately, the Bible postures the fear of the Lord as a foundational attitude that will introduce you to other principles that promote godliness and spiritual intimacy. The Bible teaches that "the fear of the LORD is the beginning of knowledge" (Prov. 1:7); "The fear of the LORD adds length to life" (Prov. 10:27); and "The fear of the LORD is the beginning of wisdom (Ps. 111:10). These are just a sampling of other truths that the fear of the Lord introduces. We will explore a few of those truths and their relationship with the fear of the Lord in the next three chapters. In this chapter, we will look at how the fear of the Lord is the beginning of wisdom.

The Importance of Wisdom

Wisdom is one of the traits God emphasizes throughout the Bible. The word "wisdom" appears some 234 times in 222 verses in the King James Version of the Bible. Is it important? You judge for yourself! We are encouraged to pursue wisdom 86 times in the three wisdom books of Psalms, Proverbs, and Ecclesiastes. When God visited King Solomon in a dream with the command, "Ask for whatever you want me to give you" (1 Kings 3:5), Solomon did not ask for riches, the heads of his enemies, or a long and luxurious life. The young king's answer to God was: "I am only a little child and do not know how to carry out my duties. Your servant is here among the people you have chosen, a great people, too numerous to count or number. So give your servant a discerning heart to govern your people and to distinguish between right and wrong. For who is able to govern this great people of yours?" (1 Kings 3:7–9).

Solomon's request pleased the Lord (v. 10). This encounter between Solomon and God is similar to what I'm hoping you experience over the course of this 40-day journey to the mountain of God. Solomon's spiritual experience was intimate, revealing, and transforming. Your anticipated experience with God will also be intimate, revealing, and transforming. Although we cannot force or guarantee any experiences with God, we can plan for them by going through the preparatory steps—such as valuing the fear of the Lord.

Solomon's experience, coupled with his later writings, demonstrates the importance of having wisdom in our daily lives. This is why he says, "For the LORD gives wisdom" (Prov. 2:6) and "Blessed is the man who finds wisdom" (Prov. 3:13). The Bible shows wisdom to come from God, and we can discover, learn, or gain it through personal or formal training. Solomon told us that regardless of *how* we get wisdom—just get it!

Wisdom Can Be Found

The psalmist declared, "The fear of the LORD is the beginning of wisdom" (Ps. 111:10). In other words, wisdom starts when the fear of the Lord is present. Solomon put it another way: "The fear of the Lord teaches a man wisdom" (Prov. 15:33). Derek Kidner, an Old Testament scholar, gives his insight into the meaning of this verse when he says "that the fear of the Lord is not merely the gateway [into wisdom] but the whole path of wisdom."[1] Kidner sees the picture: the fear of the Lord both opens the door and serves as the door of wisdom.

Wisdom speaks of insight, foresight, and hindsight. Anyone who possesses it will be benefited greatly in every area of life. I know of a pastor who has tremendous preaching, teaching, and singing gifts. One would think that his church would be bursting at the seams. But just the opposite is happening. He is unable to keep members for any meaningful length of time. The young congregation struggles to reach seventy-five people because of one principal thing: the pastor lacks wisdom. He is constantly putting his foot in his mouth by making inappropriate statements that show little regard for the congregation's feelings. Although this man is in his fifties, he lacks the pliability that wisdom brings via the fear of the Lord.

In my concern for his congregation and family, I have spoken to him on several occasions about my observation. Each time I was met with a self-assurance and reliance on his "stature" in God. I struggled to convey the difference between tenure with God and having a genuine fear of God. My point to him was: "If you truly feared the Lord—honored the Lord—you would not take such a cavalier attitude about the need to change and employ wisdom in your dealings with your congregation." But in each instance I made no headway. At this point, the matter is simply one of prayer.

Wisdom Comes Through Prayer

My thesis is: if the fear of the Lord is present, wisdom is also standing by. You cannot have one without the other. In pursuing intimacy with God, you are also seeking wisdom through the counsel that comes from the fear of the Lord. Since Solomon had a true fear of the Lord, he asked for wisdom to administer justice to God's people. Excellent request! When you find yourself experiencing sweet communion with the Lord, ask Him for wisdom. Cry out for wisdom to live, to handle people, to deal with financial matters effectively. Seek God for wisdom to treat your family in a way that reflects that the fear of God controls your actions.

The book of James tells us: "If any of you lacks wisdom, he should ask God, who gives generously to all without finding fault, and it will be given to him" (James 1:5). The fear of the Lord equips you to pray. And when you pray, you present your needs to God, even the need for wisdom. Many people are unwilling to ask for wisdom because then they must admit their ignorance or inability to find a solution to their plight. Since the fear of the Lord is a humbling force, this eliminates any inhibitions about making a request for prayer.

If you want wisdom, you must ask for it. And God promises that He won't discriminate: He will dole out wisdom to *all* who ask Him. This may sound contrary to what I stated earlier, namely, that wisdom is given to those who fear the Lord. I don't believe that it is contradictory for this reason: only those who fear the Lord will dare admit to their need for His wisdom. Still, the Lord's wisdom is available to *all those* who ask for it.

One of the lessons wisdom has taught me is to know which battles to fight. Earlier in my life, I fought every conflict that presented itself to me. Not anymore. After I sought God's face for wisdom, He taught me that not every fight is mine. It took great restraint to avoid skirmishes the first few times after I learned this tidbit of wisdom. But once I became trained in this discipline, I could just walk away from potential problems without any temptation to get involved. I remember passing on this idea to one of my senior leaders.

Frank (pseudonym) was angry because he had just received a nasty e-mail from a parent. In haste, Frank responded to this e-mail with equal venom. But before forwarding it on to the parent, he sent it to me for my blessings. I quickly shot it down with these words: "Take the high road. Don't let this person suck you into a fight. Your words will only come back to haunt you. How do you know that he won't forward your e-mail to others, who will misunderstand, judge, and condemn you? Even if you're right in feeling offended by his mean-spirited words, you're wrong in being so harsh and blunt with your retort." I then ended my response by citing a policy of President Abraham Lincoln when he dealt with critics.

Abraham Lincoln felt that it was an act of wisdom to avoid the devaluing of his subordinates based on forming a hasty perspective. Instead he expressed his angry thoughts in a lengthy letter to the erring party. G. L. McIntosh, a student of Lincoln's leadership style, wrote, "He would then hang on to the letter and read it periodically until the anger subsided, finally disposing of it, having never mailed it. It was in this way that he could vent his feelings without giving needless offense to others, which would create barriers to his leadership."[2] Frank thanked me profusely because he saw the wisdom in my response and how great leaders such as Abraham Lincoln employed that same principle.

I am sure you need the wisdom of God in some significant areas of your life. Why not take a few moments now and steal away to a private area where you can reflect on this lesson and apply the truth of it immediately to your life? Ask God for wisdom. Consider how your family would benefit by your increase of wisdom. How about the benefit that can come to your community, company, and your church? And don't forget, with more wisdom, you will personally benefit. Ask God for wisdom to pay off your debts, increase your financial strength, and to maximize the gifts and talents He has given you. All of this profit is possible because the fear of the Lord is the beginning of wisdom.

Day 13: Steps to Rehearse

The fear of the Lord is indeed the beginning of wisdom. We need God's wisdom if we want to live successful lives that exude spiritual intimacy.

1. The fear of the Lord is balanced by the wisdom it produces. This is why Solomon said, "The fear of the LORD teaches a man wisdom" (Prov. 15:33).

2. We see that wisdom is important to God and to us in that the word appears some 234 times in the Bible.

3. We can receive wisdom through prayer. Ask God for wisdom because He assures you that He will give it to you.

Day 14

Living with the
Fear of the Lord

Life can be extremely complicated. It seems that the need to make decisions—some complex, others simple—occurs almost at the speed of light. The questions we ask ourselves— *Which road do I take? What should I do with this issue? How do I respond to this unexpected problem?*—are endless. But God has instituted an internal compass that can always point us to our North Star: His will. This compass is called *the fear of the Lord*. Yielding to it will always prove to be a great blessing and a rescuer from a lot of heartaches.

Several passages of Scripture point to the benefit the fear of the Lord contributes to our lives. Each gives a slightly different perspective about the benefit, but they all work toward promoting intimacy with God. The passages are:

The fear of the LORD adds length to life,
    but the years of the wicked are cut short.
                                            (Proverbs 10:27)

The fear of the LORD is a fountain of life,
    turning a man from the snares of death.
                                            (Proverbs 14:27)

The fear of the LORD leads to life:
    Then one rests content, untouched by trouble.
                                            (Proverbs 19:23)

> *Humility and the fear of the LORD*
> *bring wealth and honor and life.*
>   (Proverbs 22:4)

The fear of the Lord provides these benefits: it adds length to life; it is a fountain of life; it leads to life; and it brings life. Keep in mind that the primary intent of examining the subject of the fear of the Lord is that God told Moses to help the children of Israel understand how to deal with Him (Exod. 19:10–13). If you want to approach God at His mountain and experience a transformation, the fear of the Lord must be at work in your life.

This sense of honor and appreciation for God—for who He is, what He's done, and what He will do for you—prepares the way to deeper spiritual intimacy. Too often we treat God like an accessory to our spiritual lives, rather than the revered King of Glory who is the Giver of all life. To gain the right perspective, let's glean from the benefits of having the fear of the Lord at work in our lives.

The Fear of the Lord Adds Length to Life

The proverbial fountain of youth does not exist. But if you're looking to eke out more days on the earth, the Bible gives a method: "The fear of the LORD adds length to life" (Prov. 10:27). When the fear (or reverence) of the Lord governs your behavior, this personal value will generate wise choices about your activities and risk tolerance for daredevil tactics.

In my twenty-plus years of pastoral experience, I have had the opportunity to counsel, pray, weep, and sometimes even laugh with people who have upset the applecart of their lives because they ignored the value of the fear of the Lord. One such case comes to mind: Philip (pseudonym)—a single, thirty-eight-year old man—kept getting himself into all kinds of desperate situations because he would not adopt the Bible's plan for money management. He was evicted from one apartment after another because of his inability to handle finances. But when it came to vacationing in the Caribbean islands and other resort places, he seemed to have no problem paying his airfare. Philip's problem was not simply a lack of financial prudence, but one where he did not personally embrace the fear of the Lord.

The fear of the Lord is a deterrent to such shortsighted behavior. Philip's actions kept him in a journey that moved constantly backward. He would save up enough money to secure an apartment but would not allow the fear of the Lord to help him properly manage his income. Consequently, the quality of his life was constantly being hampered. His goals were being delayed because he would not fall in line with this singular area of Christian living.

My desire is not just for you to journey to the mountain of God and gain a deeper intimacy with Him but to secure it for life. The fear of the Lord helps you do this. It adds length of days to your life.

The Fear of the Lord Is a Fountain of Life

Another benefit the fear of the Lord provides to your life is captured in Solomon's metaphor of a fountain. A fountain is a constant stream of water. The wise king used words to paint a picture of what the fear of the Lord produces: a constant stream of life to those who are guided by it. Solomon observed, "The fear of the LORD is a fountain of life, / turning a man from the snares of death" (Prov. 14:27).

Derek Kidner says that "evil not only attacks but attracts us."[1] How profound. It is true that evil has the ability to entice us into its grips if we are not aware of what's happening. One precious young man shared with me that he's thankful for the fear of the Lord in his life because it saved him from having an affair with a woman on the job. I asked, "How so?"

John confessed that he had become deeply attracted to the woman's beauty, and she was similarly charmed by him. He struggled in fighting the allure. But it all came to a head one night when it was his turn to tuck in the kids. As he stood over their beds, looking into the beautiful faces of his sons, the thought surfaced in his mind, "Do you want to ruin their lives and your marriage? Do you want to bring mockery to your faith?" Shocked by what was definitely a God-moment, he silently responded *no!*

That night the temptation of getting involved with the beautiful coworker was instantly broken in John's heart. The fear of the Lord welled up in him like a fountain of life. He knew that real life is enjoying the God-kind of life. It was not to be frittered away because of a momentary pleasure from a sexual encounter.

The Fear of the Lord Leads to Life

Not only is the fear of the Lord a fountain of life, but "the fear of the Lord leads to life: / Then one rests content, untouched by trouble" (Prov. 19:23). Let me complete my story about John. After his epiphany, John's love for his wife grew instantly by leaps and bounds. Had she changed? Absolutely not! The change was on John's part. The fear of the Lord gave him a greater appreciation for what he had.

The quality of his marriage improved simply because the fear of the Lord led to life—a higher and better quality of life. When the thought of infidelity threatened John's security with his wife, sobriety set in through the fear of the Lord. John started thinking clearly again. The minor problems in his marriage were not insurmountable. His roaming eyes became focused on the value of his marriage and his walk with God. The fear of the Lord helped him to focus and appreciate what God had already done in his life.

The word "life" in the text is the Hebrew word *chay* (pronounced *khah' ee*), which means "living, have life, sustain life, live prosperously, appetite, and revive from sickness."[2] With the deliverance that came through the fear of the Lord, John regained his appetite for living. In other words, the fear of the Lord revived him from his sickness. It sustained life for John. John shared with me that he felt like a man given a new lease on life. He was able to add spark to his family life and enjoy it as never before.

Who would have thought that the fear of the Lord would produce such wonderful feelings and perspective? Only God, in His infinite wisdom, would have contemplated such benefits. This is another reason why God wanted to ensure that the children of Israel understood the necessity of the fear of the Lord and cultivated that trait in their lives. Armed with reverence for God, the people would not fritter away their mountain encounter with Him as just another spiritual experience. They would treasure and guard it because they knew its value.

The Scripture was true: John was able to rest content, untouched by trouble, all because he allowed the fear of the Lord to guide his behavior and choices.

The Fear of the Lord Brings Life

Solomon proclaimed, "Humility and the fear of the LORD / bring wealth and honor and life" (Prov. 22:4). As I previously wrote, one of the definitions of the word *life* is to "live prosperously." *Prosperous* in this context does not mean that you're rolling around in money. Rather it points out that when the fear of the Lord is a guiding value in your life, you are able to come through situations successfully, reaching your fullest potential. Walking in the fear of the Lord maximizes your ability to be aligned with God and His wonderful plan for your life.

When we think of intimacy with God, we seldom apply it to the material and financial areas of our lives. If we listened solely to some of the worship gurus in our society, we would think that God doesn't care about our material needs—that all He cares about is being worshiped. On the other hand, if we listened solely to the material-wealth gurus in our midst, we would think that all God wants to do is give us wealth! Not so! Just imagine: what kind of a loving, caring person would care only about the accolades he received from his friend while his friend was in desperate straits financially and materially? I know of only a few people who would treat others that way. But then again, I would not call them "friends," nor would I pursue intimate, personal relationships with such people. It would just lead to pain and disappointment.

Fortunately God is not like that. He cares about the whole person—spirit, soul, and body. His love extends to all of our beings and not just the spiritual side, which has no material needs. God understands that our material well-being impacts our devotion to Him. Notwithstanding, our material well-being is also a proof of our spiritual wholeness and proper alignment with God. There is no way God will jeopardize the testimony He receives through the prosperity of His people. The fear of the Lord *brings* life. It brings the quality of life that shows that God honors those who honor Him. God recognizes and blesses those who take the time to discipline themselves by embracing the value of the fear of the Lord.

Be encouraged in your journey to the mountain of God. Fear the Lord because it brings life.

Day 14: Steps to Rehearse

The fear of the Lord is a personal value that has many inherent benefits. One such benefit is that it changes you to the core, thus resulting in your finding and enjoying life. In the lesson for Day 14, you learned that:

1. The fear of the Lord is a compass that points you to the North Star—the will of God.

2. The fear of the Lord adds length to life. It helps you avoid foolish mistakes and unwise decisions that may lead to disaster and an unproductive life.

3. The fear of the Lord empowers you to break free from the attacks and attractions of evil.

Day 15

God's Treasure

Everyone wants to own something priceless and unique. We pay a lot of money for such items when we come across them. My personal library has a few rare books from the seventeenth century. Although I bought them inexpensively, I treasure them dearly. Just knowing that they are in my possession gives me pride and joy.

My collection pales in comparison and value to a single leaf from the Gutenberg Bible. The Gutenberg Bible was printed in 1454–1455 by Johann Gutenberg of Mainz, Germany. It was the first substantial European book printed with moveable type. A single leaf—a sheet of paper with a page on each side—containing one of the Old Testament prophecies of the birth of Jesus of Nazareth as the Messiah was auctioned on Sotheby's Web site in December 2000 for $48,400.[1]

Can you imagine paying close to fifty thousand dollars for a two-sided sheet of paper featuring the opening verses of Isaiah 11? Call me cheap, but I'll stick with my Bible, which has all of the pages intact, and which I bought for $39.99. The point I'm making is that something that is rare is often costly. We learned earlier in our journey that we are God's treasured possession. God finds us valuable.

In order to enjoy God and attain a fruitful relationship with Him, we must note that the fear of the Lord is *a key* to both becoming and accessing God's treasure. Here is what Isaiah the prophet declared to Israel:

The LORD is exalted, for he dwells on high;
he will fill Zion with justice and righteousness.

He will be the sure foundation for your times,
   a rich store of salvation and wisdom and knowledge;
the fear of the LORD is the key to this treasure.

                                                        (Isaiah 33:5–6)

The Key to God's Treasure

Isaiah pointed out that God will be our treasure for several reasons: He's a sure foundation, He's a rich store of salvation, He's a rich store of wisdom, and He's a rich store of knowledge. Each of these assets is invaluable, unique, and much sought after. Yet, the Lord says that they are freely ours if we access them via the key labeled "the fear of the LORD." Imagine that: we are God's treasure and He is ours.

The word "treasure" in the sixth verse of Isaiah 33 is the Hebrew word *owtsar* (pronounced *o-tsaw'*), which means a depository, armory, and storehouse.[2] Hence, the fear of the Lord is not simply a key to God's treasure; it is a key to God's *treasure house*. This is far more valuable than just having access to God's sure foundation, salvation, wisdom, and knowledge. Although those elements are invaluable, God still has other treasures. Wow!

Imagine that through the fear of the Lord, you can gain access to God's compassion, mercy, joy, and even His ability to love people. The list of treasures is endless. The fear of the Lord is a key to God's *entire* storehouse. This is why this third step in the eight-step process of journeying to the mountain of God is so critical. We should not attempt to circumvent it in order to make a breakneck dash to the mountain of the Lord. An intentional process is involved in journeying to the mountain of God, the same one Moses developed in order to take the million-plus Israelites there.

What we learn from the fear of the Lord is that if we want to have a deep relational intimacy with God, we must value what He values. There is no compromise in this area. What God deems important and priceless, we must also deem important and priceless.

I became a Christian the summer before I began graduate school. I didn't have my own car, so a dear lady from church,

Ruth, always gave me a ride there. Although I was extremely grateful for the ride, I became angry every Sunday because she was late. I'm not just talking about five or ten minutes, I'm speaking of thirty to forty minutes late. She would drive up to our meeting point—the chemistry building on campus—with a big smile on her face and her young son in the backseat. I'd be so angry by the time she arrived that my hair would almost stand up like Don King's—the eccentric-looking boxing promoter. Since it was not my car, though, I couldn't complain much.

Ruth gave me every excuse in the book for her repeated tardiness. One of her excuses was: "I was born late, that's why I'm always late." Quite honestly, her repeated lateness drove me to apply my faith in God and I began praying for a car of my own. He came through for me a few months later.

Since I was friends with Ruth, I still fellowshipped with her periodically. About a year after I began driving my own car to church, Ruth married a fine gentleman who had been a drill sergeant in the United States marines. A few months later, when Ruth was to drop off some of her fine homemade bread pudding at my apartment, I was surprised when she arrived fifteen minutes early. I had to ask, "Ruth, why are you so early?" She just said two magic words, "My husband." "Say no more," I said. "I fully understand." Ruth adopted the value of punctuality that her husband cherished. No more tardiness for her; she had become a time-conscious woman.

This is what God is calling you to do regarding valuing what He values, namely the fear of the Lord. When you value the fear of the Lord—God's key to His depository of divine goodies— you will always be loaded down with heavenly treasure.

Valuing the Fear of the Lord

Values refer to interests, pleasures, likes, preferences, duties, moral obligations, desires, and wants of human beings.[3] Values also refer to preferential behavior, which helps to establish direction and mind set. Value results in the formulation of social boundaries. In other words, you tend to live based on the values you guard and support.

In a recent radio interview done via telephone about my book *Perfecting Your Purpose* (Warner Faith, 2005), the host's assistant asked to speak to me following the program. She asked if I knew a certain gentleman, but I did not. She believed that the man lived in the same region of the country as I did and said that I sounded just like him in the interview. "You guys should meet because you both value science, reason, and how that kind of outlook in life can be integrated into a vibrant faith in God." She had automatically grouped me with another Christian leader because we had the same values. That's what common values do: they unite you with others who hold the same values and priorities.

When God shared that "the fear of the LORD is the key to this treasure" (Isa. 33:6), He was communicating that we should value the fear of the Lord because it leads to His treasure. God was also sharing that if He values those things in His treasure and we value the same things, people will automatically group us together. When they see you living in the fear of the Lord, they will say that you must be a God-fearing person. They will go even one step farther and say that you must be a "child of God." This connection to God will come about simply because you share the same values as God does.

In commenting on verse 6, H. C. Leupold, the renowned Old Testament scholar, wrote, "The 'fear' is the reverence that is always basic for a right attitude toward God. . . . He [Isaiah] would seem to imply that both the Ruler (Messiah) and his people will be marked by the same noble attributes."[4] This confirms my observation of the text. We will be grouped together with God if we ascribe value to the fear of the Lord.

Adjusting Your Values

As we have explored the subject of the fear of the Lord, you must now ask yourself some fundamental questions: *Do I really*

have a genuine fear of the Lord? Have any of my actions, values, and de-
cisions changed over the past five days as I have read about the fear of
the Lord? The fear of the Lord cannot be a nice heady teaching
that you simply agree to in concept. Rather, it must be one of
the ideological filters through which you pass all of your decisions, anticipated behavior, and even financial plans. What's
your answer? Have you made any changes over the past five
days? If so, there is a growing reality of the fear of the Lord in
your life.

If you have made or contemplated no changes, then you need
to seriously consider if you're embracing the fear of the Lord as
just a concept rather than as a life value. I urge you to take it off
of the shelf of your mind and place it in your heart. Without the
application of the fear of the Lord, you remain outside of God's
armory of divine goodies. Just imagine if you truly lived, walked,
and breathed the fear of the Lord, giving Him the honor and respect He's due. If you did, there is nothing God would withhold
from you, because whoever fears the Lord is one whom the
Lord trusts. When pleasing the Lord is important to you, God
can place you in a critical position in society. You will be able to
handle material success, broad societal influence, and spiritual
power.

Why would someone hold back from embracing the fear of
the Lord? One possible answer is pride. Pride blinds. Pride deceives. Pride fools. Pride says, "You can make it on your own.
You don't need to submit to God." This reasoning won't lead
anywhere because pride is simply a time waster. It keeps you spin-
ning your wheels. The fear of the Lord is the way to progress spiritually and naturally. The fear of the Lord is a sure step toward
spiritual intimacy. Begin a life directed by the fear of the Lord.
Try it and you'll never go back.

If you have to make some changes in your behavior, family activities, or even financial choices in order to comply with the fear
of the Lord, please do not procrastinate. Just do it! And you'll find
peace and blessings.

Day 15: Steps to Rehearse

The fear of the Lord is such a powerful truth that I wonder why more church leaders do not teach on it. If you feel the same way, start teaching it in your circle of influence. Remember to bring out these points:

1. The fear of the Lord is a key to God's treasure, which includes His salvation, wisdom, and knowledge.

2. The fear of the Lord is a key to God's depository of treasures. Everything valuable to God is accessed by living in the fear of the Lord.

3. When you value the fear of the Lord, people will automatically connect you with God. Those with similar values are always associated with one another.

Step 4

A Heart of Holiness

*Shut out every other consideration and keep yourself before
God for this one thing only— "My Utmost for His Highest."
I am determined to be absolutely and entirely for Him and
for Him alone. My undeterredness for His Holiness.*
—Oswald Chambers

Moses Discovers a Holy God

Congratulations! You have completed three of the eight steps involved in journeying to the mountain of God—that place of deep communion with the Lord. This section will examine the fourth step in the process, namely, developing a heart of holiness. By way of reminder, the eight steps Moses used to navigate his congregation to the mountain of God were:

Step 1:   Invitation to the Mountain of God

Step 2:   Preparing My Heart for the Climb

Step 3:   Valuing the Fear of the Lord

Step 4:   A Heart of Holiness

Step 5:   Disciplines for Mountaintop Living

Step 6:   Ingredients for Spiritual Health

Step 7:   Unleashing God's Blessings

Step 8:   A New Beginning

Each step does a distinct work of grace in your heart so that you achieve and sustain intimacy with God if you live out the principles following the 40-day journey. When I brought my congregation through Step 4, I strived to clarify the true meaning of holiness and explain why it is so critical to have an accurate working knowledge of this biblical truth. Throughout the five chapters of this fourth step in our journey I will elaborate on my experience.

To grasp a good picture of the need for personal holiness in light of the quest for deeper intimacy with God, let's take a step back to understand why Moses thought it was necessary.

Moses Encounters a Holy God

Moses' first real encounter with God occurred some years prior to the wilderness scene depicted in Exodus 19. At the first encounter Moses was tending the flock of Jethro, his father-in-law, when he came to Horeb (later referred to as Sinai), the mountain of God (Exod. 3:1). Let's look at the biblical account:

> There the angel of the LORD appeared to him in flames of fire from within a bush. Moses saw that though the bush was on fire it did not burn up. So Moses thought, "I will go over and see this strange sight—why the bush does not burn up."
>
> When the LORD saw that he had gone over to look, God called to him from within the bush, "Moses! Moses!"
>
> And Moses said, "Here I am."
>
> "Do not come any closer," God said. "Take off your sandals, for the place where you are standing is holy ground."
>
> (Exodus 3:2–5)

Moses was simply carrying out his duties as a shepherd when he had this visit with Almighty God. As an aside, we learn from this passage that you can have a transforming encounter with God even though you have not planned for it. Similarly, you can have an encounter with God *because* you've planned for it. The latter is what Moses was doing in the Exodus 19 passage with the children of Israel, and this is what you're doing by going through this 40-day journey. You are preparing your heart to meet with God and initiate a new and more meaningful spiritual relationship with Him.

At Moses' first real encounter with God, which also happened to be at the mountain of God, holiness was extremely critical in God's willingness to commune with him. God instructed Moses to take off his sandals because he was standing on "holy ground." The question that instantly comes to mind is: where was Moses standing? The answer is simple: in the presence of God. The Old Testament scholar Walter C. Kaiser Jr. gives this response to the same question: Moses was standing where "God was present."[1] I agree. The ground was called "holy" because a holy God had manifested His presence in that place.

God Called for Holiness with Moses

This observation begs a second question: why was it necessary that Moses remove his sandals? The answer was simple: Removal of one's shoes was a symbol of reverence. This similar act occurred during the days of Joshua when the commander of the Lord's army said to him, " 'Take off your sandals, for the place where you are standing is holy.' And Joshua did so" (Josh. 5:15).

In Middle Eastern society, worshipers (regardless of their faith) had an established tradition of removing their shoes before entering into the sanctuary or onto sacred grounds. In the natural, the sandals were the dirtiest part of someone's dress, particularly when living in the desert. Arid regions get extremely dusty and this dust covered not only a person's shoes, but the exposed portion of the feet and the lower part of the leg. Although these facts are true regarding the dust covering Moses' sandals, they are not God's primary reason for asking him to remove them from his feet. I'm sure you agree that God is not offended or defiled by dust. He is spirit. And it was He who created the dust in the first place. Parenthetically, He chose to create the first human being from the dust (Gen. 2:7). God asked Moses to remove his sandals because He considered the ground Moses was standing on to be holy.

The Old Testament expositor George Rawlinson comments that the "ground was rendered holy by the presence of God upon it."[2] Apart from the presence of God, the ground was an ordinary patch of earth just like any other area in the desert. When the presence of God confronted Moses, Moses had to conform to what God desired. A meeting with God is not about us but about God. It's about what God likes and dislikes. It is about what pleases God or displeases Him.

Oftentimes, God may not even give an explanation. He just states His request and it's up to us to respond in obedience if we are to gain a deeper level of intimacy with Him. Some people try to logically decipher the requests of God, though some of these requests defy human logic. If God asked you to take off your shoes because you're on holy ground, would you do it? Or would you say, "I don't see any difference between this patch of earth versus the one twenty feet away"?

Although God's request is about reverence, more than anything else, we must obey even when some spiritual things don't compute on an intellectual level. This is why Rudolph Otto wrote, "There are essential elements in religion which cannot be comprised in any intellectual system, nor wholly exhausted in practice and conduct, and which are only faintly suggested by symbolism and sacrament. Ritual is only justified when words cannot exactly explain what it means. It is an attempt to say something which cannot otherwise be wholly expressed."[3]

Fortunately Moses obeyed God's request without a single question or act of resistance. From Moses' response, we learn that God wants us to deal with Him on His terms and not on ours. We also learn that holiness matters a great deal to God, and that we must respect that fact whether it makes sense to us or not. Moses' encounter with God further teaches us that holiness is humanity's response to the presence of God.

Experiencing God

The moment Moses complied with God's request, God began to speak. He first introduced Himself to Moses as "the God of your father, the God of Abraham, the God of Isaac and the God of Jacob" (Exod. 3:6). Since Moses had not had a personal encounter with God before, God introduced Himself by making an association with the names of the three men who were widely known to have had successful encounters with God.

The spiritual legacy of Abraham, Isaac, and Jacob was something that Moses and all the other Hebrew people learned about from childbirth. God was not ashamed to identify Himself by referring to these men's names because they had a spiritual legacy with Him. Moses was able to learn firsthand of the importance of having such a legacy.

After God introduced Himself to Moses, He connected with Moses on a deeper level by telling him the purpose behind this initial encounter. Moses automatically became hooked on the plan of God because he, too, was grieved regarding the Egyptians' horrible treatment of the Jewish people. God had a plan to bring change and freedom to the very people Moses had tried to rescue approximately forty years prior—though he had attempted it in his own strength.

Moses learned that when you do things for God, you must be willing to accept His requirement of holiness. God reiterated that truth to him years later in an effort to have him ready his congregation for a visit to the mountain of God. We have seen that God said to Moses, "Go to the people and consecrate them today and tomorrow. Have them wash their clothes and be ready by the third day, because on that day the LORD will come down on Mount Sinai in the sight of all the people" (Exod. 19:10–11).

Moses had learned from his first experience with God that if you adhere to God's request concerning holiness, you will have a transforming encounter with Him. The children of Israel's washing their clothes is a very similar act to taking off one's shoes. Both acts are a physical acknowledgment that one is in the presence of a holy God. Acts of reverence pave the way for acts of God's power.

In your own life, have you demonstrated with outward signs a true reverence for God? I mean, do you treat God in a way that is unique and special, above the way you treat everyone else? If you do, you're doing well with your journey. You are learning how to have a healthy reverence for God. This is a vital ingredient to having an audience with God at His mountain. Please continue!

Day 16: Steps to Rehearse

Moses was an encourager to the children of Israel because he was able to draw from his first encounter with God. These valuable lessons, especially on the subject of holiness, would prove useful to inspire the Hebrew people to walk in complete obedience to God. Rehearse these steps in your own life.

1. Realize that natural logic cannot decipher some spiritual things. If God invites you to do something unusual, as when he asked Moses to take off his sandals, don't argue. Just do it!

2. What experiences with God have transformed you? What can you apply from those to this 40-day journey to the mountain of God? Spiritual experiences can be evaluated on deeper levels in order to unlock their fullest strength. Do that and find a greater ease in journeying to the mountain of God.

3. In order to do great things for God, you must be willing to accept His requirement of holiness.

The Call to Holiness

Imagine overhearing the conversation Moses had with the children of Israel after he came down from meeting with God on His mountain (Exod. 19:3). A few things would have sounded unfamiliar or even strange to the Israelites. For example, God's saying "Have them wash their clothes and be ready by the third day" (Exod. 19:10–11) to meet with Him would have raised a few eyebrows. We all know human nature—the people probably became upset and argued with Moses: "Wash my clothes? What difference will it make to God if my clothes are washed or not?" They would have continued complaining until a strong corrective word came.

Some may have complained, "I am tired! I wanted to relax with the wife and kids over the next few days. Now we have to go and wash our clothes." Others may have muttered, "I wonder why God wants to meet with us? I hope it's not anything bad." I can rehearse these complaints until my fingers get tired of typing, but the reality is that the children of Israel had to learn that God wants a holy people! The idea behind the washing of the clothes, as I expressed in yesterday's lesson, was that it symbolized reverence for God just as did Moses' taking off his shoes because he was on holy ground. The people complied with Moses' request and washed their clothes as part of the consecration exercises (Exod. 19:14).

Because of Moses' successful personal encounter with God while shepherding Jethro's sheep, he could draw from his experience of removing his shoes as an act of reverence to God. Leading people into the presence of God is a lot easier if you have been there yourself. Moses knew from firsthand experience that holiness is required to commune with God!

Holiness: What Is It?

The Bible declares: "Make every effort to live in peace with all men and to be holy; without holiness no one will see the Lord" (Heb. 12:14). This is a very strong and clear statement. We can make only one interpretation of this passage: God is a holy God, and no one can see Him unless he, too, values and practices a lifestyle of holiness. For some people this requirement is rather frightening because of their pasts, for others, because of the boundaries it places on their current practices.

God is calling all of us to a place of true holiness just as He called the children of Israel in the days of Moses. Don't be frightened by that term *holiness*. The word *holy* simply means apartness; the separation of a person or thing from the common to a divine use.[1] This meaning is easily seen in the dedicated use of a certain item. For instance, if I said to you, "I wear my blue, long-sleeved shirt only to birthday parties," this would mean the blue, long-sleeved shirt has a dedicated use—it is holy. That is what the word *holy* conveys.

It is not the venue that makes the shirt holy; it is the singular fact that it has a dedicated use. It can be worn only to birthday parties, not anniversary or retirement parties. It is dedicated for only a certain type of celebration. When someone is holy, his or her life has been set apart for the full and dedicated use of God. This quality is a nonnegotiable with God. He declares that without holiness, no one will see the Lord.

Spiritual intimacy requires holiness. I hope you're not thinking about abandoning your journey to the mountain of God because you think attaining holiness is for only a small minority. If God could work through Moses to get over one million people to become consecrated within a two-day period, certainly He can help you attain the same position. There's comfort in the fact that God is able to do "immeasurably more that all we can ask or imagine" (Eph. 3:20).

Holiness Is Relevant!

The key to growing in personal holiness is to have an accurate picture of what holiness looks like, along with a working knowledge of how to promote it in your life. Just after I became a Christian I began noticing this Christian girl on my college campus. She always wore a long dress, no makeup, an old-fashioned hairdo, and a serious demeanor. This look made Jenny (pseudonym) stand out from the other girls on the campus—Christian and non-Christian alike.

Since I was just a few weeks old in my spiritual walk, I knew nothing about denominations and particularly the Holiness church. This denomination—Church of God (Holiness)—stressed the doctrine of sanctification. The emphasis on sinlessness in this life banned activities such as playing cards, social dancing, and attending the theater along with the more commonly condemned activities such as smoking, drinking alcohol, and marrying unbelievers. I later learned that Jenny was a staunch advocate of Holiness. Her definition, however, was unbiblical, antiquated, irrelevant, and nontransferable to the twenty-first century. Although Jenny was about twenty years old, she dressed and acted as if she were an old-fashioned grandmother.

Without judging her spirituality, I kept telling myself, *I hope I don't have to act and dress her vintage to be holy.* I was scared. I didn't know what to make of it. A flurry of questions entered my mind: *Jenny has few friends; will I have to give up my friends because I want to become "holy"? Do I have to become weird in order to be considered a man of God?*

These questions puzzled me until I had a heart-to-heart conversation with an older Christian. I opened up big-time. I raised all of my penetrating questions, figuring that since I had his undivided attention, I might as well learn as much as I could.

That day, I learned that all of God's Word is appropriate for New Testament believers, and we must live it out within our twenty-first-century society. Without speaking specifically to Jenny's choices on outward expressions of what she believed was holiness, my friend helped me understand that if we are to be salt and light to our culture, we must be relevant. These two metaphors of *salt* and *light* are found in the words Jesus used to describe His disciples:

> *You are the salt of the earth. But if the salt loses its saltiness, how can it be made salty again? It is no longer good for anything, except to be thrown out and trampled by men.*
> *You are the light of the world. A city on a hill cannot be hidden. Neither do people light a lamp and put it under a bowl. Instead they put it on its stand, and it gives light to everyone in the house. In the same way, let your light shine before men, that they may see your good deeds and praise your Father in heaven.*
>
> (Matthew 5:13–16)

Since we are called to be salt—a preservative to the ailing world in which we live—we must be relevant in order to get an audience. Likewise, if we are to be light—moral, ethical, and spiritual illumination—to our pluralistic society, we must not be irrelevant in nonessential things such as dress, demeanor, or other social graces. I am not suggesting that our dress should be loose or revealing. What I am saying is that we are to dress as contemporary, professional, and endemic to our sphere of influence as our budget affords us without repelling people because of this erroneous view that equates *holiness* with *old. Old* has nothing to do with *holiness.*

A few months ago, I was the keynote speaker for the fortieth anniversary of a network of churches based in New York City. During the break, while I was autographing books at my resource table, I noticed a woman in her early seventies staring at me. I felt as though she were looking at me like a piece of cheesecake. Before I could say something to stop the visual assault, she said, "I may be old, but I still got eyes!" The experience showed me that you can be old and not holy. So, it's off base for a young person to emulate the fashion of the elderly as a means of conveying holiness.

Relevant means pertinent and applicable. In order for us to embrace and practice holiness in our twenty-first-century society, we must show it to be transferable in our day without losing its potency. And I believe that just as the message of God's salvation through Christ is relevant across history, so is His call to personal holiness.

Holiness Is Achievable

The moment I started preparing my congregation to journey to the mountain of God, I knew that when we got to Step 4, many of them—like most human beings—had done things, were doing things, and would do things in the future that they would not be too proud of. And because we average approximately forty adults each Sunday making a decision to serve Jesus Christ, a teaching on holiness requires lots of gentleness, wisdom, and humor if I want to see positive change.

As I prepared my sermon during the week leading up to that Sunday, I spent much time in prayer and fasting. I really wanted God to set the people free and, more importantly, to help them choose to live in a way that pleased Him. This decision would help build a lifestyle where personal intimacy with the Lord was a daily habit and choice.

During my sermon preparation time, I also intentionally visualized some people that I knew were caught in the grips of sin. I thought about them, their situations, and how they might respond to the sermon. Like so many people, they loved God deeply and had decided to participate in our 40-day journey to the mountain of God, but they also had significant holiness issues.

To tackle the subject of holiness, I had to ensure that people knew that God's love for them was unchanging. It would never shift or alter in its commitment based on their actions. It would never quit because it is stubborn. People also needed to know that the messengers of God had also stumbled, that their lives had not been sinlessly perfect, yet God was still committed to using them to bring about a greater good in society and the church. In other words, people needed to see that holiness is achievable for anyone who wants to live a life wholly devoted to serving God.

Without getting into some of the foundational doctrine on holiness, which I will discuss in tomorrow's lesson, a lifestyle of holiness is achievable through commitment to God, commitment to character development, and commitment to transparency.

Commitment to God

As you are aware, *holiness* means to set apart and to separate oneself for a divine use. This definition is synonymous with the making of a commitment to completely surrender to God. In a surrendered state, where you go, what you do, and with whom you do it should all reflect your total allegiance to God. This kind of life is not a cumbersome one; it simply is one that demonstrates a true commitment to God.

Jesus said, "No one can serve two masters. Either he will hate the one and love the other, or he will be devoted to the one and despise the other. You cannot serve both God and Money" (Matt. 6:24). God calls for a complete loyalty. If you're going to reflect biblical holiness in your lifestyle, you must demonstrate a total commitment to God by what you do, where you go, and with whom you affiliate.

Commitment to Character Development

Intentionally working on your character is a sign that you are committed to living out the holiness of God. When the children of Israel said yes in response to God's command to wash their clothes, they were, in essence, saying yes to the invitation to work on their character. One person defined character as "who you are in the dark." In other words, a person's real character is revealed when no one else is looking.

People invest hundreds and, in some cases, thousand of dollars each year to improve their vocational abilities. But how much money do we invest each year to develop our character to more accurately model biblical holiness? The question is a very sobering one, but we need to answer it. All of us know people who once had a great platform in society to wield the sword of influence, yet because of a weak character, they tore down their own mountain of success. Charisma will bring a man to the top of his field, but character will keep him there. Focus on character development through reading, conferences, and mentoring relationships. This will equip you to maintain the blessings God gives to you.

Solomon cautioned his son:

> *Keep to a path far from her [the adulteress],*
> *do not go near the door of her house,*
> *lest you give your best strength to others*
> *and your years to one who is cruel,*
> *lest strangers feast on your wealth*
> *and your toil enrich another man's house.*
> (Proverbs 5:8–10)

The focus here is not on a loose woman or a foolish son, because the gender can easily be reversed. The focus is on the demise that can come to anyone who does not invest in the development and maintenance of his or her character.

Commitment to Transparency

Another way of establishing a lifestyle of biblical holiness is by making yourself accountable to someone. It will save you from making an impulsive decision that's steeped in temptation. A pastor friend of mine shared with me that if it weren't for his pastor, he would have succumbed to the temptation of hitting on many a secretary. "What do you mean?" I asked. "David," he said, "I found myself desiring to be with a number of secretaries under my employ over the years. But when these seductive desires mounted in my life, I went to my pastoral covering and asked for prayer and strong accountability." He shared that those times of transparency always broke the allure of being with a woman other than his wife.

I will never forget his sigh of relief and the joy he demonstrated in not having shipwrecked his family or ministry because of the power of relational transparency. This key to personal holiness is invaluable. I have enjoyed that accountability in my own life. To institute that kind of relationship requires humility. Once you have worked that out in your heart, pray that God will send the right people into your life with whom you can be transparent. Likewise, be on the lookout because people will be watching for you as the key person with whom they can be transparent.

Day 17: Steps to Rehearse

Holiness is a prerequisite to intimate fellowship with God. Because of Moses' first spiritual encounter with the Lord, he was able to glean lessons on holiness that he could transfer into his leadership of the children of Israel. What can you learn from Moses' process of consecrating the children of Israel?

1. Holiness means to be set apart; to dedicate oneself solely to God.

2. Holiness is relevant. God's Word calls us to be salt and light to our culture. Therefore, we must live in such a way that our culture can see and embrace our God. We must be relevant.

3. Holiness requires a commitment to God, a commitment to character development, and a commitment to personal transparency.

Making Sense of Holiness

The key to growing in personal holiness is to gain an accurate picture of what holiness looks like along with a working knowledge of how to promote it in your life. When I was about six months old in my relationship with Jesus, I had the awesome privilege of leading a fellow engineering student to accept Christ as his Savior. I felt somewhat responsible for his spiritual growth, so I decided to do what my church had instructed us congregants to do: I started discipling him in foundational Christianity. If that was not a sight to behold: the blind leading the blind! There I was, a babe in spiritual things, parading around like a sage to this younger babe. Since no one protested or offered to take over for me, I continued doing what I thought was best.

About twice a week I went over to his dormitory and discussed a Bible topic with him. I often just shared a lesson that my pastor recently taught in church. On one particular wintry evening, I walked through more than six inches of snow to his dorm only to find my friend sitting in his shorts with no shirt on. That wasn't so bad. The problem was that he was sitting like that in front of an open window. It was about 25 degrees Fahrenheit outside. It was freezing!

I asked, "Why are you sitting by the window, shivering?" His memorable reply was, "I'm trying to crucify my flesh." Although I was a novice myself in the things of God, I burst out laughing because I knew that achieving personal holiness—the act of crucifying the flesh—did not come that way.

Sanctification comes about in different ways: by our accepting the Christ Event, by our progressively yielding to godliness by the influence of the Holy Spirit, and by our being made perfect upon our deaths.

Sanctified by the Christ Event

The term *Christ Event* captures the significance and value of Christ's death, burial, and resurrection. Together, these three acts completed God's plan of salvation for the entire human race. When Christ died on the cross, He was paying a debt the human race owed God. The Bible says "The wages of sin is death, but the gift of God is eternal life in Christ Jesus our Lord" (Rom. 6:23). Jesus' death replaced the need for our deaths. Hence His death became the full payment *we* were obligated to give for our sins against God. We were not only freed from our indebtedness toward God, but we were also given eternal life. We received God's salvation from eternal damnation.

We receive the gift of salvation once we accept Jesus Christ as our Savior. In our acceptance of Christ, we are also saying, "Lord, please forgive us of our sins." This request for forgiveness is captured in the act of repentance. We are making a deliberate change of mind and purpose concerning the direction of our lives. A repentant person claims: "I am wrong! God is right! I need to live in a way that pleases God!" This change of view regarding life's values is an acknowledgment of the gift of God's salvation.

Along with this free gift come other benefits, such as sanctification. When we accept Christ as Savior, we are, in essence, accepting the position His death, burial, and resurrection have earned us before God. Therefore, we are *positionally* sanctified before God. The Christ Event *positioned* us before God as holy. A good illustration of this point is captured in Paul's conversion experience. Jesus said to Paul: "I will rescue you from your own people and from the Gentiles. I am sending you to them to open their eyes and turn them from darkness to light, and from the power of Satan to God, so that they may receive forgiveness of sins and a place among those who are sanctified by faith in me" (Acts 26:17–18).

We are told that all those who accept Jesus Christ as Savior are sanctified by faith in Him. Because of the Christ Event, God has granted us forgiveness. We can do nothing to become *more* acceptable or *less* acceptable to God in terms of our positional holiness.

God has already given us the ability to stand before Him with the assurance of full acceptability. We do not have to cower in shame, fear, or guilt. In fact, we are instructed: "Let us then approach the throne of grace with confidence, so that we may receive mercy and find grace to help us in our time of need" (Heb. 4:16).

Our state of mind when we approach God in prayer should be one of confidence. Don't confuse confidence with arrogance or pride; it is rather a psychological state of mind that communicates that our heavenly Father is full of grace and love toward us—God sees us through the filter of the Christ Event. God loves us with an eternal love, which makes us acceptable before Him. R. C. Sproul, the renowned professor of theology, wrote: "God does not love us because we are lovely. He loves us because Christ is lovely. He loves us in Christ."[1]

Positional sanctification also is the starting point of personal holiness. The moment you accept Christ as Savior, a moral change should also occur in your heart. The apostle John wrote: "No one who is born of God will continue to sin, because God's seed remains in him; he cannot go on sinning, because he has been born of God" (1 John 3:9). In other words, salvation removes the appetite for sin. Positional sanctification is a break with sin as well as the desire to continue sinning. This break puts us in a great position with God.

Progressive Sanctification

The next step in the process of personal holiness is commonly referred to as *progressive sanctification*. This fancy theological term simply means that now that God has made you positionally holy through salvation, you have to yield to the Holy Spirit so that you make progress in your personal holiness. This is an extremely critical point to consider if you want to achieve intimacy with God. Progressing in holiness means that you have chosen to keep on cleaning your heart, motives, and actions in order to keep the line of communication open between you and a holy God.

Paul told us how he felt about progressive sanctification:

In the same way, count yourselves dead to sin but alive to God in Christ Jesus. Therefore do not let sin reign in your mortal body so that you obey its evil desires. Do not offer the parts of your body to sin, as instruments of wickedness, but rather offer yourselves to God, as those who have been brought from death to life; and offer the parts of your body to him as instruments of righteousness. For sin shall not be your master, because you are not under law, but under grace.

(Romans 6:11–14)

Paul offered the Roman Christians a strong word when he encouraged them to consider themselves *dead* to sin. This meant they were not to keep promoting sin, engaging in sinful practices, or doing things that would awaken an appetite for sin in their lives. Not only should they consider themselves dead toward sin, Paul said, they ought to count themselves alive to God. This is where we see the whole idea of ongoing relationship with God. If you are alive to God, you show that relating to God is so important that you will totally build your life on that foundation. No longer will you associate it with the platform of sin and its pleasures. God now takes the number-one seat in your life.

Progressive sanctification is about developing your personal relationship with God through your commitment to live in a way that pleases Him. This commitment to ongoing holiness and a lifestyle of purity does not mean that you never sin. In fact, John addressed the very point in his letter to one of the early Christian community: "If we claim to be without sin, we deceive ourselves and the truth is not in us" (1 John 1:8). John openly acknowledged that although Christians have positional sanctification before God and they are practicing progressive sanctification, the reality is that they still sin. The issue is that they do not commit this kind of sinning—that of people who practice their faith and enjoy a life of progressive sanctification—willfully or in a premeditated way.

To enjoy progressive sanctification means that you have agreed with God's desire for you to live with certain values, morals, and ethics. You no longer struggle in your heart about choosing your own moral or ethical path. Your choice is God's choice. You have aligned yourself with God. This is why the step of holiness is so instrumental in moving you along the road to the mountain of God.

Agreeing to live and walk holy before God is one of the most honoring things you could ever do. It signifies that you are aware that God is a holy God. The writer of Hebrews put it this way: "Make every effort to live in peace with all men and to be holy; without holiness no one will see the Lord" (Heb. 12:14).

Making an effort to live holy is what progressive sanctification is all about. You take on the mind set of a person desirous of achieving a certain outcome. The goal in this area just happens to be personal holiness, without which, the Bible says, no one will see God. God is a holy God and all who desire to fellowship with Him, enjoy a growing relationship with Him, and have the benefit of attaining a deep level of spiritual intimacy with Him must intentionally discipline themselves so that their lives reflect personal holiness. This is not a onetime decision or action. It is a daily walk that stems from the frequent decision to live in a way that pleases God.

Eugene Peterson, the author of the popular *Message* (a modern translation of the Bible) wrote:

> *In our kind of culture anything, even news about God, can be sold if it is packaged right; but when it loses its novelty, it goes on the garbage*

heap. There is a great market for religious experience in our world, but there is little enthusiasm for the patient acquisition of virtue, and little inclination to sign up for a long apprenticeship in what earlier generations of Christians called holiness.[2]

Choosing to live holy is not a popular decision, but it is the only road to travel if your destination is intimacy with God. God lives in light—moral light. We cannot "claim to have fellowship with Him, yet walk in the darkness" (1 John 1:6). I encourage you to make the decision to live holy and let it have an ongoing impact upon the choices you make each day.

You cannot go wrong with this advice. Living holy before God is the best quality-of-life decision you can ever make. You will enjoy sweet communion with God amidst the blessings that will follow, because your holy life becomes quite attractive to success.

Sanctification Is Perfected at Death

Once you die, you will no longer continue in progressive sanctification. The process of becoming like Christ is over at death. You will be like Him (1 John 3:2)! The purpose of sanctification is to purify us from sin while we're in the physical body. When death occurs, sin ends. There will be no more temptation. No more stumbling and falling in moral failure. No more anger issues to work through. No more personality clashes that challenge us to be more patient. Since heaven is a perfect place, only those whom a loving God has made perfect (Heb. 12:23) will enter into its gates.

I look forward to that time. When you get to heaven, I will be the one dancing and shouting at the top of my voice, "I am free! Free from temptations. Free from my own weakness to sin. I am free!" When you see me, please leave me alone. Let me enjoy myself. And if I were you, I would find my own spot to shout and dance as well.

Day 18: Steps to Rehearse

Holiness is a prerequisite to intimate fellowship with God. The process to attaining complete sanctification is outlined below.

1. We are positionally sanctified because of the Christ Event.

2. We are progressively sanctified as we choose to yield our lives to the leadership of the Holy Spirit and God's word.

3. We will be completely sanctified when we die. Death is the entrance into the perfect place called heaven where sin and its enticement do not exist.

Day 19

Flirting with Temptation

I must admit, sometimes living on the edge is fun. Quite a number of people just love extreme sports or scary movies. They get a little buzz from fear—or at least what appears to be controlled fear. Other times, though, living on the edge is not what it appears to be. It's disappointing and unfulfilling.

Last summer my family and I went on a one-day outing to New York City. The trip ended at the famous Madame Tussaud's Interactive Wax Museum. This museum located in the heart of Manhattan features life-sized statues of famous people including actors, political leaders, and athletes. At the ticket counter we were offered the opportunity to walk through a haunted house area for a slightly higher fee. My wife, Marlinda, my fourteen-year old daughter, Jessica, and I were not interested. We conceded to the tour, however, when our seventeen-year-old daughter, Danielle, excitedly said she wanted to experience it. Danielle was the brave one that evening.

Before we went into the haunted house, the sign at the entrance boldly stated: *Do not touch anyone because they—the ghosts— will not touch you.* I walked in first with Marlinda following me and Jessica following her. Danielle chose to be at the back of the pack. After all, it was her event.

As we walked through the haunted area, we saw subtle movements of shadows and objects—typical of a haunted house. People were dressed in white sheets to simulate ghosts. In about five minutes we heard a loud, heartrending scream. I looked back and saw Danielle with her two eyes wide like saucers. She said that she felt a touch on her shoulders. In less than one minute the event ended and we were in the general area of the museum where all of the wax figures were located. Everyone was excited and talkative—everyone except Danielle. She was uncharacteristically quiet for the next hour. None of us were sure that someone had actually touched her shoulder, but her previous fascination with touring the haunted house was over.

In fact, as we drove home, Danielle was totally quiet. We started teasing her because she was the one who practically demanded that we walk through the haunted house. No one else wanted to go! Now that she had had a taste of it, she was frightened into complete silence and reflection. The advertisement of the haunted house had seemed so alluring to Danielle, but the experience did not fit its promise.

This is what temptation to sin is like. Prior to our performing the actual sinful act, the temptation seems to promise lasting pleasure. However, committing the sin is never the way we fantasized or imagined it would be.

This is like making your selection for a meal based on the photograph on the restaurant's menu. The photo makes the dish appear sumptuous, mouthwatering, and irresistible. But in many restaurants, when the dish comes, it seldom looks or tastes like what the picture depicted. When temptation seduces you, it appeals to your flesh by promising delightful sensations. The tragedy is that these promises cannot be attained or sustained. They may simply offer a momentary pleasure. The stark reality is: temptation deceives.

Learning How to Live Holy

Learning how to live holy is synonymous with learning how to recognize and avoid the temptation of sin. Although the word *sin* in our culture sounds quite ugly and distasteful, in reality sin offers momentary pleasure. The Bible admits that sin offers enjoyment—the caveat is that the enjoyment lasts only a short time (Heb. 11:25). The word translated "pleasure" is the Greek word *hedone* (pronounced *hay-don-ay'*), which means "sensual delight, lust, and desire."[1] If you notice, our English words *hedonism* and *hedonistic* have their origin in the word *hedone*. Hedonism is the pursuit of or devotion to pleasure. If your philosophical outlook on life is entirely centered on momentary pleasure, you will not discipline yourself to live a life of personal holiness.

The Practice of Holiness

We can draw powerful principles about the practice of holiness from God's command to Moses regarding the need to prepare the Israelites to meet at His mountain. When God told Moses to consecrate the people, that simple yet direct command points out that personal holiness must be sought. It does not occur in a haphazard manner while you're going about your regular routine. An outside stimulus or a prompting from God helps to initiate the process of sanctification.

The children of Israel were not thinking about becoming consecrated. They did not even know they needed consecration. Since God can fellowship only with those who share in His holiness, He had to initiate the process by calling for their cleansing.

As a pastor, I realize that the people in my congregation often become caught up in their individual lives. Some may be newlyweds, others may be striving for job promotions, and still others may be grieving due to the loss of a loved one. A child may be a victim of the fact that her parents fight all the time. In other words, everyone is busy living. Life happens! Our natural lives distract us from real life in the Spirit.

For this reason, periodically I make a public call for the congregation to join me in a special weeklong or three-day-long consecration. During this period, we begin a fast and conduct special corporate times of prayer. My invitation usually says, "Come join me in seeking the Lord." Truthfully, when my own life is filled with mundane things and I'm not seeking the Lord the way I should, or the way I desire, I don't recognize the need for a consecration. Looking back, I have come to realize that only those who are pursuing God can help shake others out of their spiritual stupor. The practice of holiness stems from a heart that is inclined to respond to God's invitation to spiritual intimacy.

At first, this desire is buttressed by sheer discipline. You begin practicing holiness by making an ongoing commitment to live holy before God. You achieve discipline through repetition. You repeatedly agree that living holy is both honorable before God and is the most reasonable way you can openly demonstrate your gratitude for salvation. God's free gift of salvation does not have a repayment plan; however, you can show how much you value the death of His one and only Son by choosing to deliberately avoid temptation.

Brian Whitlow, former rector of Christ Church Cathedral in British Columbia, wrote in his book *Hurdles to Heaven*: "Temptation then is not the same thing as sin. It is a testing, a trial of strength, and, by steadily resisting it, the soul can grow firm and strong."[2] Repeatedly resisting temptation is one of the ways you discipline yourself to live holy. I recognize that this process seems difficult, yet it is the way to go. In my preparation to compete in the New York City Marathon, I've learned that experts advise joggers to perform *tempo runs* each week during the four months leading up to a marathon. A tempo run is one where you run for fifteen minutes at a comfortable pace and then for the next five minutes increase to a much faster pace, perhaps two miles per hour more. Afterward, you slow down to the original pace for one to two minutes. At the end of the two-minute period you resume the fast pace for another five minutes. You may alternate the five-minute fast pace with the two-minute slower pace several times before you close out your run with a fifteen-minute jog at the original starting pace. The purpose of the tempo run is for your body to learn how to run with the painful burning sensation stemming from lactic acid. Lactic acid is produced and begins to accumulate in the muscles when there isn't enough oxygen available to meet your energy needs during rigorous exercise. Learning to run in this oxygen-depleted state will ensure that you do not drop out of the race due to pain.

Practicing handling pain helps you become skillful at handling

pain. In the same way, learning repeatedly how to handle temptation enhances your ability to practice holiness because you have
disciplined yourself by repeatedly overcoming temptation. While
avoiding temptation appears complicated, if your goal is achieving intimacy with God, you will find the power to escape its
seductive grip.

The Pleasure of Holiness

Do not equate a life of holiness with a life of misery. This simply is not the case! If it were true, we would have to conclude that
God has no pleasures because He is holy and He epitomizes holiness. How could God have no pleasure amidst His awesome creation of the earth's unique animal, aquatic, and plant life? Can
you fathom God sulking and complaining that He's bored—that
He has no pleasure with the splendor of the galaxies, solar system,
sun, moon, and stars? Or picture God not having any amusement
with human beings—the highest order of His creation—
especially when He's observing all of the antics and drama we
human beings create! It is unfathomable. If a holy God can find
pleasure in being holy, why can't we find pleasure in walking in
holiness?

During our church's 40-day journey to the mountain of God,
we distributed prayer request cards. One woman asked that the
Lord give her the joy that comes from holy living. My heart
leaped with excitement as I thought about the mental picture this
woman had formulated in her heart. She had recognized that her
lifestyle of moral inconsistency had brought her unhappiness.
And she recognized that the opposite response would bring her
satisfaction.

Sadly, most people unconsciously believe that holy living is
synonymous with boring living. It's as if they believe only sin is
pleasurable. This thinking is destructive to the goal of attaining a
deeper personal relationship with God. You cannot subconsciously despise holiness while at the same time strive to relate
more intimately with a holy God.

The fact is, living beneath God's moral standard is not going to bring lasting pleasure. Consider all the pain a morally inconsistent life yields. Whether the moral problems stem from the inability to properly manage your emotions or address behavioral problems, these problems will ultimately cost you—relationally, monetarily, or physically. Sinfulness cannot generate greater blessings than holiness can.

Holiness becomes pleasurable when you see your relationship with God deepen in quality due to your renewed commitment to living a holy life. I have seen failing marriages make 180-degree turnarounds all because one or both parties decided to walk holy before the Lord. No amount of money could pay for the joy these families now experience.

The reverse is equally true. We have all seen good marriages erode to the point of divorce because one or both parties chose to live in an unholy manner. This is a terrible sight to behold. Yet it reinforces the truth that unholy living has negative repercussions. The point that often goes overlooked, however, is the reverse one: holy living has positive repercussions. Choosing to live holy not only is a godly action, it is also a less-complicated way of life that brings a number of instant pleasures.

The pleasure generated from holiness is apparent in your state of mind, your key relationships, and even your financial where-withal. When your state of mind moves from distress to peace, the value of holiness becomes extremely apparent on an intraper-sonal level. Likewise, when holiness contributes to your family life's improving in quality, warmth, love, and enjoyment of one another, this is a priceless benefit to a lifestyle change.

Sin costs. No matter what the intensity of the unacceptable be-havioral practice is, a financial string is always attached to it. Therefore, choosing to live holy before the Lord brings with it a financial remuneration that will be greatly enjoyed.

Another way of looking at things is this: God is the Creator of all things, even the things that bring satisfaction and pleasure. In my book *Secrets of a Satisfying Life*, I drew rich information from the Bible and connected it with findings of behavioral scientists.[3] The outcome of a poll taken by the noted George Gallup regarding the habits of happy people demonstrated that living a life of genuine faith is far more satisfying than living a life of insincerity or compromise.[4]

Make a concerted effort to walk in holiness before God. It will not only be more fulfilling spiritually, but as a practical matter, you will have a more satisfying life.

Day 19: Steps to Rehearse

Most people look at holiness as a chore rather than as a discipline that produces quite a number of benefits.

1. The practice of personal holiness originates from a heart that is open to spiritual intimacy with God.

2. You can achieve the discipline of holy living by committing to overcome temptation. When you deliberately avoid temptation, you become morally stronger. This process makes the holiness walk easier and more natural.

3. Holiness becomes pleasurable when you see your relationship with God deepening in its spiritual intimacy.

The Beauty of Holiness

I wish you had been at Christ Church to experience the end of our first 40-day journey to the mountain of God. We planned a special service entitled *Encounter with God* as the culminating event. The congregation was filled with great expectation in the weeks leading up to the meeting. Throughout the 40-day journey I had been encouraging everyone to attend this special service because God was going to meet us in a phenomenal way. In reality, I did not know what God was going to do, if anything at all. I was simply speaking it by faith. I knew the nature of God is to bless His people so I did not feel my exhortation was disingenuous.

Apart from my pastoral encouragement, the people in my congregation exhibited a genuine desire to meet with God. The heightening of the spiritual temperature was very noticeable, even midway through the journey. It had moved from a nominal sense of expectation to a roaring fire that communicated radical faith, passionate worship, and an intense anticipation for God to manifest His presence in our midst.

I witnessed people speaking to one another about their hunger for God. They sought the forgiveness of those they had offended. Those who are normally very reserved in their public expressions of love for God were now being expressive and emotive. It was a sight to behold. I was pleasantly surprised.

I realize that we each worship God in a way that is comfortable. But there must come a time when we are not afraid to put our affection for God on display. The psalmist wrote: "I do not hide your righteousness in my heart; / I speak of your faithfulness and salvation. / I do not conceal your love and your truth / from the great assembly" (Ps. 40:10). I was seeing this passage come alive in my midst. People were beginning to reveal their love for God in a way they had never done before.

With this kind of spiritual momentum as a backdrop to our Encounter with God service, something powerful was sure to occur. When Friday night came, the entire building was packed—the main sanctuary and three overflow rooms were filled to capacity. People were even in the lobbies watching by closed-circuit television. People were hungry for God. The preservice prayer was electric.

As soon as worship began, the presence of God enveloped the entire building. The songs we had sung dozens of times before now seemed to create an unusual atmosphere—one where the presence of God seemed almost tangible. The Holy Spirit was definitely at work in the hearts and lives of the people that night. About twenty minutes into our worship, people began to weep uncontrollably. Some positioned themselves on the floor where they lay crying out to God. The glory of God had filled the cathedral.

This is similar to what happened in the days of Solomon when the temple had been completed. The Bible states: "All the priests who were there had consecrated themselves, regardless of their divisions. . . . Then the temple of the LORD was filled with a cloud, and the priests could not perform their service because of the cloud, for the glory of the LORD filled the temple of God" (2 Chron. 5:11, 13–14).

My experience that Friday night sealed some precious lessons about the holiness of God. Because we had systematically worked on our progressive state of sanctification, our personal holiness gave God access into our lives, our lives of holiness created a hunger for intimacy with God, and God responded to our holiness.

Holiness Is God's Access Card

In the days of King Solomon, the priests took time to consecrate themselves for the service of God. These men demonstrated a sincere value of their priestly roles as God's liaison to the people and as the people's liaison to God. The priests were to model God's character, His justice, His compassion, His wisdom, and His nature. This would allow the people to have a visible representation of the nature and temperament of the invisible God.

Moses discovered the value and priority of this priestly requirement the hard way. At a critical juncture in his leading the people to the promised land, the children of Israel had become very thirsty. God heard their complaint and offered this response:

> *The LORD said to Moses, "Take the staff, and you and your brother Aaron gather the assembly together. Speak to that rock before their eyes and it will pour out its water. You will bring water out of the rock for the community so they and their livestock can drink."*
>
> *So Moses took the staff from the LORD's presence, just as he commanded him. He and Aaron gathered the assembly together in front of the rock and Moses said to them, "Listen, you rebels, must we bring you water out of this rock?" Then Moses raised his arm and struck the rock twice with his staff. Water gushed out, and the community and their livestock drank.*
>
> *But the LORD said to Moses and Aaron, "Because you did not trust in me enough to honor me as holy in the sight of the Israelites, you will not bring this community into the land I give them."*
>
> (Numbers 20:7–12)

God's instruction to Moses was crystal clear: he was to speak to the rock and water would pour out. In anger, Moses struck the rock twice. Although water was produced miraculously, God said Moses' act of anger dishonored Him before the people. We extract from this passage a clear understanding that Moses—a priest and spiritual leader—was God's liaison before the people. Moses' actions could easily misrepresent God's righteous and holy qualities. This annoyed God greatly, to the point where He punished Moses. He would not allow Moses to enter into or enjoy the promised land.

The other aspect of the Old Testament priest's role is to function as the people's liaison before Almighty God. The people needed a voice that could be heard on high. The reality is that a holy God can hear only the voices of those who have consecrated themselves. The willing consecration of the priests in the time of Solomon, this action of personal holiness, gave them full access to the throne of the holy God. So when the dedication event took place, God showed up in a clear and distinguishable way. His glory became apparent like a thick cloud. The lesson was cemented in my mind during our Encounter with God service. The glory of the Lord had filled our cathedral because the people had voluntarily consecrated themselves before God over a 40-day period.

Do not ignore these days when you are consistently working on the holiness portion of your life. Although we have received positional sanctification by the work of the cross, progressive sanctification means a lot to God.

Holiness Creates a Hunger for Spiritual Intimacy

When you willingly choose to sanctify yourself before God, it puts you on a trajectory that says: *I want to be like my heavenly Father—holy.* Valuing the moral quality of holiness creates an appetite for the one who epitomizes holiness. Your consecration enables you to see the value of holiness.

We can draw this insight from the priests at Solomon's dedicatory event: their consecration evoked a deeper appreciation for God. Consequently, the priests, along with the temple singers and musicians, "joined in unison, as with one voice, to give praise and thanks to the LORD. . . . They raised their voices in praise to the LORD and sang: / 'He is good; / his love endures forever' " (2 Chron. 5:13).

This spontaneous song conveyed more than just a joyful heart; it signified that the priests, singers, and musicians could not help but express their desire for intimacy with God. This expression had a direct correlation to their time of consecration. Again, holiness creates a hunger for intimacy with God.

This is what my congregation was worshipfully conveying at

the Encounter with God service. Our postures of weeping, passionate worship, and intense intercession revealed that we were connecting with God on a deeper level. We were not afraid to put our emotions for God on display. We were not concerned with what anyone thought or how we appeared. That night our hearts were bursting with the desire for deep intimacy and fellowship with God. Holiness and extended times of consecration create that kind of spiritual appetite.

God Responds to Holiness

Throughout the Bible, we see a pattern that God responds to repentance and the personal pursuit of holiness. Luke wrote, "Repent, then, and turn to God, so that your sins may be wiped out, that times of refreshing may come from the Lord" (Acts 3:19). In the historical account of the early days of the Christian church, Luke—the author of the book of Acts—pointed out that God is moved by our repentance, and our repentance is like a key to releasing a fresh touch of the Holy Spirit.

When our church was receiving "times of refreshing" throughout the 40-day journey, and even at the culminating event, the glory of God was evident to all. *Glory* means weight, wealth, or worthiness.[1] Hence, when we speak of the "glory of God," we're saying God has revealed His worthiness or wealth to humanity. God's glory would not have been revealed if our repentance had not preceded it.

In Psalm 15 we learn once again of the necessity of holiness as a precursor to experiencing a response from God. The response in this case is the granting of a secure position in God's sanctuary.

> LORD, *who may dwell in your sanctuary?*
> *Who may live on your holy hill?*
> *He whose walk is blameless*
> *and who does what is righteous,*
> *who speaks the truth from his heart*
> *and has no slander on his tongue,*

who does his neighbor no wrong
and casts no slur on his fellowman,
who despises a vile man
but honors those who fear the LORD,
who keeps his oath
even when it hurts,
who lends his money without usury
and does not accept a bribe against the innocent.
He who does these things
will never be shaken.

Holiness is so powerful that God sees it as the dividing factor for spiritual intimacy. Those who walk with God continuously, or those who, in the words of Psalm 15, "live on [His] holy hill," must have a blameless lifestyle. The reward of such a lifestyle is that you dwell in the presence of God.

In the dedicatory event of Solomon, we see how the glory of God was a revelation of the presence of God. God's glory was so powerfully apparent that the priests could not perform their duties. This expression of the Holy Spirit is not just for Bible characters, it is also for us. The key, however, is to make a concerted effort to walk holy before the Lord. When you do, you will share in the benefits of times of refreshing and intimate worship opportunities. These experiences will enrich and deepen your relationship with God.

Experiences like the one at our Encounter with God service and Solomon's dedicatory event occur when you work systematically to follow the eight steps that lead to the mountain of God. Each step along the way allows you to become increasingly vulnerable to the Holy Spirit. As it is happening, you hardly recognize the change because it is so subtle. But don't mistake it—there is a definite change going on in your heart and soul in regard to how you relate to God.

Congratulations! You have just completed Step 4—A Heart of Holiness—in your journey to the mountain of God. You're now about to begin the second half of the journey. Be encouraged.

You've come a long way, and the second half is where you will see the greatest growth in personal intimacy with God.

Day 20: Steps to Rehearse

Holiness is a doorway into intimacy with God. If you really want to gain a closer walk with the Lord, make a concerted effort to:

1. Give God access into your heart by voluntarily consecrating yourself daily to the Lord. Volunteering to walk in holiness is very different from making a change under duress or due to obligation.

2. Develop an appetite for spiritual intimacy by practicing personal holiness. When you value the moral quality of holiness, it gives you hunger pangs for the presence of God.

3. Position yourself to experience times of refreshing that come from the Lord via repentance.

Step 5

Disciplines for Mountaintop Living

Who may ascend the hill of the LORD?
Who may stand in his holy place?
He who has clean hands and a pure heart,
who does not lift up his soul to an idol
or swear by what is false.
(Psalm 24:3–4)

Obedience: The Breakfast of Champions

In journeying to the mountain of God, I find myself wondering what kind of discipline I will need to sustain my life on God's mountain. This question introduces the fifth in our eight-step journey. Over the next chapters we will explore disciplines that will enable you to enjoy a growing relationship with the Lord: obedience to God's will, faith in God, sensitivity to the Holy Spirit, humility, and being teachable. These spiritual disciplines will anchor us in living successfully in the presence of God.

Let's explore the subject of obedience.

Eat, Drink, and Sleep Obedience

Show me a champion and I'll show you someone who has a deep devotion to obedience. Regardless of the sport or field, a person rises from obscurity to enjoy championship status by becoming fully obedient to his or her coach's training advice. Coaches bring a historical objectivity to the table when mentoring a protégé. A coach's ability to draw from a wealth of knowledge and experience is invaluable to someone who is young and inexperienced, even though a raw gift may be present.

In journeying to the mountain of God, we will face a time when God gives us a test in obedience. He tests every worshiper because our obedience impacts our true fellowship with Him. *Obedience* simply means *the act of obeying*. The word suggests that you have heard God's request, instruction, or command and you choose to obey Him. Obedience is what God expects from us and, frankly, it is our reasonable act of service.

Since God expects this kind of compliance from us, He will test us. But God is not walking around with a big stick waiting to pop us whenever He finds us walking in disobedience. Rather, God is seeking relationship with us. Without our obedience to His Word, He is unable to deepen those relational bonds.

If intimacy with God is your goal, obedience cannot be one of your low-level concerns. It must be up there at the top along with holiness and cherishing the fear of the Lord.

Obedience vs. Disobedience

The question that God puts to each of us is: what type of worshiper do you want to be—an obedient or a disobedient one? Granted, God will *not* articulate the question as something critical to your development. The question surfaces in a nonchalant way while you're going about life, minding your own business. In fact, you may be facing the question right now. Or you may have just wrestled with the question last week or last year. Regardless of the timing, you *will* face this question.

God gave the test to Saul, the first king of Israel, and he failed terribly. Consequently, the Lord took the kingdom of Israel from him. God's thinking was: *I cannot have someone representing Me who is unwilling to follow basic orders.*

The Value of Obedience

After Saul committed a willful act of disobedience, God sent the prophet Samuel to pronounce His judgment. Samuel said: "Does the LORD delight in burnt offerings and sacrifices / as much as in obeying the voice of the LORD? / To obey is better than sacrifice, and to heed is better than the fat of rams" (1 Sam. 15:22).

This statement was a direct response to Saul's attempt to justify his disobedience by claiming that he was going to worship God with the animals he had retrieved as part of the spoils of battle. The problem was that God had given strict orders to kill the people *and* their animals as an act of judgment against the Amalekites. Since Old Testament worship incorporated animal sacrifice as an act of atonement, Saul tried to hide his disobedience under the pretense that his soldiers wanted to sacrifice the animals as an obedient act, and he was simply complying with their desire.

Samuel cut through both of Saul's feeble excuses and communicated God's perspective on the matter. Saul's feigned excuse that he was simply trying to please his men, along with his flawed logic that partial obedience is identical to full obedience, did not hold water in the eyes of God or His prophet. The conclusion was that "to obey is better than sacrifice." Ronald F. Youngblood, an Old Testament scholar, offers this comment regarding Saul's action of disobedience: "Practically speaking, this means that sacrifice must be offered to the Lord on his terms, not ours. Saul's postponement of the commanded destruction, however well meaning, constituted flagrant violation of God's will."[1]

God is not looking for excuses. He is looking for obedience. God is not even looking for perfection. He is looking for integrity and honesty. Sinless perfection is flawless living, but no one can achieve this except the Lord Jesus Christ. What we can do is to take responsibility for our sin and disobedience by admitting to God what we have done. This means that you ought not attempt to cover up or rationalize your acts of disobedience. Humbly admit to them and ask God for forgiveness. If Saul had done this prior to Samuel's confrontation, I believe God's judgment against him would have been gracious and compassionate. Saul would probably have kept his job as king.

The famous televangelist Jim Bakker related his thought process leading up to his affair with Jessica Hahn by writing:

> *As I said, I knew I was wrong the moment I entered the hotel room. I should have run out of that place. Nobody forced me into the room or to stay once I was there. Yet I rationalized the situation: I was feeling rejected by my wife; I knew that Tammy Faye was seeing an-*

other man; I was wondering whether I was much of a man at all.
Suddenly, I felt as though I were an adolescent boy who had to prove
he was a man by having sex. I willfully crossed the line and went
through with it.[2]

Hearing Bakker's sequence of mental steps helps us learn from his failure how to avoid falling into the trap of rationalizing away our disobedience to God. Our minds have a wonderful way of making us see only the pleasurable side of disobedience—not the full consequences of our poor choices. This is why Solomon cautioned his son against falling into the disobedient act of adultery by saying: "For the lips of an adulteress drip honey, / and her speech is smoother than oil; / but in the end she is bitter as gall, / sharp as a double-edged sword" (Prov. 5:3–4). The stark reality, Solomon asserted, is that the end is going to be devastating despite the exciting beginning.

How to View Obedience

Disobedience offers false hope because it usually promises feelings of pleasure yet oftentimes delivers only a big mess. The reverse is worth meditating on, however. Obedience may appear at the onset to be an undesirable chore, but in the end you will have great pleasure and lasting blessings.

Frankly, if Saul had obeyed God's initial commands, we would not have to conjecture as to what might have happened had he repented from his disobedience. The historical account clearly demonstrates that there is an inherent benefit to obedience. Referring back to verse 22 of 1 Samuel 15, we learn that God delights more in our obedience than in our worship soaked with disobedience. He does not delight in worship to the point that He overlooks our disobedience. Worship is acceptable and satisfying to God only when it stems from someone who is walking in obedience to His will. God's value system emphasizes private integrity over public displays of spiritual intimacy. Political correctness with God is about doing the right thing, not about making public or private pretenses.

Obedience Training

A year ago my family purchased a Yorkshire terrier puppy. At maturity she will weigh no more than four pounds. Star Mocha is the name my daughters gave her. We've had the toughest time training this dog in basic obedience. I'm not even expecting the crowd-pleasing stunts, such as fetching, lying down, or rolling over. I'm just asking Star not to relieve herself in the house, and I want her to come when I call! I want her to accomplish the basic skills needed to survive in the Ireland household.

In this painstaking trial of teaching Star to obey, I've learned that obedience training for dogs occurs when you reward—not scold or punish—them. In other words, you ought to praise the dog when it does what you want so that the positive reinforcement gets it to repeat the action. If you scold the dog all the time for not doing as you ask, it tends to shut down emotionally. Although I'm not a dog expert, I have learned that much from my canine friend Star.

You reinforce a behavior with praise, not threats. Threats and punishment may come in when you have to become more aggressive just to get the dog's attention. A friend of mine, who is a professional dog trainer, told me a story that's worth repeating. Someone brought a massive Rottweiler to him for obedience training. This 140-pound dog always broke off the leash and chased people and cars while barking ferociously. The owner had tried everything and was at his wits' end. The problem had to be solved before someone got hurt.

The trainer began working with the dog, teaching it how to sit and not bolt at the sight of cars. Yet all the praising and rewarding in the world did not win over the dog to the desired responses.

As a final measure, before recommending that the dog be put to sleep, my friend retrieved a collar from the back of his closet that received electrical charges from a wireless remote device. Once he'd placed the collar on the dog, he set the current to the mildest voltage. Yet when my friend shocked this particular dog, it still refused to heed the training prompts. Even after a few shocks at a stronger voltage, the dog still did not obey. Finally, my friend cranked the mechanism up to the highest voltage. As soon as the next car passed by, when the Rottweiler jumped up and started running after it while barking ferociously, my friend pressed the button to release the electrical current. This time the shock knocked the dog off his feet. When the dog regained his composure and got up from the ground, he was fully obedient. The dog finally got the picture: he was not the master! He was to obey his master's commands.

What about you? If you struggle with learning how to walk in obedience to your heavenly Master, will His simply praising you get you to fall in line? I hope that is the case. I know in my own life, after a few praises by God, I fell in line and opted to live in a way that pleased Him. I must confess, however, there was one time God used the shock treatment on me. And it worked quickly.

Prior to the jolt, I had rationalized away my disobedience. It seemed more logical, more cost-effective, and even timelier to approach things the way I had planned. Yet, no matter how I tried to justify my disobedience, I knew deep in my heart that I was doing things the wrong way. Fortunately, God was patient with me.

His patience did not mean, however, that He was not going to punish me. The Scripture is true, regardless of the person involved or the story we concoct to shirk our responsibility to comply with God's will: "My son, do not make light of the Lord's discipline, / and do not lose heart when he rebukes you, / because the Lord disciplines those he loves, / and he punishes everyone he accepts as a son" (Heb. 12:5–6). Another way of saying *discipline,* at least from my experience, is to say "shock." In other words, the Lord "shocks" those He loves. And He shocked me. Everything became crystal clear. I shunned my disobedient approach and quickly adopted the obedient direction.

Spiritual development and intimacy with God occur in direct proportion to our willingness to walk in obedience to God's will. There is no way around it. Disobedience is a dead-end street. It will lead only to failure in your spiritual life and cause you to abandon your journey to the mountain of God. Fortunately, your appetite for intimacy with God should outweigh the temptation to disobedient living.

Day 21: Steps to Rehearse

Obedience to God's will is the diet of spiritual champions. Incredible men and women of God intentionally make up their minds that regardless of the task, occasion, or circumstance, the benefits of obedience outweigh disobedience. Let's rehearse these facts:

1. Obedience is what God expects from us, and it is the least we can do to convey our appreciation to the Lord for all He has done for us.

2. What type of worshiper do you want to be—an obedient or a disobedient one?

3. Obedience training can take place through a barrage of praise from God or via strong "shocks," or acts of discipline. What has been your experience? And what do you want your future to be like in this area of your spiritual development?

Faith: The Fuel
of Champions

The Lord issues a clarion call regarding the importance of faith when He says, "Without faith it is impossible to please God, because anyone who comes to him must believe that he exists and that he rewards those who earnestly seek him" (Heb. 11:6). This is one of my favorite Bible passages on faith because God lets us know that the absence of it is a deal breaker for anyone who attempts to earnestly seek Him.

Journeying to the mountain of God is all about undergoing an intentional process to diligently seek the Lord. Throughout the first half of the 40-day journey, you probably made significant changes in your heart regarding the way you relate to the Lord. More than likely, these changes have increased your understanding of the Lord, heightened your spiritual passion, and enabled you to choose to guard the growth you have made. You also may have made a personal promise never to return to your former spiritual condition. If all this took place, I want to congratulate you at this juncture. If nothing like this has occurred in your heart, press on—it should occur before the end of the journey.

The Importance of Faith

God set up the whole notion of the importance of faith. He also is the one who instituted a faith environment where rewards are doled out. The word *rewards* covers the entire gamut of gifts, blessings, and answered prayers. You name it, and I'm sure God has included it in His reward system for those who use their faith and earnestly seek Him. One reward I'm certain is included in the list is spiritual intimacy. If spiritual intimacy with God is not a reward, then I don't know what is. God speaks to us: "Draw near to Me; I want you close to Me." In other words, God has given us the thumbs-up. We pass the test.

"What test?" you may ask. The test of preparing your heart for the spiritual journey into intimacy with God; the test of adjusting your lifestyle for the climb; the test of valuing the fear of the Lord; the test of growing in progressive holiness; and now you're finishing up the test on how to develop spiritual disciplines that can sustain mountaintop living.

I have much to say on the topic of faith, having recently written a book on the subject entitled *Why Drown When You Can Walk on Water?*[1] In that work, I addressed what faith is, and how you distinguish between authentic faith and mystical faith or presumption. I also give a great strategy for how to grow your faith in order to obtain God's promises for your life. I will limit my instructional comments, however, in this book to these areas: faith is an anchor, and faith talk is relational language.

Faith Is an Anchor

The writer of the book of Hebrews noted that "anyone who comes to him [God] must believe that he exists" (Heb. 11:6). Desiring a more intimate relationship with God must first be rooted in the premise that you believe in the existence of God. And you must believe that God can relate to His creation.

The first statement of belief seems like a no-brainer. You may be saying, "Of course I believe God exists! That's why I am reading this book to draw closer to Him!" Great! We're on the same page. The second statement of belief, however, suggests that you must believe that God is a *relatable* God. This point is not a play on words. It says we should not doubt God's concern when we find ourselves struggling and in need of faith. God made it clear up-front: you must believe that He exists and that He cares about you.

We can look at the word *faith* as an acronym in order to gain a full understanding of its meaning. I have learned to see the word FAITH as: **F**ull **A**ssurance **I**n **T**he **H**eart. When you apply faith in your crisis or in order to appropriate a new promise of God, you must have **f**ull **a**ssurance **i**n **t**he **h**eart that God is able to do exceedingly and abundantly above all that you can ask or think. During a crisis, when you resolve *My God is able—despite my inability to recognize how, when, or where the answer is going to come from,* your faith has anchored you to the Lord.

We are to believe God by faith when we make our requests in prayer: "But when he [the person in a crisis] asks, he must believe and not doubt, because he who doubts is like a wave of the sea, blown and tossed by the wind. That man should not think he will receive anything from the Lord; he is a double-minded man, unstable in all he does" (James 1:6–8). Doubting people are unstable people. Faith people are stable people anchored in God.

God placed on the heart of the great English preacher Charles Haddon Spurgeon the need for building an orphanage. After the orphanage was built, financial shortfalls arose from time to time. On such occasions Mr. Spurgeon prayed and God always provided. One night the minister asked the Lord to send gifts to supply the needs of the orphanage. At the same time a man walking the foggy streets of London was suddenly impressed to visit the Tabernacle preacher and make a donation to his church work. He had never met Mr. Spurgeon or read any of his sermons, but so strong was the impression that he went to the door that very night, insisted on seeing Mr. Spurgeon, and gave a large sum of money. He refused to give his name, but later he sent another large sum, declaring that the other donation had been the best investment of his life.[2] As Spurgeon's story illuminates, faith anchors us with God.

Faith Talk Is Relational Language

In order to have a meaningful relationship with someone, even with God, you must become vulnerable with that person. Vulnerability can be expressed in myriad ways. For example, intimate questions such as: "What can I do to please you?" "What are your personal goals?" should be part of the normal dialogue if you want to move the relationship along growth lines.

If you're not interested in developing a deeper relationship, simply continue being preoccupied with your own life and world. This perspective is what creates individualism. Individualism is the preoccupation with the freedom of individuals to make their own decisions, live the way they want to live, and to believe anything that violates this view of life "is sacrilegious."[3]

Fortunately, God wants to have a growing relationship with us. He becomes vulnerable by communicating to us: "And without faith it is impossible to please God" (Heb. 11:6). This portion of verse 6 tells us that God can be pleased. The word *please* means "to gratify entirely."[4] We know that God can be pleased because the Bible says that Enoch was "one who pleased God" (Heb. 11:5). The idea of God being pleased is not a mere concept, it is a historical reality. If Enoch could please God, so can you.

Learning what pleases God from God Himself is quite revealing. When my wife tells me about the specific things I can do to please her, I want to do them because of my love for her. Likewise, when God shares His heart with us, we can't continue doing only what we want to in the hopes that we will please God that way. Why guess when the Bible has given us the information?

God is pleased by faith. When we trust in and rely upon Him in all areas of our lives, we please Him. When God is pleased He brings us closer to Him, as He did with Enoch. God also rewards those who through their faith pursue a deeper relationship with Him. The renowned Greek scholar Kenneth Wuest makes this observation regarding Hebrews 11:6: "The idea is not merely that God exists as a rewarder, but that He will prove Himself to be a rewarder of that person who diligently seeks Him."[5]

God advertises beforehand that blessings await the person who pleases Him by walking in faith. God wants us to be able to please Him. He doesn't hide His desires. This example of faith talk conveys the path to deepen our relationship with God. Hence, faith talk is really a relational language that God instituted in order for us to grow closer to Him.

If faith talk deepens our relationship with God and results in rewards, doubt talk must fray our relationship and hinder our receiving anything from the Lord. This is why James says that a double-minded, doubting man "should not think he will receive anything from the Lord" (1:7). The opposite of faith is doubt. Faith strengthens our relationship with God while doubt weakens it. If I am doing specific things that weaken my relationship with my wife, wisdom says I should cease doing those things immediately. The knowledge of what pleases her is a form of relational communication.

In some relationships, you have to search hard to catch the signals that can tell you how better to relate with the other person. And, even with an observant demeanor, you may still not recognize those signals. In our relationship with the Lord, it's not like that. God openly communicates that faith talk pleases Him. We are then instructed to speak often in that language and we will be rewarded for our continued diligence in seeking His face.

If you choose to speak in doubt talk, don't expect God to respond. This is not His language. There are some people who will connect relationally only with others who speak doubt language. It is as if faith talk—the kind of speech that claims God's promises for the present time and season of life—frightens them. If you start speaking faith, they distance themselves from you because it makes them nervous. Perhaps the reason is that they don't know how to use faith or they don't believe that God exists. Whatever their reason, when faith talk is introduced, you must be careful that you don't abandon the language of God to fit within the environment of doubt-talkers.

When she was fifteen, Linda Stafford announced to her English class that she would someday write and illustrate her own books. Half of the class sneered and the remainder just laughed at her prophecy. To make matters worse, her English teacher responded that only geniuses became writers and then smugly announced that Linda was on track to receive a D for the semester. Stafford broke into tears.

She went home and wrote a sad, short poem about broken dreams and mailed it to a weekly paper. To her astonishment, the newspaper not only chose to print the poem but also sent her a two-dollar check. When Linda shared the news with her teacher, her only reply was that "everybody experiences some blind luck from time to time in his or her life." During the next two years, Linda sold dozen of poems, letters, jokes, and recipes. By the time she graduated from high school, she had a scrapbook filled with her published writing—but she never again mentioned it to her teachers, fellow students, or even to her family. Such people were "dream-busters." Stafford recently stated, "If you have to choose between your friends or your dreams, always go with your dreams."[6]

Like Linda Stafford, learn the language of faith and use it to draw closer to the Lord and to fulfill His dreams for your life.

Day 22: Steps to Rehearse

God clearly states that without faith it is impossible to please Him. It's one thing to journey to the mountain of God; it's quite another thing to dwell on the mountain of God. A lifestyle of faith will keep you relationally connected with the Lord. Learning to walk in faith is an important discipline to growing in the Lord.

1. A great way to remember the meaning of the word faith is to use it as an acronym: **F**ull **A**ssurance **I**n **T**he **H**eart.

2. Faith anchors you to God and keeps you properly focused during life's storms.

3. Faith talk is a relational language God instituted. When you use faith in your quest to seek God, you are able to readily connect with the Lord.

Sensitivity: The Touch
of Champions

Champions have great finesse. Whether you're watching a concert pianist or a boxer at work in the ring, the common denominator is his or her skill in executing his or her craft. The countless number of hours these people have given to practicing and preparing for the actual performance has made them lithe, nimble, and sensitive. The pianist is sensitive to the feel of the keys on the piano while the boxer is acutely aware of the type of punch he throws at different points in the fight. Without sensitivity, these champions will lose their status. Sensitivity is a significant part of the skillfulness of champions.

In a similar manner, spiritual champions must also know how to handle the presence of God in a sensitive way. I'm not suggesting that God is skittish. What I am suggesting is that we can unknowingly do things that grieve the Spirit of God. Journeying to the mountain of God is not about the actual journey, it's about the relationship that you formulate and maintain with the Lord en route and once you get to God's mountain.

That proverbial mountain is a place where passionate worship, intense intercession, and true spiritual communion occur. God does not need to make any movement on His part. Nor does He need to learn how to handle the atmosphere of passionate worship because that's where He permanently lives. The ball is in your court regarding the need to make adjustments in your behavior once in the atmosphere of the manifest presence of God. The wrong moves on your part, or perhaps the wrong statements, can break the mood and disrupt what God had intended to do.

The Skilled Worshiper

Do you recall the dedicatory service regarding Solomon's temple? Another scene in the event clearly depicted an excellent example of passionate worship. The Scriptures declare:

When Solomon finished praying, fire came down from heaven and consumed the burnt offering and the sacrifices, and the glory of the LORD filled the temple. The priests could not enter the temple of the LORD because the glory of the LORD filled it. When all the Israelites saw the fire coming down and the glory of the LORD above the temple, they knelt on the pavement with their faces to the ground, and they worshiped and gave thanks to the LORD, saying,

"He is good;

his love endures forever."

Then the king and all the people offered sacrifices before the LORD.

(2 Chronicles 7:1–4)

Let's not even address the supernatural portion of the event, namely, that fire came down from heaven and consumed the sacrifices. Instead, notice the actions of the people the moment the glory of the Lord filled the temple. First, the priests could not enter the temple. Second, the entire congregation knelt on the pavement, faces to the ground. Third, they all worshiped and gave thanks to God. Fourth, they spontaneously and in unison sang a new song. These four actions demonstrate that the people knew how to sensitively handle the moment that was pregnant with passion for God.

Spiritual Leaders Must Lead

Oftentimes we look to our spiritual leaders to teach us about God and His Word. This is a must. But their leadership should not be limited to knowledge they have gained by reading books and dialoguing with their own teachers. Rather, their leadership must also stem from spiritual sensitivity gained in personal experience with the Spirit of God.

In the dedicatory event, the priests could not enter the temple of the Lord because of the glory of the Lord. The priests recognized that they *should not* continue with their normal priestly routine as if nothing special were occurring. Just as in every area of life, people always look to certain leaders when facing new or awkward situations. This event was no different. And priests are no different. My experiences in spiritual things tell me that someone had to lead the response of the priests. One of the priests, one that the others deeply respected because of his spiritual maturity and sensitivity, had to first stop proceeding into the temple.

As soon as that first priest stopped, the others followed suit. Their actions were not based just on the actions of the one man, but their spiritual keenness bore witness to the accuracy of the first priest's sensitive response to the manifestation of the glory of the Lord. I suppose that the same process occurred with the entire congregation of Israelites when they knelt on the pavement with their faces to the ground.

In our church, we call the posture of lying on the floor facedown "carpet time." Although the Israelites did not have the luxury of carpet, without hesitation they buried their faces in the ground in awe of the presence of God. They demonstrated their sensitivity to God in that all recognized a need for a posture of reverence. Although no official leader articulated a verbal call, the people knew how to respond when the manifest presence of God was present. They knelt in awe, reverence, and deep honor of God.

What would the scene have looked like if a number of the priests or even the congregants did their own thing? If the insensitive priests went into the temple because it was the official routine, it would show that something was amiss in their spiritual lives. Though they may have been well-suited for the priestly role, and though they may have had the knowledge of the commandments down pat, their sensitivity toward the Spirit of God would have been a missing factor. And if we take this conjecture a step farther, we can conclude that an insensitive priest would not reap the experience or blessings God wanted to give him at this dedicatory event.

We can draw the same observation concerning the greater congregation. If a portion of the crowd ignored the promptings of the Holy Spirit because the promptings didn't make sense to them, or they could not interpret the mood of the meeting, what would have happened? I suspect that the insensitive congregants would have remained spiritually unfulfilled because of their lack of sensitivity. Fortunately, the priests and the congregation responded both sensitively and sensibly to the desires of the Spirit of God.

As a pastor, I try to help those in my congregation grow in their sensitivity to the Holy Spirit. Periodically, when the mood of the service calls for repeating a song because it elicits introspection and thankfulness to the Lord, I call attention to it with a pastoral exhortation: "We are repeating this song because the touch of God is upon it for this service. God is doing something in the lives of people through the lyrics, melody, and mood this song creates." I want my comments to train them on how to be sensitive to the Holy Spirit. Without these kinds of unplanned training opportunities, people who are prone to mechanical actions and strict, analytical thinking would continue plodding along without experiencing a fresh touch of God.

Now, don't misunderstand, these are fine people who live consistent moral lives before the Lord. They enjoy holiness, the fear of the Lord, and even the idea of pursuing God. But the fact of the matter is that these people adhere to biblical principles in a limited way. If the service or worship goes what they consider "over the top," they will dig in their mental heels and mechanically continue with the process of worship. Consequently, people need leaders to help coach them in how to become sensitive to the Holy Spirit.

Techniques of Spiritual Coaching

Sensitivity is the key to abiding in the atmosphere that true worship creates. If you're sensitive to the presence of God, you know how to carry yourself in the atmosphere of intimacy. Spiritual coaches have the same base of experience as natural coaches: they are experts at the task in front of them. In the same way that you observe the need to go to school for academic training in a certain field, you also need to get training in understanding the dynamics of the Holy Spirit.

When I train leaders in our church to draw closer to the Spirit of God, I take a number of months to walk them through fasting, waiting on God, and learning to yield to God's desires.

Fasting

Throughout the Bible we read of the spiritual discipline of fasting. Fasting means "to abstain from eating."[1] It calls for the abstaining from eating for a period of time. The Bible outlines a number of reasons for participating in the discipline of fasting. Fasting humbles us (Isa. 58:3; Ps. 35:13), causes our voices to be heard on high (Isa. 58:3–4), facilitates a great deliverance (Ezra 8:21–23), and produces a more intimate relationship with God (Acts 9:7–11). This last benefit of fasting is what I emphasize with my leaders as I coach them in becoming more sensitive to the Lord.

As part of my teaching on fasting, we actually go on a fast. Before beginning, I caution the men to ensure that their motives are pure. The idea of fasting is not to twist God's arm—and we cannot, anyway. But the discipline should result in our drawing nearer to God by emptying ourselves of all of the junk and distractions that life brings.

Before we start the fast, I encourage the group to prepare their bodies for the experience. I also mention the need to establish a reason for the fast. In other words, I want them to think about what they're asking God to do: what is the nature of their prayer request? These preparatory steps heighten their sensitivity to spiritual things. In an effortless way, the layers of spiritual numbness are being peeled away so that they become in tune with the desires of the Spirit of God.

Waiting on God

The phrase *waiting on God* simply captures the experience of a worshiper who postures himself in a receptive position to hear from the Lord. This person finds a quiet place and begins to pray, read the Scriptures, repent of his sins where needed, and—without putting a strict time frame on the moment—wait for God to respond to him. The Bible illustrates how Daniel waited on God for twenty-one days (Dan. 10:2–6); Paul waited on God for three days following his conversion (Acts 9:1–19); and Anna, the prophetess, often waited on God with prayer and fasting (Luke 2:36–38).

The purpose of waiting on God is to get an answer from the Lord regarding a heart matter or a major life decision. Rarely do people understand that this discipline is still for today. We are used to getting quick answers. Ours is a fast-paced society. We have microwave ovens, cell phones, the Internet, fast cars, and jet planes to take us to international destinations in a few hours. With all of this twenty-first-century technology at our fingertips, it is going to take good coaching for the principle of waiting on God to be resurrected in the American church.

The stark reality, however, is that waiting on God is vital to spiritual growth and developing the muscle of sensitivity toward the Spirit of God. The more you learn how to patiently wait on God, the more you know how to follow the Lord's direction when you find yourself in meetings where the presence of God calls for unplanned responses from the worshipers.

During the waiting-on-God period, there usually are times when your praying becomes intense or quiet. And then there are times when you know the Lord wants you to read a certain Bible passage and reflect on it. These reflective times endear you to the Lord, and they sensitize you to His desires and moods. Almost unconsciously you will grow in spiritual sensitivity.

Yielding to God's Desires

Once you've started a life of prayer and fasting then added times of waiting on God, the next step is yielding to God's desires. This spiritual discipline includes an obedient response to God's promptings in your worship posture, vocational goals, family plans, and overall life decisions. Since God is a speaking God, He will not be quiet when He has something to say (Heb. 1:1–2). Further, you will not have a deafened ear toward Him when you have voluntarily positioned yourself not only to wait on Him but commit to yielding to His desires.

Hudson Taylor, the famed missionary to China, had this experience of yielding to God:

> He [Hudson Taylor] had come to an end of himself, to a place where God only could deliver, where he must have His succor, His saving strength. If God would but work on his behalf, would break the power of sin, giving him inward victory in Christ, he would renounce all earthly prospects, he would go anywhere, do anything, suffer whatever His cause might demand and be wholly at His disposal. This was the cry of his heart, if God would but sanctify him and keep him from falling.[2]

Although Hudson Taylor is a famous believer, he was not extraordinary. What he did is what God calls all of us to do: obey His promptings by being spiritually sensitive. What good is knowing how to fast and wait on God in prayer if you yet remain unwilling to follow through on His desires? You must go for the whole package.

Make a commitment today to adhere to God's stated desires. And if you find yourself in a spiritually moving service as did the people in Solomon's day, don't hesitate to do some carpet time. If you are in a church where the people are too proud to respond to the desires of the Holy Spirit in such outward gestures, you may need to be the trendsetter and break out of that stifling box and become a radical believer in Jesus. You also may enjoy those gestures in the privacy of your own home during your personal devotional times.

Day 23: Steps to Rehearse

Dwelling in the presence of God calls for real sensitivity to the Holy Spirit. In the same way that you have to learn how to study the Bible, you also have to learn how to be sensitive to spiritual promptings from the Spirit of God. Remember these teaching elements:

1. The skilled worshiper is unafraid to respond in an unplanned way to the promptings of the Holy Spirit.

2. You learn to be sensitive to the Holy Spirit by emulating leaders who have learned how to be spiritually sensitive.

3. You can develop sensitivity to the Holy Spirit through intentional spiritual coaching, which may include elements of fasting, waiting on God, and yielding to the stated desires of the Lord.

Humility: The Attitude of Champions

A disappointing sight is a champion boasting about how good he is. This person is showing his true colors: pride. His ego is so large that he constantly needs attention. Some celebrities misbehave to draw media attention. Others glean the spotlight because of their extramarital affairs, drug-induced behavior, and tempter tantrums. When this happens, we consider them spoiled or starved for attention. But Cornell University psychiatrist Robert B. Millman says they're not spoiled, they're sick. The affliction is Acquired Situational Narcissism (ASN).

ASN develops when ordinary people achieve extraordinary success, such as winning an Oscar or being named Rookie of the Year. This double dose of adulation loosens people's grip on reality, and they become, according to Millman, "unbelievably self-involved because of the attention from us. We make it so." Now there's a unique twist: Millman says it's *our* fault celebrities act that way! Even though most of us will never be at risk of acquiring ASN because our lives are far too ordinary, we all struggle with the temptation to become overly self-involved. We sometimes imagine minor-league celebrity status for ourselves and become prima donnas in the workplace, at church, or at home.[1]

Although celebrities are particularly prone to ASN, we are all aware of noncelebrities who are guilty of it. The Bible uses a single word to describe such behavior: pride. Pride refers to having an excessively high opinion of oneself; conceit; and haughtiness. The Bible says: "God opposes the proud / but gives grace to the humble" (James 4:6). This boundary to the presence of God is quite clear. Pride has no audience with God—only humility is at home in the presence of the Lord. This verse communicates that you must work on bringing your opinion of yourself into proper focus so that humility reigns in your life.

Humility is a relational anchor with the Lord. The person who willingly chooses to walk in humility before the Lord will be a recipient, as the verse says, of "grace." According to New Testament scholar Leon Morris, "God in grace gives his people the help they need to resist the appeal of the world and to remain loyal to him."[2] In a contrasting way, pride is a relational killer because God says He "resists the proud." In *The Message* Bible by Eugene Peterson, verse 6 is translated this way: "God goes against the willful proud; God gives grace to the willing humble."

Walking in humility is a conscious choice you must make if you aspire to dwell on the mountain of the Lord. Humility is a discipline for those who desire spiritual intimacy with God. In order to grow in humility, you must adapt God's standards in especially these areas: your view of others, and your view of yourself.

Your View of Others

The apostle Paul dealt with the topic of pride by cautioning the church at Philippi, "Do nothing out of selfish ambition or vain conceit, but in humility consider others better than yourselves. Each of you should look not only to your own interests, but also to the interests of others" (Phil. 2:3–4). At the core of pride is self-centeredness. To monitor how well you are defeating pride in your life, you must notice how much *your* goals, *your* plans, *your* feelings, and *your* desires consume you. To be anchored in a passionate relationship with God, you must learn to think and feel this way: *It's not about me! It's about the Lord!*

According to Paul, you should focus on *others'* interests. This takes practice. A single person has the freedom to come and go as he pleases; to cook if he wants to, to clean his home if he so desires. Now, a child in a family of six—mother and father with four children—has limited freedoms and others to consider in every decision he makes. How would you handle having to share your bedroom with two or three other children? Prior to the question, you may have said that you had no struggles with pride, but after some consideration of your new living situation, you may begin to question your humility. If you were humble, you would be able to live in that home—considering others better than yourself. I'm not saying you wouldn't have challenging moments. You would. But the predisposition of humble people is to put the spotlight on others while taking it off of themselves.

Your View of Yourself

Harvey Penick was a golf pro whose biggest success came late in his career. He is best known for his "little books" on golf. Penick never wrote with the intention of making money. In the 1920s, he purchased a red spiral notebook in which he recorded his observations on golf. He kept this notebook for decades. In 1991 he showed his notebook to a writer and asked if he thought it was worth publishing. The writer said yes and agreed to help him find a publisher. A short time later, the man sent Harvey a letter telling him that Simon and Schuster had agreed to an advance of ninety thousand dollars.

The next time these two met, Harvey was troubled. He told his writer friend that with all his medical bills there was no way he could advance the publishing house that much money. The writer had to explain to Harvey that it was he who would be receiving the ninety thousand dollars! The book was titled *Harvey Penick's Little Red Book,* and it sold more than a million copies.[3]

Harvey Penick did not have a haughty view of himself, and the Scripture calls us to view ourselves in the same way. Peter said, "Humble yourselves, therefore, under God's mighty hand, that he may lift you up in due time" (1 Pet. 5:6). Peter was not saying that we ought to think we are nobodies, people with nothing to offer the world. Rather, the apostle was saying that we must view ourselves in a way that is not exaggerated or dishonoring to God. If we honor God, we must see ourselves in *His* light.

Seeing yourself in the way God does helps you to walk gingerly. If you don't maintain an attitude of sobriety, pride can easily sneak into your heart. Richard Dortch, the executive of PTL during the time that Jim Bakker fell morally, cautions us:

> *The fascinating aura surrounding television can suck you in like quicksand if you let it. Almost every time I went to PTL for a board meeting, I made a television appearance. It didn't take long for me to be captivated and enchanted by the experience. Surrounded by cameramen and sound people who focused on my every word and movement, I enjoyed the exposure and attention of television—not realizing its dangers.*[4]

Dortch's honesty is sobering because any one of us can easily find ourselves in the same trap. I have to constantly monitor myself because of the measure of success God has given me. Sometimes, even as a pastor, you can start believing your own press releases. A few months ago my barber asked, "How do you keep yourself humble, given your accomplishments?" I laughed. The question was funny to me because I don't see myself as having achieved many great accomplishments. There are so many things I want to do for God that I cannot allow a false sense of pride to set in my mind. In response to my barber's question, I said, "The devil is still trying his best to sabotage God's plans for my life. And that keeps me sober and open-minded about my need to walk in humility before the Lord and before people."

On a practical level, in order to maintain humility in my life, I have to look to role models. These people have accomplished, in my estimation, so much for the Lord, but they don't behave in a way that is haughty or self-absorbed. A second thing I do is keep people in my life who simply see me as David—not the man of God or the successful pastor—but as an ordinary guy who is trying to build a peaceful life for his wife and children. This is healthy. Without this commitment, you can get a whole entourage to follow you around, singing your praises.

Another practical solution to maintaining a growing sense of personal humility is to have people in your life who hold you accountable to biblical definitions of morality and ethics. This accountability team is not there just to confront you when you veer off track; they are there to keep you sober about who you are and who you are not.

Billy Graham shared how the counsel of the bishop of Barking, Hugh Gough, a graduate of Cambridge, helped him as he prepared to preach at Cambridge University many years ago. Gough's letter to Graham stated:

> *I can well understand your feelings of apprehension about Cambridge, but Billy do not worry. God has opened up the way so wonderfully & has called you to it & so all will be well. . . . Do not regard these men as "intellectuals." Appeal to their conscience. They are sinners, needing a Savior. Conviction of sin, not intellectual persuasion, is the need. So many preachers fail at this point when they speak to university men. So, Billy, keep to the wonderful clear simple message God has qualified you to preach.*[5]

Incorporating these kinds of protective measures in your life will ensure that your view of yourself is not over the top. In order to enjoy the presence of God in your life, you have to carry yourself as someone whom God has gifted, elevated in stature, and given grace. If you think that you pulled yourself up by your bootstraps, you will be the next victim of pride.

The discipline of humility is vital to mountaintop living. Humility anchors you in your relationship with God.

Day 24: Steps to Rehearse

In walking with the Lord, Peter told us to "humble [our]selves." It is our responsibility to voluntarily do this while purposefully avoiding the tentacles of pride. Here are a few helpful hints for achieving a growing state of humility.

1. Humility anchors your relationship with the Lord; pride functions as a relational killer.

2. Pride, at its core, reflects selfishness. Humility, at its core, reflects consideration of others.

3. Your view of yourself should not be haughty but one that is God-honoring. Then God can lift you up in due time.

Learning: The Commitment of Champions

A friend of mine in her late sixties is completing her doctorate in ministry. Although she has a number of other degrees, including a PhD in psychology, her writing, according to her divinity professor, needs some improvement. After getting grades of C+ and B- on a number of essays, she asked her professor what was wrong with her work. He said that her information was brilliant and doctrinally correct. The problem was her grammar. He recommended that she get tutoring on her grammar skills.

Armed with that advice, she signed up at one of the neighborhood learning centers. To appreciate this story, you have to formulate a mental picture of my friend. She looks like the proverbial grandma with her hair in a bun, and she calls everyone "sweetie." The first week at the learning center, a ten-year-old boy was leaving the tutoring room when he happened to see my friend waiting in the lobby. The little boy stared at her and said, "Oh no!" She didn't know what was going on in his mind, so she asked, "What's the matter, sweetie?" His response: "I'll never finish school!" The boy figured that since my friend was so old and still in need of tutoring, what hope did he have ever to stop having to be a student?

Although this illustration is comical, the point is that we should all make the voluntary choice to be lifelong learners. In order to be a learner, you must become teachable. A know-it-all cannot abide in the presence of God. This type of person will not posture himself to hear from the Lord or let the Lord shape him. Only a perpetual student will allow God to keep molding him into a person who is growing relationally deeper with the Lord.

When the apostle Paul was in the winter season of his ministry, his second letter to Timothy pointed out his passion for learning: "When I was in Troas, I left my coat there with Carpus. So when you come, bring it to me, along with my books, particularly the ones written on parchment" (2 Tim. 4:13 NCV). At that juncture Paul had accomplished many things, including writing most of the books in the New Testament, leading thousands to salvation in Christ, and planting a number of new churches. Yet, this high achiever was still exhibiting a passion for learning. He wanted his books, "particularly the ones written on parchment." Paul was a reader. It has been said that readers are leaders. So, if you want to be a leader—in any sphere of life—choose to be a reader. Keep your mind alert by learning, no matter how old you are or feel.

In his book *The Wonders of the Word of God,* evangelist Robert L. Sumner tells about a man who was severely injured in a terrible explosion. The man's face was badly disfigured and he lost his eyesight as well as both hands. He had recently become a new Christian, and one of his greatest disappointments was that he could no longer read the Bible. Then he heard about a lady in England who read Braille with her lips. Hoping to do the same, he sent for some books of the Bible in Braille. Much to his dismay, however, he discovered that the explosion had also destroyed the nerve endings in his lips. But one day, as he brought one of the Braille pages to his lips, his tongue happened to touch a few of the raised characters and he could feel them. In a flash he thought, *I can read the Bible using my tongue.*[1] At the time Robert Sumner wrote his book, the man had "read" through the entire Bible four times.

If this man could read the Braille Bible using his tongue, we have no excuse for not reading it or learning from other books. Since the journey to the mountain of God is about deepening your relationship with the Lord, you must love learning—fellowship with the consummate Teacher will offer the greatest of learning opportunities.

A lifelong learner is skillful in learning from the past and is willing to learn from others.

Learn from the Past

Many people despise their pasts, which means they ignore great learning opportunities. If you are going to be a consummate learner, you must view the past as an invaluable classroom that presents principles for successful living. The cliché that says history repeats itself tells us that life has cyclical patterns. Past experiences may turn up again in the future. The Bible puts it this way: "What has been will be again, / what has been done will be done again; / there is nothing new under the sun" (Eccl. 1:9). With this axiom as a benchmark to our thinking, we must embrace the past—especially the lessons it teaches us.

The past tells us what to avoid, what to focus on, and what to embrace. If you position yourself to learn from the past, you can avoid repeating its mistakes. As a pastor, I'm often surprised to see the great number of people who consistently repeat the same mistakes. For example, if you never invest in your spiritual life, you may find yourself becoming indifferent, grumpy, and unfulfilled. To mask those disturbing feelings, you may pour yourself into your career, entertainment opportunities, and time-consuming activities in hopes that the spiritual vacuum will eventually just go away. Although you know that the only way to enjoy life as a Christian is to have ample fellowship with the Lord, you keep hoping it will be different for you. So, while your choices lead only to more emptiness, you continue to pursue nonspiritual activity.

The future will be exactly like the past if you make no changes. Learn from the past by analyzing what elements produced good/bad actions, blessings, and successes. This exercise will give you clear marching orders to move into a bright future.

Learn from Others

It takes a secure person to ask this question of another: "How did you get where you are?" I recently had lunch with the mayor of my city. We had known of one another through mutual associates but had never taken the opportunity to engage in a face-to-face encounter. As we explored our likes and dislikes, I recall the mayor asking, "In terms of your success, how did you get to where you are?" When I answered him, he fired off another penetrating question: "Who are the people you look up to as role models?" After I answered, he asked one more heart-searching question: "What books have you read that shaped the way you think?"

After lunch, I walked away with yet another picture of what a learner is. This man, successful in every definition of the word, was a consummate learner. His questions were not just conversation-fillers, they reflected his commitment to being a lifelong learner. The answers he gave to the questions I put to him confirmed my observation. I learned that he tries to read one book each week of his life. Wow! Talk about learning from others. There is no better way to learn than by reading and talking to others while being a student of life.

One problem I see within our schooling programs is that they do not offer courses or training on how to become a lifelong learner. That's why many people stop reading and growing the moment they finish their formal educational training. In some homes, the only literature the adults read is the television guide. Their biggest intellectual question is "What's on the television tonight?" This mind set fails to create an atmosphere that fosters ongoing personal development.

Charles Haddon Spurgeon, the great English preacher, taught young clergy to grow intellectually:

We must, I say, make every effort to acquire information, especially of a Biblical kind. We must not confine ourselves to one topic of study, or we shall not exercise our whole mental manhood. God made the world

for man, and He made man with a mind intended to occupy and use
all the world; he is the tenant, and nature is for a while his house; why
should he shut himself out of any of its rooms?[2]

Spurgeon was a brilliant man who had a unique perspective on what the mind set of clergy—or anyone, for that matter—ought to be regarding learning. The preacher should be a walking commentary on many types of information, not just theological. To become this informed person, he must make a true commitment to quarantine himself in a room with books, journals, and other teaching implements. This type of thirst for knowledge must include some discrimination, however. The information you choose should be theologically sound to ensure its doctrinal safety.

A few years ago, I had lunch with a pastor friend at a restaurant near his church. Afterward, he took me to his office to show me some additions to his library. He was so proud—until I asked some theological questions about the content of his books. Although he had been a pastor for years, he had not completed formal theological training in seminary. He was an excellent pastor, a man who knew how to care for the sheep, but he tended to look for quick answers that he offered up via pithy statements. He did not want to wrestle with the difficult passages of the Bible that were not necessarily black and white.

Without trying to be a killjoy regarding his library, I responded honestly to what I saw. With his permission, I showed him some of the major theological problems with some of the authors whose books graced his shelves. I then suggested authors who could provide a good biblical base for their positions. I told him that a minister must know his technical doctrine and be aware of the scholarly arguments surrounding the subject before he presents a sermon to the congregation.

Preaching should not be a time for the preacher to work out what he or she believes in front of the congregation. He or she should do this in the private study and in the prayer closet. Public presentations should reflect deep conviction one has formed through scholarship.

Your appetite for learning will motivate you to keep seeking the Lord. Walking with the Lord is about learning more about Him . . . His ways . . . His will . . . and His plan for the world. You will never tire of the knowledge you will gain about the Lord. It is inexhaustible and unfathomable. But it is worth searching out.

Day 25: Steps to Rehearse

Learning is a part of growing in intimacy with Christ. Abiding in His presence comes as you deepen your knowledge about God. Learners must be teachable; this shapes them into instruments of worship in the hands of God. A learner must make clear commitments to:

1. Develop a great appetite for reading and gathering pertinent information.

2. Learn from the past.

3. Learn from others.

Step 6

Ingredients for Spiritual Health

It is when we face ourselves and face Christ, that we are lost in wonder, love, and praise. We need to rediscover the almost lost discipline of self-examination; and then a re-awakened sense of sin will beget a re-awakened sense of wonder.
—Andrew Murray

The Fire of Worship

Over the twenty-five years that I've enjoyed relationship with Christ, I have learned that the Christian walk is a marathon, not a sixty-yard dash. You have to know how to stay focused and institute biblical principles that keep you spiritually healthy and moving toward the heart of Jesus each step of the way. I regularly do certain things to keep my relationship with God healthy and vibrant with spiritual passion. These actions have become values that I guard dearly.

Over the next five chapters, I will elaborate on each of these values: worship and praise, the power of prayer, the need for fellowship, adventures with the Holy Spirit, and fresh times of surrender to the Lord. My intent in this sixth step of our journey—Ingredients for Spiritual Health—is to offer you a perspective that is sure to help you maintain passion for and intimacy with God.

When I first came to Christ I was extremely stoic—emotive expressions came few and far between in my life. I wasn't trying to be cool or reserved in my display of affection toward the Lord. I simply did not realize that I had been that way my entire life. But it eventually became apparent to me, and others close to me, because worship is a transparent activity. People who know God will know your struggles by worshiping with you. Observers are sure to notice the lack of freedom you exhibit in worship, whether you like it or not. I always say that worship is like an x-ray machine: it will disclose all of your personal struggles and issues.

Worship Must Become a Personal Value

I just didn't know that I needed to learn how to engage myself emotionally with the one who died for my sins. The Bible says: "I will declare your name to my brothers; / in the congregation I will praise you" (Ps. 22:22). The word "praise" in this verse means "to celebrate; to cause to shine."[1] God views worship as an action that is showy to the point of foolishness. Redeemed men and women like you and me are to be so thankful for God's love expressed through Jesus' death on the cross that they do not hesitate to show their appreciation for salvation. Although I knew this responsibility doctrinally, I was still not walking in the reality of its truth as a worshiper should.

This emotionless worship pattern followed me into the ministry. When Christ Church began in 1986, the first few months of our worship meetings were extremely unfulfilling for me *and* the fledgling church. I recall thinking one Sunday, *Our worship is boring!* The moment I said that to myself, the Holy Spirit spoke to my heart and said: "David, you're the reason the worship is boring. You have not modeled biblical worship to the congregation."

The moment I heard that, I knew I needed to repent. Before I delivered the sermon that morning, I made the following statement: "I want to apologize to you for not modeling biblical worship. I have been too reserved and lax in expressing the emotions or portraying the physical gestures the Bible calls for from worshipers." It took a lot of humility on my part to say that. Frankly, I was not even thinking about the humility issue. I was just eager to make things right before God and my tiny congregation.

I was so desperate to have a strong presence of God in our congregation that I was willing to do anything to please Him. With my limited pastoral experience, I wasn't even sure that my public confession was correct. I spontaneously responded with what I thought was the right thing to do.

Please understand that I really loved God and wanted to magnify Him. But I was being more of a spectator in worship, having convinced myself that a pastor's job is to watch over the service to ensure it goes in the right direction. Certainly that is one of the jobs of the pastor, but it shouldn't deter the environment that fiery worship creates or eliminate the pastor's participation in public worship.

The following week, I started to enter into worship with my heart, mind, and body. I didn't become some pew-jumping, chandelier-swinging pastor, but one who engaged his emotions in the worship experience in such a way that it conveyed to God that I truly loved Him and was in awe of His love for me. Remarkably, the presence of God filled that small sanctuary and the worship at Christ Church moved instantly from lifeless and unfulfilling to vibrant and engaging. A new beginning to the worship environment of our church was sprung that very Sunday.

I learned that the actions and values of the senior pastor have a direct correlation to the actions and values of the rest of the congregation. Since that time, I have kept growing in my personal worship practices because it is my reasonable act of service toward the one who bore my sins on His shoulders and gave me access to God's eternal forgiveness.

Since that time our church has earned a reputation as a people who really know how to worship God. We certainly are not perfect, but we are hungry to convey our love and affection for God. Not only do I preach annually on worship, we also host a three-day worship event we call Spring Conference. This conference attracts people from around the nation who enjoy learning about worship and, more particularly, who enjoy hanging out with people that have become addicts to the presence of God.

Worship: A Way to Exalt God

To get a good picture of true worship I like to look at the heavenly worship pattern depicted in the book of Revelation. It reveals that intimacy with God is attained via fiery, heart-revealing worship. For example, John wrote:

> *After this I looked and there before me was a great multitude that no one could count, from every nation, tribe, people, and language, standing before the throne and in front of the Lamb. They were wearing white robes and were holding palm branches in their hands. And they cried out in a loud voice:*
> *"Salvation belongs to our God,*
> *who sits on the throne,*
> *and to the Lamb."*
>
> (7:9–10)

This vision of heavenly worship captures redeemed people who are eternally thrilled about God's love and forgiveness. They express this appreciation verbally, with physical gestures, in symbolic clothing, and in confession. These heavenly believers were on fire for God. No holding back on their part. They unabashedly put their emotions for God on display. This glimpse of heavenly worship should be what we earthy Christians emulate as best we can.

When you worship God without hesitation or emotional restraints, you learn more and more that He has created us to worship Him. When you're in worship, you're doing what you have been designed to do. Robert E. Webber, the author of dozens of books on the subject of worship, writes, "The focus of worship . . . is not human experience, not a lecture, not entertainment, but Jesus Christ—his life, death, and resurrection."[2] Terry Wardle, a church planter and former professor at Alliance Theological Seminary, adds, "The corporate worship service is an act of adoration in which God's people seek to please Him with praise. They seek to bless Him, honor Him, extol Him, glorify Him."[3]

Wardle is pointing out that our language and actions should converge in worship to honor God. Worship is the enactment of an event—the Christ Event. Our corporate worship should retell the story of God's love for humanity, which became fully visible and evident in the death, burial, and resurrection of His Son.

Therefore, we should not leave the organization of worship to the whim of creative people or community consensus. Theologically sensitive people should participate in the design of the worship service so that the message of God's love can be embodied in ways that contemporary people can understand. In preaching, we retell the story. In the Eucharist—Holy Communion—we dramatize the event. Even worship on Sunday has significance in terms of enactment, for this is the day of the resurrection of Christ.

Worship also entails reaching out to God to fill the hunger in the soul of humanity. The psalmist David wrote,

> *O God, you are my God,*
> *earnestly I seek you;*
> *my soul thirsts for you,*
> *my body longs for you,*
> *in a dry and weary land*
> *where there is no water.*
> (Psalm 63:1)

Since worship satisfies our hearts' desires to commune with God, you must make worship a priority in your life. Worshiping the Lord will keep you fresh spiritually. In the natural, if you don't eat you will lack the energy to function properly. You will become lethargic and eventually die of malnourishment. It's not just the idea of eating that makes one healthy; it's the idea of eating a nutritious and well-balanced meal. Similarly, without a proper spiritual diet, you will eventually get lazy, lacking the spiritual vibrancy and motivation to do anything for God—even worship Him. This is why worship is a fundamental necessity if you are to stay fueled in your passion to commune with God.

I love a good metaphor. It provides a word picture that simple words alone cannot convey. I've put together a few metaphors that explain what worship is. Perhaps they will help stir you into a fiery devotion toward the Lord so that you'll always strive to maintain a spiritual vitality. Worship is like a nutritious meal—it's healthy and fulfilling. Worship is like a pit stop in a car race—it gives you strength to finish the race. Worship is like winning the championship—it's victorious and validating. Worship is like bungee jumping—it's exciting. Worship is like intimacy in marriage—it's passionate. Worship is like playing—it's fun. Worship is like a tall glass of water on a hot summer day—it's satisfying and refreshing.

I urge you to set aside some daily time to worship God. Incorporate into your devotional time an opportunity for worship. Purchase a few CDs of some of your favorite Christian artists and put your emotions for the Lord on display in the privacy of your home. You will be surprised that only a few minutes in the presence of God will give you a clearer perspective regarding your life, your aspirations, and even your problems. Your voluntary desire to grow in personal worship is going to prove an invaluable part of your journeying to the mountain of God. In fact, when worship is embraced as a personal value, it will prove to be an effective anchor to *keep* you at the mountain of God.

Day 26: Steps to Rehearse

Personal values can enrich your spiritual life and keep you fresh for the long haul. We can view our relationship with Christ and our quest to go to heaven as a race. The reality is that this race is not a sixty-yard dash, it is a marathon. To go the distance, the benefit of a life of worship will prove to be a great spiritual sustenance.

1. Worship occurs when the created thing does what he or she has been created to do.

2. Heavenly worship is typified in the book of Revelation. Here, hearts are vulnerable to God and gestures accompany the words that confess believers' sincerity and appreciation for salvation.

3. Newcomers to a true worship environment should be able to understand the Christ Event through the songs, lyrics, gestures, and the overall atmosphere of love they see at work in their midst. People should recognize that the worshipers are saying, "Christ died, He was buried, and He arose triumphantly on the third day for our salvation."

Day 27

The Power of Prayer

One of the most vital ingredients to staying fresh in your relationship with God comes from a daily time of prayer. Prayer is more than simply placing a request before a generous God with the expectation of receiving a positive answer. It is a way you fellowship with the Lord. Prayer is communion. Communion is the act of sharing one's intimate thoughts and feelings with another. It's important that you understand that when you pray to God, you're drawing closer to Him on a relational level.

We see this truth fleshed out in the intercessory dialogue God held with Abraham regarding the anticipated judgment against Sodom and Gomorrah.

> Then the LORD said, "Shall I hide from Abraham what I am about to do? Abraham will surely become a great and powerful nation, and all nations on earth will be blessed through him. For I have chosen him, so that he will direct his children and his household after him to keep the way of the LORD by doing what is right and just, so that the LORD will bring about for Abraham what he has promised him."
>
> Then the LORD said, "The outcry against Sodom and Gomorrah is so great and their sin so grievous that I will go down and see if what they have done is as bad as the outcry that has reached me. If not, I will know." . . . Abraham remained standing before the LORD.

(Genesis 18:17–22)

God was sharing with Abraham His personal plans before they were to occur. These plans dealt with the welfare of two major cities that were caught up in rampant sin. God did not speak in a monologue. God expected feedback from His friend, Abraham. In fact, Abraham's future was so promising, God felt that sharing this anticipated plan was not only a relational move, but also a strategic one to hear Abraham's feedback.

Abraham did not hold back. He took a posture of compassion toward the inhabitants of Sodom and Gomorrah by pleading to God, asking that He refrain from commingling the righteous with the unrighteous when He doled out judgment.

Although God honored Abraham's request, He still released judgment on the two cities. But the righteous people, namely Lot (Abraham's nephew) and his family, were taken out of the city prior to its destruction.

How to Make Prayer a Priority

Getting men to pray has always been a daunting task. I suspect that we men like to talk to God on our own terms. Plus, the whole notion of *relational connection* is always frightening to us. Although quite a number of men feel this way, many women also struggle with the notion of building lives of prayer. As a pastor, I make teaching men and women how to pray part of the church's annual teaching calendar.

Last year I designed a ten-lesson course for men. I titled it "The Kneeling Warrior." Since I was dealing exclusively with men, I used military nomenclature to label the topics and overall course so that men *would not* consider prayer merely a feminine practice.

I asked for one hundred men to meet with me for ten sessions. One of the prerequisites for participation was that they had to be deeply interested in being trained to take their post as commandos in prayer. I set a modest twenty-five-dollar registration fee to help ensure that I drew serious men. To my delight, 138 registered for the course. These men were husbands, fathers, sons, and brothers who wanted to build solid lives of prayer. Additionally, they shared the common bond of sincerely wanting to see results in their spiritual development as Christians.

At the first session, the men were teeming with excitement. To their surprise I gave out military hats. After everyone greeted each other, I announced the title of my first training topic, "Can Rambo Learn to Pray?" Rambo, of course, is the name of the tough guy character Sylvester Stallone played in several action movies. This Hollywood-created mythical character fights villains in order to earn respect and to exact justice and revenge. The problem is that movie perpetuates a myth that men are two-fisted, rough, crude, and nonspiritual creatures who take what they want from anyone. Can you imagine Rambo walking into your church today, asking, "Can you teach me how to pray?"

Still, if you cannot envision someone like that becoming converted to Christ, why even contemplate the necessity of prayer as a vital ingredient to maintaining passion with God? God can do the impossible. But we must offer prayer to get His power released.

Making Prayer Easy

I recommended that the men look at prayer in a disciplined way. I encouraged them to start with a commitment to prayer of just thirty minutes each day, telling them that they would surely experience a continued surge in their spiritual growth and development.

I developed and used the following diagram to outline six areas of life that are in constant need of prayer. The idea was to spend five minutes per day praying for each of these areas so that in thirty minutes the men would have erected a prayer shield around their families, church, or communities.

The same is true for you. If you intercede for the passions, people, possessions, purpose, and problems that you or a family member is facing, you will maintain freshness in your relationship with God.

PROBLEMS
Pray that God's wisdom will combat every problem in your life.

PASSIONS
Pray that your passions, cravings, and desires come under the lordship of Christ.

30 MINUTES OF PRAYER

PURPOSE
Pray that you will discover and serve the purpose of God.

PEOPLE
Pray for God to bring people into your life who are a source of blessing and not a bad influence.

POSSESSIONS
Pray that possessions will not own you, but you will increase in wealth and resources.

If you're new to daily prayer, this diagram will help you practice. As you mature in prayer, you may no longer need this guide. The relational dialogue between you and Jesus will deepen to such a point that you will simply know how to pray what is on the Father's heart because He gives you a holy concern for such things. According to E. M. Bounds, a man noted for his life of prayer, "Prayer is a trade to be learned. We must be apprentices and serve our time at it. Painstaking care, much thought, practice and labour are required to be a skilful tradesman in praying."[1]

Crying Out to God

To maintain an ongoing freshness in your relationship with Christ, where mountaintop living is normal, you will have to mature in prayer. The thirty-minute structured prayer format I provided will not be adequate to anchor you on the mountain of the Lord. You will have to ascend to another level, which some refer to as *intercession*. This does not necessarily translate to more time in daily prayer, just a more singular focus of prayer. The word *intercession* means "to intercede for or in the behalf of someone, to plead for someone."[2]

The Bible uses different metaphors to illustrate how this form of prayer is different from the devotional prayer. The apostle Paul wrote about Epaphras, an intercessor who, he told the Colossians, "is always wrestling in prayer for you, that you may stand firm in all the will of God, mature and fully assured" (Col. 4:12).

In order to wrestle in prayer, you are obligated to expend a great degree of emotional and perhaps physical energy often on a singular topic each prayer session. It is not a cute prayer in which you are emotionally disconnected. This kind of prayer usually includes crying out to God. Paul said, "In the same way, the Spirit helps us in our weakness. We do not know what we ought to pray for, but the Spirit himself intercedes for us with groans that words cannot express" (Rom. 8:26). This verse helps us understand that intercession occurs when we express a great degree of emotion regarding a specific topic and a desired outcome. The intercessor feels the burden. You release this burden only as you cry out to God for His intervention or His wisdom.

When you feel an emotional anguish about something, a righteous anger often wells up within you that says, "I will not rest until I see God's plan come to pass in this matter." Your soul is grieved over acts of injustice or a loved one's foolish decisions. Your only recourse is to ask the Lord to break through in the midst of the situation. A divine disruption is the sole answer for many of the things going on in the world around us. Sometimes communication, legal solutions, or even attempts to offer healthy compromise cannot remedy matters. You often need a word from the Lord to be the cure for the spiritual or natural ailment.

Anyone can become an effective intercessor. It simply requires a heart that is ablaze for the will and plan of God. Most Christians recognize the name of the famous American evangelist, Charles G. Finney, but few have heard of the humble intercessor, Father Nash. Father Nash was a simple man of God who arose from a backslidden state to become a powerful pray-er. Nash labored in obscurity alongside the nineteenth-century American revivalist, Charles Finney. Father Nash's continuous cry in prayer was for Finney's effectiveness in preaching. Finney wrote of Nash:

He would pray until he got an assurance in his mind that God would be with me in preaching, and sometimes he would pray himself ill. I have known the time when he has been in darkness for a season, while the people were gathering, and his mind was full of anxiety, and he would go again and again to pray, till finally he would come into the room with a placid face, and say: "The Lord has come, and He will be with us."[3]

Father Nash often traveled to the towns several weeks prior to Finney's preaching engagement. Nash locked himself in a hotel room and cried out to God in prayer and fasting for the salvation of the lost people of that town. He was known to establish a prayer list of the "rankest" sinners of the town and pray specifically for their conversion. This man knew how to abide on the mountain of God by making intercessory prayer a part of his lifestyle.

Don't let the famous televangelists be the only models of men and women of God. People like Father Nash, and others who are powerful in prayer, are also to be our mentors and role models. I have learned that E. M. Bounds is correct:

Eminent Christians have been eminent in prayer. The deep things of God are learned nowhere else. Great things for God are done through great prayers. He who prays much, studies much, loves much, works much, does much for God and humanity. The execution of the Gospel, the vigour of faith, the maturity and excellence of spiritual graces wait on prayer.[4]

Day 27: Steps to Rehearse

How can anyone grow spiritually without including daily prayer as a life priority? My question is rhetorical. Prayer is essential as part of the diet of spiritual development. In order to enjoy mountaintop living, prayer should accomplish much in your life.

1. In order to make prayer easy, try spending thirty minutes each day communing with God. Pray about the passions, people, possessions, purpose, and problems that you or your family may be facing right now.

2. The only way to learn how to pray is by praying.

3. Intercession is a way to maintain an ongoing freshness in your relationship to the Lord. Intercession is to take the place of someone else by arguing his or her case before God. When you intercede, you will expend emotional and physical energy in an attempt to secure the answers to your prayers. Crying out before God often accompanies true intercession.

The Need for Relationships

One of the things we seldom do these days is make time for fellowship with other believers. People in our contemporary society rarely use the word *fellowship*. But it simply means to *share in something with someone*. The word describes the common experience of salvation (the something) enjoyed by people who have had this same experience (Jesus, the Someone). Hence, fellowship is not just a social outing with the guys or with your coworkers. Fellowship is social, but it revolves around Jesus and others who have met Him at the cross.

Still, I am not suggesting that Christians should not connect with non-Christians socially or otherwise. The Bible states that we are called to be salt and light to the world. The metaphor of salt reflects the fact that believers in Jesus are to preserve the culture, while the metaphor of light signifies that we are to illuminate the world through our righteous living. You could not possibly fulfill this requirement of being salt and light if you never socialized with non-Christians. Plus, you would never be able to win them to Christ if you did not get actively involved in their lives.

Fellowshipping with another believer accomplishes something quite deeper than participating in a mere social activity. When you fellowship with another Christian you experience communion—a deep sense of connection that runs beyond the natural parameters of earthly relationship to the core of something that is a glimpse of heaven. The shared salvation experience makes you both open to discuss what Jesus means to you and why you love Him so. The apostle John described fellowship in this light: "We proclaim to you what we have seen and heard, so that you also may have fellowship with us. And our fellowship is with the Father and with his Son, Jesus Christ. We write this to make our joy complete" (1 John 1:3–4).

The New Testament scholar Amos N. Wilder offered these comments on these verses: "Man seeks fellowship on various levels—of self-interest, hobbies, cultural tastes and intellectual interests, political affiliation, patriotic loyalty, causes of social good will. But fellowship of men with God and with one another through Christ is the richest fellowship, and alone fulfills the purpose of life as fellowship."[1]

How true. Understanding the theological truth of the need for fellowship should help you see the need to begin guarding your time. This will afford you the opportunity to regularly enjoy the benefits that fellowship with other believers provides.

The Importance of Fellowship

We're so busy working, seeking God, and raising our families that when we finally get a minute of free time, all we can think about is getting to the nearest bed. This kind of fast-paced life can transform the best-intentioned person into a social and spiritual dwarf. God has made us social creatures. This means that all work-related activities or even spiritual activities cannot meet all of our needs. Although work and spiritual pursuits are good, if they absorb all of our time, we will lack the balance that promotes healthy Christianity. The early church understood this reality, and that is why "they devoted themselves to the apostles' teaching and to the fellowship, to the breaking of bread and to prayer" (Acts 2:42).

In order to keep sober, healthy, and continuously growing, the Jerusalem Christian community made time for these things: the apostles' teaching, fellowship, the breaking of bread (Holy Communion), and prayer. As you can see, participating in fellowship opportunities was a devotional activity in the early church. Those first believers considered fellowship a lifeline to ongoing spiritual growth.

The early church also understood that Christianity is a communal faith. You cannot practice Christianity by yourself. Jesus said, "A new command I give you: Love one another. As I have loved you, so you must love one another. By this all men will know that you are my disciples, if you love one another" (John 13:34–35). How much clearer could He be? Loving each other is one of the principal ways unbelievers recognize that we are Christ's disciples. You cannot live in isolation, ignoring the need for fellowship, and at the same time adequately demonstrate New Testament Christianity.

From a psychological perspective, Drs. Henry Cloud and John Townsend pointed out that Christians experience God's grace in two unique ways:

> *We can certainly connect to God "vertically" through prayer, but to feel his grace completely we have to open our hearts to the full expression of it "horizontally" through other people. To connect fully with the grace of God, we have to go to where it is, and he has chosen to put it into other people. So those who only study the "facts" of the grace of God and do not experience other people loving them, as Peter directs us, will fall short in their realization of that grace.[2]*

Journey to the Mountain of God is about growing. Growth should occur spiritually, devotionally, and passionately. But this growth cannot occur in a healthy way if you make no time to share this growth with God's people. You cannot love God without loving His people. Fellowshipping with the body of Christ is a way you share your love for God. This love must eventually have physical and tangible actions that often incorporate people.

The Components of Fellowship

One of the toughest things for people to do is become vulnerable with one another. Without this letting down of your emotional barriers and dropping of your defense mechanisms, though, you will never benefit from fellowship opportunities. Remember,

Christianity is a communal faith. We have to share our lives with one another in a real and vulnerable sense.

I will not be able to help you if I don't know that you need help. I will not be able to pray for you if you're experiencing marital problems, financial pressures, or unresolved conflicts with your boss or children unless you open your heart and share these prayer needs. To do this will require taking a risk on your part.

This kind of unveiling of personal information is more difficult for some people than others. For example, I grew up in New York City, and in that urban environment you have to be emotionally tough to survive. If you are a single parent, and you've had to learn how to rough it without the help of a spouse, you may need more time to become vulnerable within a fellowship relationship. I have not even broached the category of the person who has been emotionally wounded from a close relationship, be it marriage or a church-based friendship. This person also may find laying down his or her tough exterior to be very challenging.

Without sounding unkind or insensitive, let me say this: whatever may have happened to you, you are still required as a Christian to spend regular times in fellowship. The key components to having great fellowship are common experience, openness, and healthy boundaries.

Common Experience

In order to benefit from fellowship, the people who are a part of the social group must share in the common salvation experience. When serving Jesus is the top priority in your life, you can easily detect if it is the same in the lives of those who you connect with. If it is not, you must view the relationship as a ministry opportunity and not necessarily a true fellowship time. Although you can socialize with practically anyone, the rich benefit of enjoying Jesus together in a peer relationship will be slightly skewed if the other parties are not fully walking with the Lord.

If the reverse is your situation, that is, people you connect with are 100 percent sold out to serving Jesus, then you can receive the benefits that fellowship produces. When you fellowship with other believers you are also building community. Community is a place of belonging; a safe place, and a place of realism. It is a place of inclusivity and consensus.[3] It is the kind of environment the Jerusalem church enjoyed: "Every day they continued to meet together in the temple courts. They broke bread in their homes and ate together with glad and sincere hearts, praising God and enjoying the favor of all the people" (Acts 2:46–47).

If establishing community is to be the outcome of fellowshipping around the common experience of salvation, we must answer two important questions: Why are we together, and how are we to be together?[4] The first question points to vision, while the second addresses the quality of relationship. The answer to the vision question is: Jesus is the reason why we meet purposefully. You and your fellowship group have made a deep commitment to live in a community of knitted relationships. Apart from the experience of community, we all know that living as a Christian would not be as easy.

In answer to the second question, the quality of relationships within the community hinges on the moral, ethical, and relational treatment inherent in Christianity and embraced by the members of the community. In other words, how should I treat you and how should you treat me if we are going to walk together in a vulnerable way? The common experience of salvation helps us look to the Bible and hold it up as the final basis for addressing relational issues.

Openness

A one-sided vulnerability will never provide the relational satisfaction needed to experience true fellowship. Drs. Cloud and Townsend wrote:

To connect with God's love, however, we not only need people, but also need our hearts to be available to those people. We have to be open and vulnerable for the grace and acceptance to do any good. Many people "fellowship" with others, but they share so little as they fellowship that nothing happens at the heart level. As Paul told the Corinthians, "We have spoken freely to you, Corinthians, and opened wide our hearts to you. We are not withholding our affection from you, but you are withholding yours from us. As a fair exchange—I speak as to my children—open wide your hearts also."

(2 Cor. 6:11–13)[5]

All of us are guilty of holding back in relational settings from time to time. But in order to establish true fellowship, you must acknowledge that vulnerability and openness are foundational to the relationship. One of the things I have learned in building fellowship communities is that I start off slow in becoming vulnerable. Then, when I feel it's safe, I venture into other deeper levels of vulnerability. No matter how busy and time constrained I am, I usually walk away from a fellowship time feeling rejuvenated in my desire to live out my faith in this broken society.

It is as if journeying to the mountain of God becomes more pleasurable and meaningful when I learn that other believers are trying to pursue intimacy with God the way I am. This knowledge makes my relationship with God even more satisfying. In fellowship with other believers, I am really getting a chance to meet God's other friends. They, too, are pursuing intimacy with the one with whom I'm seeking to commune with on a deeper level.

Healthy Boundaries

You're always going to find people who misconstrue what biblical fellowship is all about. They may want to cheapen it because of their own spiritual and natural immaturity in handling relational issues. Some may try to make it into a gossip center with your private information placed in the middle of the discussion. This is where healthy boundaries come in. A boundary is simply a guideline or a limit to people's access into your life. Every one of us needs boundaries in all of our relationships.

Some people struggle in saying no to others. Or they delay confronting people about inappropriate situations. If you fall into either category, you need to erect a boundary so that people will not repeatedly take advantage of you by crossing the line marked *Private*. In a relational environment, you need to erect signposts so that people understand that you want to be vulnerable and you want to maximize the benefits of fellowship, but not by building dysfunctional relationships. Since the word *fellowship* is the Greek word *koinonia*, some people jokingly call dysfunctional fellowship *koinonitis*. This is supposed to sound like a sickness.

Once you have set clear boundaries in your community, you will find that people will respect them. It is important that you have a few people that are able to access your life *beyond* those boundaries. These individuals will help you preserve healthy accountability, which is slightly different from fellowship. An accountability team can be made up of close friends, some of whom should be farther along the Christian walk than you are. This team can be there for you when temptation rears its ugly head. To avoid falling morally, or in any other way, you call upon members of this team and engage in honest dialogue.

The whole idea of establishing fellowship opportunities is that you want to grow in your walk with the Lord in such a way that you bring greater honor to His kingdom. This kind of growth helps you to become a stronger disciple in Christ. A disciple is a disciplined follower of Jesus Christ; you learn discipleship through lifestyle. Fellowship circles give you an opportunity to come up close to the lives of other believers. This way, you not only fulfill your relational needs and those of others, but you have an opportunity to exercise the biblical and spiritual lessons learned through community.

I encourage you to experience true fellowship by forming a healthy spiritual community with members of your church or among Christians in your neighborhood. In so doing, you will be able to sustain mountaintop living.

Day 28: Steps to Rehearse

Relating to God vertically is great! But relating to His people horizontally is also important to growing in your walk with the Lord. Fellowship—the sharing of our lives with people of like precious faith—is a vital ingredient to living in the presence of God. Here's why:

1. As social creatures, we need to connect beyond the surface level and enjoy community with people who have experienced the common salvation established in Jesus Christ.

2. Christianity is a communal faith. Living an isolated life will not aid you in achieving spiritually healthy growth.

3. In order to benefit from fellowship opportunities, you must be genuinely vulnerable. God's love flows through others to you when you are vulnerable and open.

Day 29

Spiritual Adventures

If you do the same things every day, life will be extremely boring. I enjoy talking to interesting people. My fascination often stems from the fact that they are avid travelers, or have interesting jobs, tell great stories, or just have captivating personalities. Whatever the reason, it's a lot of fun being with them. In the same way, serving Jesus is a lot of fun, especially when you invite the Holy Spirit to include you in the activities God is doing on the earth. God is always at work around you. Our job is to try to get involved in some of those assignments.

What good is journeying to the mountain of God if, at the end of the day, you're bored out of your mind because you don't know how to participate in the adventures of the Holy Spirit? The worst thing is to be bored while living for the one who epitomizes creativity and excitement. Some people spend a lot of time in prayer and in fasting, yet their lives are dull. My question is this: what have they been praying and fasting about? If you want to be a part of God's spiritual adventures, you must start expecting them to happen. Your prayers and times of fasting should reflect this desire.

If you want your life to be predictable, neat, and sterile, then mountaintop living is not for you. Mountaintop living is for people who are spiritual adventurers. These adventures help to fuel your passion for God. When you meet people who are on fire for God, they always have a fantastic story to tell about something exciting God just did or is in the middle of completing. I believe that anyone who walks closely with God will find that He regularly sends them on spiritual adventures.

The Holy Spirit and You

The Holy Spirit has a job description that includes interfacing with you. Jesus said, "I have much more to say to you, more than you can now bear. But when he, the Spirit of truth, comes, he will guide you into all truth. He will not speak on his own; he will speak only what he hears, and he will tell you what is yet to come. He will bring glory to me by taking from what is mine and making it known to you" (John 16:12–13). Jesus indicated that the Holy Spirit is to provide several unique functions in your life, namely, guide you into all truth, speak to you regarding what He hears, tell you what is to come, and glorify the Son by revealing things to you. Anytime you are receiving news and directions supernaturally, you have to conclude that those are ingredients for a spiritual adventure.

All the things you have learned on this 40-day journey up to this point have prepared you to participate with the Holy Spirit in the lives of people and in the broader society. Now you must learn how to yield yourself to the Holy Spirit's leadership role in your life. The Holy Spirit will not force or bully you into doing anything. The relationship we have with the Holy Spirit is a voluntary one—just like the one we have with God the Father and Jesus, the Son. We voluntarily agreed to repent of our sins to the Father. Similarly, we have voluntarily agreed to accept Jesus as our Savior. In the same manner, you must voluntarily submit to the Holy Spirit.

This means that you must make plans that include space for the Holy Spirit to make His adjustments. For example, when you wake up tomorrow and prepare for work or school, stop a few minutes prior to leaving the house and pray, "Lord, I know I will meet people whom You are dealing with today. Whatever You want me to say to them or do for them, please let me know. Your work is very much a part of my agenda today."

This prayer communicates a readiness to take a detour from your plan in order to actively participate in God's work that is occurring all around you. God is always busy doing something spectacular. The psalmist wrote, "He will not let your foot slip— / he who watches over you will not slumber; / indeed, he who watches over Israel / will neither slumber nor sleep" (Ps. 121:3–4). Since this omnipotent God doesn't sleep, the work He does is immeasureable. He is actively at work on all levels—from the grandiose to the seemingly inconsequential. Because we human beings are finite in our thinking, we tend to think that only what we know reflects the sum total of the work of God. How pompous of us to think that way.

Becoming a Spiritual Adventurer

People like to be informed about the subjects of their interest. Think about all of the millions of books we buy every year, place on our bookcases, and never read. We've all been guilty of this practice at some time or another. The sad reality is that a lot of people like to think that being aware of an idea is the same as executing the idea. I'm sure you've read the numerous biblical examples of spiritual adventures and thought: *What will it take for me to be like that?* Whether you connect with the bravery of David as he slew Goliath, or you resonate with Rahab, the harlot who was able to keep a secret and it secured her deliverance, you must ask yourself: *What are the qualities God looks for in spiritual adventurers?* I believe God looks for ordinary people, available people, and obedient people.

God Uses Ordinary People

Sometimes we disqualify ourselves from becoming spiritual adventurers by thinking that we're not dynamic enough, or tall enough, or smart enough, or experienced enough. This is not biblical. The apostle Paul shed light on the heart of God when he wrote:

> *Brothers, think of what you were when you were called. Not many of you were wise by human standards; not many were influential; not many were of noble birth. But God chose the foolish things of the*

world to shame the wise; God chose the weak things of the world to
shame the strong. He chose the lowly things of this world and the
despised things—and the things that are not—to nullify the things
that are, so that no one may boast before him.

(1 Corinthians 1:26–29)

God uses ordinary people so that all glory goes to Him. Ordinary people may not stand out. Their high school graduating classes did not vote them the most likely to succeed. In fact, they were not even in the running. This is the picture of an ordinary person.

Although by some people's standards you are ordinary, you are just the person God is looking to use. Consider David. He was the youngest of Jesse's eight sons. When Samuel came unannounced to Bethlehem to anoint one of Jesse's sons as king, Jesse didn't even call David to the event. Samuel was the most renowned man of God in that day, yet David was not even afforded an opportunity to turn down an invitation.

Samuel looked first at Eliab, who he thought—from all outward appearances—would make a fitting king. But God said to Samuel, "Do not consider his appearance or his height, for I have rejected him. The LORD does not look at the things man looks at. Man looks at the outward appearance, but the LORD looks at the heart" (1 Sam. 16:7).

After that quick lesson on how to look for God's choice of leader, Samuel was able to finally select David, an ordinary person. In order to become a spiritual adventurer like David, you need to get God's attention with your quality of life and willingness to be used by Him. Don't look to please people or be in the "in" crowd. Look only to God and He'll begin to take you on adventures with Him.

God Uses Available People

A second trait in the spiritual adventurers God uses is available people. These individuals willingly adjust their lives to honor God's desire to use them. Oftentimes, the way God intends to use them are not ways they previously contemplated.

Consider Elisha, whom the prophet Elijah found plowing a field with twelve yoke of oxen. Elisha had his own farm, and he was working alongside the employees. Although Elisha had a successful business, he was still available to pursue God's plans. In fact, as Elisha was plowing the field, Elijah "went up to him and threw his cloak around him" (1 Kings 19:19). This gesture symbolized that Elijah was to mentor Elisha to eventually do what he did.

Elisha received the message and abandoned his profession instantly in order to be a protégé to the great prophet Elijah. Elisha is an example of a real man of humility and wisdom. It took humility to walk away from a thriving business where he was overseeing his own staff to become a servant to Elijah. It also took wisdom on the part of Elisha to recognize God's invitation to a spiritual adventure even though all he knew was the security of his job and business.

Would you be able to recognize the involvement of God, should He try to turn your life completely around in one day? If you make yourself fully available to God, you will always be enjoying spiritual adventures. Learn to pray: "God, all that I have and all that I am, I freely give to You."

God Uses Obedient People

It takes a big God to use ordinary people who make themselves available to Him. On the flip side of that coin, it will take people who are fully obedient to God's plan to become spiritual adventurers. Obedience is the ability to honor God's request in the face of difficulty and the lack of popularity. A lot of people start off making promises to God about how He can trust them and use them for His purpose. But when the rubber meets the road, the numbers drop off significantly. Some people quit because of the fear of failure while others quit because they like some plan other than God's.

The temptation to veer off course must be overcome. My counsel is to stay the course and demonstrate a true obedience to God. In order to see how well you're obeying God, ask yourself some hard questions. For example: *Is there anything that God has asked of me that I have not completed? If so, why have I left it incomplete?*

My concern is that God may not want to issue new instructions for you if you have not followed the previous ones. You must be a steward of the grace of God. This means that you must treasure the plans and purposes of God. In treasuring them, the actual executing of these plans will convey to God that you can be trusted. Even if these areas of action may seem small, the best policy is to complete them. Jesus said, "You have been faithful with a few things; I will put you in charge of many things" (Matt. 25:21). God is watching what we do in order to promote us to bigger and better things. If we are not faithful in handling small things, we should not expect Him to entrusted us with larger things.

This message should spur us on to complete all the little assignments we have been given so that we position ourselves to handle God's larger spiritual adventures. Since the Holy Spirit is charged to speak to us what He hears from Jesus, we can ask God to provide spiritual adventures that bring glory to His kingdom. Why not take a moment right now and pray this prayer?

Heavenly Father, I long to participate in the fantastic plans You're executing around me. Please include me. Whatever You would like me to do, please let me know. I will prepare my heart and life to carry out all of Your orders. Just tell me what is on Your heart, Lord, and I will fulfill it. I will go where You want me to go. I will do what You want me to do. I will speak to whom You want me to speak. I am Your servant—send me. These things I ask in Jesus' name. Amen.

Day 29: Steps to Rehearse

Spiritual adventures are a by-product of your journey to the mountain of God. Adventures can start when you decide to yield to the leadership of the Holy Spirit. Fresh commitment to walk in a new level of obedience, repentance, or consecration marked by prayer and fasting will also go a long way in fostering spiritual adventures.

1. The Holy Spirit will not force or bully you into submitting to His leadership. You must voluntarily agree to submit to the Holy Spirit just as you voluntarily submitted to accept Jesus as your Savior.

2. God looks for ordinary, available, and obedient people to take on spiritual adventures.

3. In making yourself available to God, learn to pray: "God, all that I have and all that I am, I freely give to You."

Total Surrender

The call to follow Jesus is a call to die. You are called to die to selfish desires . . . to die to your own will . . . to die to your own preferences. If you are not totally surrendered to the Lord, this probably sounds like brutality. But this is just another way of saying that you are called to be a true disciple of Christ. A disciple—a disciplined follower—is one who finds total pleasure in ensuring that his master is completely satisfied.

The journey to the mountain of God is not about you; it's about God and what He wants for you. Remember what the apostle John wrote: "Thou art worthy, O Lord, to receive glory and honour and power: for thou hast created all things, and for thy pleasure they are and were created" (Rev. 4:11 KJV). You have been created for the total pleasure of God. With that said, what must you do to convey total surrender to Jesus?

The apostle Paul answered the question with this statement: "I have been crucified with Christ and I no longer live, but Christ lives in me. The life I live in the body, I live by faith in the Son of God, who loved me and gave himself for me" (Gal. 2:20). In other words, you best demonstrate living totally for Christ when you return your life to Christ by saying, "Lord, I surrender my body, soul, and spirit to You. Please live Your life through me." People who desire this exhibit their posture in these principal ways: they surrender their wills, they surrender their interests, and they surrender their lives—forever.

I Have Surrendered My Will

Throughout the Bible we learn of a term that is associated with someone who speaks and lives for God: "servant." Paul referred to himself as a "servant of God" (Titus 1:1). Paul perceived the title as a badge of honor and not something negative or belittling. The word we translate "servant" from the Greek, in which the New Testament was written, is *doulos,* which means "a bond slave."[1] This particular class of servant voluntarily puts his will— his mental faculties—in submission to the will of his master. In other words, the master's choices are now the servant's choices.

This is no light matter. Imagine if you placed all of your choices and courses of action into someone else's hands while saying, "Whatever decision you make in these matters, I'll freely go along with it." Fortunately, God did not call us to offer up our wills in that manner to another human being. He alone is to receive that gift from us. True surrender to God must include the voluntary yielding of our wills. In order to have an intimate relationship with the Lord, we have to trust Him completely. This trust must extend into every area of our lives, even those areas that make us feel uncomfortable. If we trust God, we must trust Him with our wills.

This yielding of the will to the will of God means that your choice of mate, choice of home, career, and even church affiliation must all be God's choice. In essence, the will of God must become your will in every area of your life. A surrendered person strives to live the will of God because he recognizes that God has created him for His pleasure. Saint Augustine voiced his view of humanity's purpose this way: "You [God] have formed us for Yourself, and our hearts are restless till they find rest in You." In response to the question "What is the chief end of man?" The Westminster Catechism answers: "The chief end of man is to glorify God and enjoy Him forever."[2] This truth must ultimately translate into you voluntarily placing your will into the hands of God.

I Have Surrendered My Interests

If you have surrendered your interests to the Lord, you have made a conscious and voluntary effort to commit your curiosities, concerns, and attention to His purposes. While some have made a clear commitment to submitting their wills to God, they still are curious about the things they feel they are missing. Their interests vacillate between the desires of God and the desires of the world. It's like a newlywed husband who spends all his time wondering if he chose the right woman. Although he's at home in bed with his bride, he is curious about Mary on the job, questioning whether she would have been a better selection.

Surrendering of our interests to the Lord means that we must also die to our own selfish desires. We must completely accept God's will and plan for our lives without any second thoughts. For example, my first two degrees were in the field of engineering. After graduate school, I worked for a consulting engineering firm as an environmental engineer. When the Lord called me into the ministry, I worked part-time as an engineer while attending seminary. After Christ Church was planted, I still worked part-time as an engineer. When I transitioned, eighteen months later, into full-time Christian ministry, I knew I was in the will of God. I did not look back, wondering if I had missed something.

This vocational transition also helped me transition emotionally and spiritually. My interests were no longer linked to engineering issues, but to ministry and people issues. Some seventeen years out of the engineering profession, I have not had one day where I wanted to leave the ministry and return to the field of engineering.

The only accomplishment I sometimes wish I had achieved is my professional engineering license. In order to receive that impressive designation, a person has to pass two exams. The Engineering in Training exam covers the theoretical topics found in undergraduate-level studies. One can take the second exam, Principles and Practice, after attaining four years of approved

work experience in the field. I passed the first exam and had qual-
ified to take the second one. But it was during a review course for
the Principles and Practice test that my calling to the ministry
compelled me to serve Christ Church in a full-time capacity.
Thus, I never took the second exam. Although sometimes I think
about the fact that I had never completed a stated goal, I've surrendered myself to the Lord's will.

Through this and other experiences, I learned how to submit
my interests to God voluntarily. I learned the joy of obedience.
When you know what God's will is, your heart should not struggle to comply with it. You should freely obey, knowing that obedience is precious to God. This act of obedience will ultimately
result in joy springing up in your heart.

You should not only surrender your will, but also your interests
to the interest of God. By transitioning into the ministry I realized that God has great plans for my life, and that having a professional engineering designation pales in comparison to my new
designation: David Ireland, a servant of Jesus Christ.

I Have Surrendered My Life

In the last chapter, I made a statement that bears repeating—
especially in light of the need for you to surrender your life to
Christ. I said that we must all be willing to pray: "All that I have
and all that I am, I freely give to You, Lórd." Making this statement is more than just a poetic gesture. It must consume your
heart, mind, and soul with the reality that the best thing you can
do to show that you are a fully devoted follower of Christ is to
give Him your life.

Paul wrote: "Therefore, I urge you, brothers, in view of God's
mercy, to offer your bodies as living sacrifices, holy and pleasing
to God—this is your spiritual act of worship" (Rom. 12:1). In
The Message, a modern translation of the Bible by Eugene Peterson, the same verse reads this way: "So here's what I want you to
do, God helping you: Take your everyday, ordinary life—your
sleeping, eating, going-to-work, and walking-around life—and

place it before God as an offering." A surrendered life is a life dedicated to God. When you present your life to God as an offering—a prized gift—you are saying, "God, I love You. The best way to show You that I love You is by giving You my life. Use me, Lord, for Your purpose. I give myself to You as a living gift."

This dedicatory act will be well received by God. If you are honest and sincere, God will start to align your life with His plans. Get ready to be used by God. He may start by pouring out the Holy Spirit upon your life so that you will learn to enjoy supernatural experiences. God uses these experiences to sharpen your effectiveness in helping others come to know and serve Jesus Christ.

Dwight L. Moody, the famed American evangelist, recounted a supernatural experience he had following his fresh commitment to live for God:

> One day in New York—what a day! I can't describe it! I seldom refer to it! It is almost too sacred to name! I can only say God revealed Himself to me! I had such an experience of love that I had to ask Him to stay His hand! I went to preaching again. The sermons were no different. I did not present any new truth. Yet hundreds were converted. I would not be back where I was before that blessed experience.[3]

Moody is no different from you or me. He was just hungry to live for God. A fresh surrender on his part positioned him to be more effective in ministry. Why not make a fresh commitment today? Let this renewed desire to serve Christ be marked with the investment of your time, talent, and treasure. When you spend your time for God's purpose, you employ your talents in the work of the Lord, and you've given your resources freely to God's house, you will demonstrate to God that you have freshly surrendered yourself to Him. Go for it! Give in all the way to God's plan for your life. You'll never regret it!

Day 30: Steps to Rehearse

One of the ways you keep your spiritual fire burning is to initiate times of fresh surrender to the Lord. Oftentimes the novelty of walking with Jesus wears off. This lull should evoke a new action that says: *I mean business for God.* Your actions may include the following:

1. Renew the surrender of your will to God. Declare to the Lord that His will is your will.

2. Surrender your interests to God. Communicate in a fresh way to the Lord that you will not give your curiosities, concerns, and attention to things outside of His will.

3. In making yourself available to God, learn to pray: "God, all that I have and all that I am, I freely give to You."

Step 7

Unleashing God's Blessings

God is more anxious to bestow his blessings on us than we are to receive them.

—Saint Augustine

The Power of Faith

Congratulations! You have made it to Step 7 in the journey to the mountain of God. At this point, you should be experiencing substantial growth in your personal worship and prayer habits. Your intimacy level with Christ should have also increased to the point where you're starting to ask such questions as, *How do I unleash God's blessings in my life and in the lives of those around me?* My focus for the next chapters will be to answer that question. Five power bases unleash the blessings of God, namely: the power of faith, the power of persistence, the power of unity, the power of agreement, and the power of spiritual warfare. Let's examine the power of faith.

Applying Faith in Life

We learned in an earlier lesson that we should embrace faith as a personal value if we are to achieve intimacy with the Lord. Faith, however, is more than a value system. It is the means God has instituted for us to appropriate His promises into our lives. The writer of Hebrews said, "We do not want you to become lazy, but to imitate those who through faith and patience inherit what has been promised" (6:12). While God has already announced His promises for us, we must exercise faith in Him to realize those promises. This verse also teaches us that the testimony of others can stimulate the muscle of faith in our lives.

Hudson Taylor, the famed missionary to China, commented in a letter to his mother about the role of faith in his life:

I felt that one's spiritual muscles required strengthening for such an undertaking [referring to his trip to China]. There was no doubt that if faith did not fail, God would not fail. But what if one's faith should prove insufficient? I had not at that time learned that even "if we believe not, yet he abideth faithful; he cannot deny himself." It was consequently a very serious matter to my mind, not whether He was faithful, but whether I had strong enough faith to warrant my embarking on the enterprise set before me. "When I get out to China," I thought to myself, "I shall have no claim on anyone for anything. My only claim will be on God. How important to learn, before leaving England, to move man, through God, by prayer alone."[1]

Hudson Taylor learned how faith worked when his back was pressed to the wall. He needed daily provision, resources, and favor with people who were ethnically different from himself. He needed the Lord to make a way out of no way for him once he was in China. You practice faith when you recognize that you have come to the end of your abilities and only God can make up what's lacking.

The writer of Hebrews told us that we are to imitate people like Hudson Taylor, who through faith enjoyed the promise of God. This simple man of faith pioneered the China Inland Mission organization that led thousands to Christ and was instrumental in bringing missionaries into that nation.

You may be facing a very difficult trial right now, yet you are pursuing intimacy with God. I commend you for the pursuit, but you also need to know how to fight the good fight of faith. One approach to engaging your faith in this trial is to find a promise of God that speaks to your situation and hold on to it. Hold on to it in prayer. Hold on to it in meditation. Hold on to it in your heart. The means of standing on God's Word for a promise to come to pass is spiritual warfare. Paul told us "to put on the full armor of God, so that when the day of evil comes, you may be able to stand your ground" (Eph. 6:13).

Your motives must be pure when you pursue God's promises in prayer. John Owen, a Puritan writer, said, "If we would pray for the things God has promised, we must ask for that which he has promised for the same reason that God gave us the promise and not to spend it on satisfying our own lusts."[2]

Once you've discerned that your motives are pure, spend some time in prayer concerning that promise. Whether you're praying for the salvation of your spouse or a new job for your adult child, stand on the fact that God loves you and will demonstrate His love. To secure the promise, you may also use the prayer of thanksgiving. Paul said to the Philippian Christians, "Do not be anxious about anything, but in everything, by prayer and petition, with thanksgiving, present your requests to God" (Phil. 4:6). This verse teaches us that after we've prayed and prayed about something, we should stop praying and start thanking God for His promises; we should tell the Lord, "Thank You that my spouse will be saved. Thank You for the new job for my son."

Giving thanks suggests that we know that God is able to do exceedingly, abundantly above all that we can ask or imagine. Therefore, we have ceased asking and have started thanking. In other words, God has heard our requests, so we move on to a place of confidence in God's abilities. Give Him thanks and leave the matter alone. This is where we exhibit true faith.

Do you recall Daniel when he was placed in the lions' den? At some point, he had to relax and say, *My life is in God's hands.* There was no way he could ward off hungry lions all night. Certainly if he had cried out in desperation all night, it would have shown that he was not sure if God was listening to his previous prayers.

People have a tendency to not believe something until they can see it. And people within certain cultures tend to be unsure that you're listening to them unless you're looking right into their eyes when they're speaking. Since we cannot see God, we don't know if He's listening to our prayers. So, what do we do? We keep praying the same prayers over and over, as if we'll one day see God standing in front of us, listening intently to our repetitious request. Our Savior is greater than we are. He does not need to have face time with us in order to hear us or to answer our prayer requests. Pray in faith and maintain a thankful heart as you await God's reply.

Faith Makes God Look Good

God does not need anyone's approval. He is secure in who He is. But for our sake He declares: "The people that do know their God shall be strong, and do *exploits*" (Dan. 11:32 KJV, italics mine). God expects us to use our faith and secure powerful promises as proof that we know Him. Have you considered how God can get glory out of your current dilemma?

A large portion of Psalm 96 captures the intent of God to receive glory out of every family and nation that serves Him.

> *Declare his glory among the nations,*
> *his marvelous deeds among all peoples.*
> *For great is the LORD and most worthy of praise;*
> *he is to be feared above all gods.*
> *For all the gods of the nations are idols,*
> *but the LORD made the heavens.*
> *Splendor and majesty are before him;*
> *strength and glory are in his sanctuary.*
> *Ascribe to the LORD, O families of nations,*
> *ascribe to the LORD glory and strength.*
> *Ascribe to the LORD the glory due his name;*
> *bring an offering and come into his courts.*
> *Worship the LORD in the splendor of his holiness;*
> *tremble before him, all the earth.*
>
> (Psalm 96:3–9)

Your present situation has potential to bring glory and honor to God. How you apply your faith is the decisive issue. You call upon faith in times of crisis. In fact, crisis is the building block of faith. The famous German theologian Dietrich Bonhoeffer taught a Sunday school class in an African-American church in Harlem while studying at Union Theological Seminary in New York City (1930–1931). That experience of interfacing with people who had learned how to be resilient from the devastation of past enslavement proved to be a powerful lesson on how people could endure dehumanizing oppression by exercising childlike, biblical faith, particularly in praise and worship. Unquestionably, that exposure strengthened Bonhoeffer in his struggle against Nazi power in Germany.[3]

Even in the midst of Nazi-inflicted pain, Bonhoeffer was able to bring glory to God. No matter your situation, you can still draw closer to God while exercising strong faith in God's abilities. Ask God to show you how to view your situation. He is faithful; He will show you. This faith request is not just a positive approach to handling problems; it is a biblical method of dealing with difficult situations. James said:

> *If any of you lacks wisdom, he should ask God, who gives generously to all without finding fault, and it will be given to him. But when he asks, he must believe and not doubt, because he who doubts is like a wave of the sea, blown and tossed by the wind. That man should not think he will receive anything from the Lord; he is a double-minded man, unstable in all he does.*
>
> (James 1:5–8)

The faith approach in difficult times is to ask God to bring you through successfully. You should also ask for the wisdom to understand why you're in the trial. If God does not address that point, then aim your prayer strategy at gaining wisdom to handle the emotional, physical, and spiritual ramifications of the crisis. You ought never to think that God doesn't care about your situation, or that He is powerless to bring change. Your mind set should be: *I am going to enjoy the Lord even in the midst of this unpleasant situation.* This is a faith sentiment that declares: *No matter what situation is at work in my life, my resolve is to enjoy mountaintop living and try my best to let this situation generate some glory to God.*

Faith is an invaluable ingredient to pursuing spiritual intimacy. Passion for God brings you closer to Him, while faith in God helps you to execute the plans of God. Both are necessary to become the mature disciple Christ is calling you to be.

Day 31: Steps to Rehearse

Mountaintop dwellers are also powerful in the exercise of their faith. Faith in God is a transforming force that passionate believers must wield. The power of faith goes into effect when:

1. Your back is pressed against the wall due to a trial.

2. You find a promise of God that fits your situation and you hold onto it in faith until the heavens release God's blessings.

3. You start giving thanks to God. After you have prayed intently, switch gears by thanking Him for the resolution to the conflict.

Day 32

The Power of Persistence

Patience comes as a by-product of spiritual intimacy, as you learn to persist to obtain the blessings of God. The blessings of God often follow the successful completion of intense trials. Without the power of persistence, these trying situations may get the best of you, causing you to give up before receiving the reward of your faith.

Fortunately, patience—which is a form of persistence—is one of the nine fruits of the Spirit (Gal. 5:22). The fruit of the Spirit ripens in our lives as we abide in fellowship with the Lord and yield to His leadership. Your journey to the mountain of God is building a greater level of spiritual passion in your life. At the same time, this spiritual passion is also making you more Christlike, which is another way of saying that the fruit of patience is maturing in your life.

To patiently persist en route to the blessings of God is not a novel idea. The Bible declares: "We do not want you to become lazy, but to imitate those who through faith and patience inherit what has been promised" (Heb. 6:12). As I shared in the previous chapter, God's promises—namely His many blessings—await those who utilize the twin weapons of faith and patience. We have already looked at the power of faith, so now let's explore how the power of patience, or put another way, the power of *persistence,* works.

The Call of Persistence

I don't know about you, but the question of when to persist has always been a puzzle to me. Fortunately, I have discovered a few parameters that have helped me to decipher the situations in which I should unleash the power of persistence. Apart from this method of analysis, it would be extremely difficult to discern when to continue plugging away at a trial or at some course of action that doesn't seem to be leading anywhere. Sometimes problems can morph into deeper problems while we're exercising persistence. To avoid the unwise use of patience, follow this helpful guideline.

The power of persistence is best used when your position in the situation reflects righteousness, you continuously bathe the matter in prayer, and your persistence is in direct response to a word from the Lord.

Persistence Works Through Righteousness

In Luke 18, Jesus shared the parable of the persistent widow. Read on and then let me discuss the approach of persistence. Jesus said:

> *"In a certain town there was a judge who neither feared God nor cared about men. And there was a widow in that town who kept coming to him with the plea, 'Grant me justice against my adversary.'*
>
> *"For some time he refused. But finally he said to himself, 'Even though I don't fear God or care about men, yet because this widow keeps bothering me, I will see that she gets justice, so that she won't eventually wear me out with her coming!'"*
>
> *And the Lord said, "Listen to what the unjust judge says. And will not God bring about justice for his chosen ones, who cry out to him day and night? Will he keep putting them off? I tell you, he will see that they get justice, and quickly. However, when the Son of Man comes, will he find faith on the earth?"*

(Luke 18:2–8)

We shouldn't think of this widow as an old woman. Girls in the New Testament era usually married between the ages of thirteen and fourteen, so this widow could have been very young. Widows in that day, however, were very poor. They usually fell in the same economic ranking as orphans. Because this widow had to go before a single judge, and not a tribunal in search of justice against her adversary, the scholarly community has drawn the conclusion that her case was a financial matter. Someone either owed her a debt, a pledge, or a portion of an inheritance. Hence, a single judge could hear the matter and grant her justice.

Unfortunately, the judge she stood before was an unjust one. He was unethical. Nonetheless, the widow was persistent in pursuing a just decision. Even if she was inclined to offer him a bribe, she was too poor. Persistence was her only solution to secure God's blessings. Her persistence eventually wore the judge down and he granted her a just verdict, albeit to get rid of her.

What made this widow maintain her stance? One reason was that she was holding onto a position of righteousness in this matter. Archbishop Desmond Tutu wrote:

> *During the darkest days of apartheid I used to say to P. W. Botha, the president of South Africa, that we had already won, and I invited him and other white South Africans to join the winning side. All the "objective" facts were against us—the pass laws, the imprisonments, the tear gassing, the massacres, the murder of political activists—but my confidence was not in the present circumstances but in the laws of God's universe. This is a moral universe, which means that, despite all the evidence that seems to be to the contrary, there is no way that evil and injustice and oppression and lies can have the last word. God is a God who cares about right and wrong.*[1]

Bishop Tutu's experience with apartheid and how South Africa was able to overcome this insidious poison affirms that we should use the power of persistence when we are in the position of righteousness.

Persistence Works Through Prayer

Jesus introduced the parable of the persistent widow by stating to His disciples that they should "always pray and not give up" (Luke 18:1). The parable is about the role of prayer alongside persistence. One without the other is futile. Prayer is a means of dialoguing with God. But it also is a way of gauging the wisdom of God. In other words, if you're constantly in prayer, you will be able to tap into God's wisdom. In fact, James told us, "Perseverance must finish its work so that you may be mature and complete, not lacking anything. If any of you lacks wisdom, he should ask God, who gives generously to all without finding fault, and it will be given to him" (James 1:4–5).

The apostle James was speaking about how to deal with trials that never seem to end. James used the word "perseverance," which is just another way of saying persistence. He instructed us that if we lack wisdom and we're doggedly plowing through a trial, we should ask God for wisdom. And God, who is not stingy with His insights, foresight, and perception, will certainly give us a generous dose of wisdom so we can navigate all of the complexities of our trials. Wisdom fuels persistence. Wisdom helps you realize that what you're fighting for is worth the fight. So, you persistently continue in the process of the trial in order to gain the desired prize.

In 1955, when Colonel Harland Sanders retired at the age of 65, he had little to show for himself, except an old Caddie roadster, a $105 monthly pension check, and a recipe for chicken. Knowing he couldn't live on his pension, he took his chicken recipe in hand, got behind the wheel of his clunker, and set out to make his fortune. His first plan was to sell his chicken recipe to restaurant owners, who would in turn give him a residual for every piece of chicken they sold—5 cents per chicken. The first restaurateur he called on turned him down.

So did the second. So did the third. In fact, the first 1,000 sales calls Colonel Sanders made ended in rejection. Still, he continued to call on owners as he traveled across the USA, sleeping in his car to save money. Prospect number 1,009 finally gave him his first "yes." After two years of making daily calls he had signed up a total of five restaurants. Still the Colonel pressed on, knowing that he had a great chicken recipe and that someday the idea would catch on. Of course, you know how the story ends. The idea DID catch on.

By 1963 the Colonel had 600 restaurants across the country selling his secret recipe of Kentucky Fried Chicken (with 11 herbs and spices). In 1964 he was bought out by future Kentucky governor John Brown. Even though the sale made him a multi-millionaire, he continued to represent and promote KFC until his death in 1980.[2]

Just the way Colonel Sanders used wisdom to fuel his persistence, you can get the wisdom that you need from the Lord through prayer. Ask God for wisdom and let it feed your persistence until you secure His blessings in the matter at hand.

Persistence Is Based on a Word from the Lord

In the final words of the parable of the persistent widow, Jesus said: "When the Son of Man comes, will he find faith on the earth?" (Luke 18:8). This verse speaks of His second coming. His question connects the subject of faith with the parable of persistence. Faith is vital to maintaining persistence. Paul added that "faith comes from hearing the message, and the message is heard through the word of Christ" (Rom. 10:17). The word "message" in this passage means "the thing heard." The New Testament Greek scholar Kenneth Wuest said that this passage can be translated this way: "Faith is out of the source of that which is heard."[3]

When you connect the lessons in both passages, you see that persistence is based on faith that originates in what you hear from the Lord. Put another way: persistence is based on a word from the Lord. In order to decide whether or not you are to keep hanging in there, you should seek to hear a word from the Lord. In other words, what is God saying about the matter? If, while you're in prayer, you hear the Lord tell you to be patient and pursue persistently, then you should obey without questioning. On the other hand, if you have not heard a word from God and your situation does not meet the first two parameters that support persistence, then you should seriously consider yielding.

As a pastor, I have seen so many people confuse having a strong will with the Bible's meaning of persistence. They are two entirely different things. One is based on socialization and personality while the other is a fruit of the Spirit that we learn by forging a relationship with God. If being persistent is simply another way to save face, it is not biblical persistence. Biblical persistence is about the Lord's plan to bring blessings to the lives of people who are committed to serving and living for Him.

Biblical persistence is also about our commitment to seeing God's plan lived out in this broken world. If your persistence is all about you and your plans, your pursuit is an exercise in selfishness. Your persistence should reflect your commitment to pursuing a deeper relationship with the Lord. Don't confuse that with any earthly achievement.

Day 32: Steps to Rehearse

The power of persistence is a quality that God has told us directly to cultivate in our lives. We need faith and patience if we are to obtain the promises of God.

1. The power of persistence is best used when your position is one that fits God's definition of righteousness.

2. Persistence works through prayer. Through prayer you receive an opportunity to hear God's wisdom, which you can apply to your situation.

3. Before you dig in your heels through persistence, remember that persistence is based on hearing a word from the Lord. Faith to stay under a trial must be based on God's word to you.

Day 33

The Power of Agreement

What releases God's blessings? *Unity.* I have seen spiritually passionate people who could not experience the blessings of God in their families, finances, or their areas of influence because they just could not cooperate with anyone. They had become islands unto themselves. They did not find pleasure in making the critical adjustments needed to facilitate healthy compromise and concession, which are the ingredients of teamwork.

The Bible is clear: Christianity is a communal faith. God calls us to be a part of a body that is "built up until we all reach unity in the faith and in the knowledge of the Son of God and become mature" (Eph. 4:12–13). Furthermore, Paul continued his address to the Ephesian Christians by saying, "Speaking the truth in love, we will in all things grow up into him who is the Head, that is, Christ. From him the whole body, joined and held together by every supporting ligament, grows and builds itself up in love, as each part does its work" (Eph. 4:15–16). These passages point out that we are not to live isolated lives. Our lives must be integrated in an active way within a local fellowship of Christians so that we can supply spiritual nutrients to the group, and they to us.

The commingling of our lives, gifts, resources, personalities, and overall strength of relationship with God is important to the process of spiritual development. Paul used words such as: "grows up," "joined," "held together," and "builds itself up" in a manner that speaks of the necessity of working in harmony so that we can experience the fullness of God's blessings in our lives.

The Call to Unity

You would be hard-pressed to find someone who would say that the Bible doesn't call believers to walk in unity. The King James Version of the Bible shows a total of five hundred times the words "unity," "agreement," "agree," and "together" appear in the Scriptures. Although your relationship with God is primarily dependent upon how you personally invest in your spiritual development, you must not ignore the value and contribution that unity with other believers can add to your life.

I have learned over the years that unity can come about in many different ways. God can use crises, projects, or goals to establish a sense of shared destiny. In 1994, when our church purchased our current facility—a cathedral built in 1911—we were five hundred in number. Previously, we had worshiped in numerous rental facilities. The pressure of having to assemble and disassemble the chairs, the public address system, and the music equipment each week had galvanized us into a powerful team. Unbeknownst to us, amidst our complaints, we were being molded into a close-knit and unified group through those weekly chores.

In my naiveté as a pastor, I was praying for unity and expecting it to occur miraculously. I didn't realize that it had occurred slowly and subtly. Once we occupied the newly purchased cathedral, everything was in place. We didn't have to put away the children's church materials. We did not need to fold up and store the chairs. The public address system had a permanent home. Having our own building provided a greater sense of stability to families who needed the brick and mortar in order to make their decisions about joining our church. Consequently, we grew rapidly to one thousand people within the first year and doubled again in the second year.

Soon, I started noticing a marked difference between the hundreds of newcomers and the ones who had been part of the ministry prior to purchasing the cathedral. The "before cathedral," or BC, members, were more sociable and committed to the local church than the AC—after cathedral—members. The preservice and postservice setup requirements in the rental halls had created a deep unity and a shared sense of purpose. Many AC members showed a nominal sense of commitment to the church family.

I prayed feverishly about the need to mold both groups into one. With all of the preaching, teaching, and other kinds of ministry presentation, we were not fully attaining the goal. It took a building fund project to galvanize the hearts of the BC and AC members into becoming one united congregation. People became united around a common need. Our one-hundred-year-old cathedral needed air conditioning, a new heating system, and some major renovation work. The building fund put everyone on the same page, which cemented our hearts together, resulting in a deep relational commitment and a united vision.

The Need for Unity

After growing to over five thousand members and having five worship services each Sunday, we had essentially grown into five different congregations. Without any intentionality on the part of our leadership team, the dynamics of each service are different. Although I speak at each service and we offer the same song selections, albeit with a couple of rotating worship teams, each service still turns out differently. I found myself returning to praying for unity. I wanted to see the church experience unity, despite the space limitations we now faced.

You can feel disunity. You can lie in bed with your spouse and feel alienation. It is a feeling that says, "I don't see things quite the way you see things" or "We are looking for two different things. We used to connect emotionally and relationally, but time, pressure, experiences, and/or poor decisions have divided us." Given that emotional and spiritual reality, I learned that in order to regain unity, I needed to introduce a spiritual action.

Jesus used remembrance and repentance as means of engaging

the church at Ephesus to regain its spiritual passion for Him, saying: "You have forsaken your first love. Remember the height from which you have fallen! Repent and do the things you did at first" (Rev. 2:4–5). In some instances, disunity is the direct result of sin. In this case, repentance is required. In the case of what I was experiencing in my local church, disunity was a result of numerical growth and the lack of relational opportunities.

We had to remember what it was like to spend quality time with one another prior to the time demands of five services. We had to come up with different structures and concepts of ministry that facilitated small group gatherings. This had to become a value that we embraced and guarded if we were going to experience unity again.

Repentance for us centered on the fact that we had not made relationships a high enough priority in the church. We thought that they would naturally evolve as they had in the years prior. We had unconsciously made organizational efficiency and excellence a high priority, and rightly so, but we should have made an equal investment of time and effort in building knitted relationships. Unity in relationships can only come about by spending time with one another around a worthy cause.

Tools for Achieving Unity

We can use significant tools to achieve unity on a personal or organizational level: acceptance, accountability, and agreement. Let's explore each one.

Acceptance: The Mark of a Healthy Relationship

Good relationships are intentional. You cannot have a meaningful relationship that deepens over time if you don't intentionally invest in its development and maturation. You have to convey worth and value to the person in the relationship by spending time with him or her. Often, this may require time that you don't have. But building a healthy relationship with another requires a commitment to keeping a portion of your schedule clear for that other person. Even in marriage, there must be a concerted effort to guard your schedule so that personal time with each other is a priority.

In counseling engaged couples or newlyweds, I warn that one of the greatest mistakes in marriage is neglecting to grow *together.* You cannot delegate your need to build a strong, healthy relationship to someone else. You must be personally involved. This is critical to walking in unity. And your personal involvement is a result of your being accepted by those around you. Acceptance is critical to healthy relationships. A true friend looks beyond your flaws and shortcomings and wants to spend valuable time with you because of you. He is not in the relationship because you're perfect. He is committed to the relationship because he enjoys your presence in his life.

Take a moment right now and put a plan together to call, e-mail, or write a friend and say: "Can we get together soon? I need some face time just to reconnect as friends." I guarantee that that person is more than likely in the same boat as you are, busy journeying to the mountain of God but lacking the blessings that come from walking in the power of agreement.

Accountability: The Ingredient of a Lasting Relationship

Lasting relationships are built on sincerity. A genuine trustworthiness must flow from you to your friend. You are not trying to impress each other but rather to get to know one another around the shared values of honesty and trust. Trust speaks of reliance upon that person's word or stated actions. Honesty, uprightness, and ethics must be at work in the relationship if trust is going to exist. People must understand and trust each other in order to work well together.[1]

When you trust each other, it's easy to hold one another accountable. Because accountability is an ingredient that helps secure relationships for the long haul, your friend must let you into his life and vice versa. You must be able to discuss vocational desires, life's ambitions, joys, fears, and even frustrations. This helps to build a relationship that has a wide base of fellowship topics and issues. Accountability occurs best when your friend knows your world. This keeps the friendship growing. Open the door of your heart and let friends in so that they can love you for you, and you can become vulnerable and transparent—a sign of true accountability.

Agreement: The Power Behind Good Relationships

David the psalmist wrote, "How good and pleasant it is / when brothers live together in unity!" (Ps. 133:1). This verse affirms how potent and life-transforming unity and agreement are in the lives of believers. In order to walk in agreement, you must identify with a common need. Whatever that need may be, it must be common to all parties involved and articulated in such a way that each person can hear what is being asked of him or her. In some cases, the need may simply be: "I need prayer about my relationship with my children." Whatever the request, it must be plainly stated and easy for others to grasp.

In order to achieve a state of agreement in your relationships, you must clearly convey your appreciation of that other person. Everyone wants to be valued and cherished—even men in their friendships with other men. When you convey appreciation to the other person for being in your life, you are saying that you enjoy walking together down the road of life.

This principle of agreement also conveys the fact that you resonate with one another's needs. You may find yourself purchasing two of the same book—one for you, and one for your friend—because you share the same interests. These little tokens of appreciation go a long way in securing true friendships.

Make a list of the people with whom you want to establish deeper relationships. What will you do over the next several days to see this come about? Take the next step and unleash the power of unity by building great friendships. Remember the words of Solomon: "A man that hath friends must shew himself friendly" (Prov. 18:24 KJV).

Day 33: Steps to Rehearse

We often overlook the power of unity. But fortunately, every day we can decide to start a new relationship by showing ourselves friendly. In order to release the power in agreement, consider engaging yourself in the following practices.

1. Recognize and accept the reality that you need others in your life to help you become the person that God wants you to be. Know that others need you for the same reason.

2. Agreement and unity must become values that you intentionally pursue.

3. Acceptance, accountability, and agreement are three significant steps to achieving unity on a personal and organizational level.

The Power of Love

Of all the powers available in the world, the power of love is the most transforming. When you consider the power of electricity, water, or nuclear weapons, it cannot compare with what true love can produce. While electricity can light up an entire city, love can light up the soul of each person in the city. While water can sustain each person's natural life, love can make each person want to live. The power of love is unfathomable. This is why Paul wrote: "And now these three remain: faith, hope and love. But the greatest of these is love" (1 Cor. 13:13).

The first time I ever heard the reading of the great chapter on love—1 Corinthians 13—I was a new Christian attending a Bible study in the dorm of a fellow engineering student. When she read the words of that passage, I was spellbound. I had never heard such a beautiful sentiment. After the study let out, I ran to my dorm room and searched my Bible for that passage. When I found it, I sat down and read over and over this portion of Scripture:

If I speak in the tongues of men and of angels, but have not love, I am only a resounding gong or a clanging cymbal. If I have the gift of prophecy and can fathom all mysteries and all knowledge, and if I have a faith that can move mountains, but have not love, I am nothing. If I give all I possess to the poor and surrender my body to the flames, but have not love, I gain nothing.

Love is patient, love is kind. It does not envy, it does not boast, it is not proud. It is not rude, it is not self-seeking, it is not easily angered, it keeps no record of wrongs. Love does not delight in evil but rejoices with the truth. It always protects, always trusts, always hopes, always perseveres.

Love never fails. But where there are prophecies, they will cease; where there are tongues, they will be stilled; where there is knowledge, it will pass away.

(1 Corinthians 13:1–8)

Love Defined

Paul presented fourteen different descriptive terms for love in these verses. Each term broadens our perspective and opens another window in our minds as to how God's love ought to be viewed. We learn that love:

1. Is Patient.

2. Is Kind.

3. Does not envy.

4. Does not boast.

5. Is not proud.

6. Is not self-seeking.

7. Is not easily angered.

8. Keeps no record of wrong.

9. Does not delight itself in evil.

10. Rejoices with the truth.

11. Always protects.

12. Always hopes.

13. Always perseveres.

14. Never fails.

I don't know about you, but I struggle to love in this manner. I am committed to reaching toward this standard, however. For some, loving another person is quite frightening. For others, receiving love is the most difficult thing in the world. The one constant, however, is that each of us needs to be a giver and a receiver of love if we are going to live satisfying lives.

The Shades of Love

There are different kinds of love, yet these fourteen traits should be your aim. Since the New Testament was written in classical Greek, in order to fully understand what Paul or any other writer truly meant, you can consult a concordance. In the 1 Corinthians passage, Paul used the Greek word *agape* wherever you see the English word "love." *Agape* means "A love which is awakened by a sense of value in an object; a love that puts self aside in an effort to help and bless others, yes, a love that goes to the point of suffering if that is necessary in order to bless others."[1] If *agape* is the way God loves us, we must do our best to love others in that same fashion.

Another type of love is captured in the word *phileo,* where we get the English word "Philadelphia." This is the love which is "the response of the human spirit to what appeals to it as pleasurable [i.e., friendship, friendly love, etc.]. This love takes pleasure in the person loved."[2] We use *phileo* to describe friendship and friendly love.

A third type of love is *stergo.* This Greek word captures the love that parents have for their children and children have for their parents. Husbands and wives also have this kind of love for one another. The final type of love described in the Bible is *eros,* where we get the word *erotic.* This fourth type of love has its basis in passion; sex love; it speaks of the blind impulse produced by passion.[3]

The love I'm referring to in this chapter is *agape*—the God-kind of love. This is the love Paul was describing in 1 Corinthians 13. This type of love, like all the others, requires vulnerability. One writer described agape love with these words:

To love all is to be vulnerable. Love anything, and your heart will certainly be wrung and possibly broken. If you want to make sure of keeping it intact, you must give your heart to no one. . . . Wrap it carefully round with hobbies and little luxuries; avoid all entanglements; lock it safe in a casket or coffin of your selfishness. But in that casket—safe, dark, motionless, airless—it will change. It will become unbreakable, impenetrable, irredeemable. . . . The only place outside heaven where you can be perfectly safe from all the dangers of love is—hell.[4]

I would also add that the closer you walk with Christ, the more you will create a heavenly environment in the lives of those you touch because of His love working through you.

Love Released

The power of love must be released in our lives and in the lives of those we influence. John declared: "Dear children, let us not love with words or tongue but with actions and in truth. This then is how we know that we belong to the truth, and how we set our hearts at rest in his presence" (1 John 3:18–19). Moreover, you cannot journey to the mountain of God without getting infected by the very thing that God is—love. Not only does God have love and give love, He also *is* love (1 John 4:8, 16). John said that "love comes from God" (1 John 4:7). When the power of *agape* love has filled your life and you release it, certain qualities should be evident: compassion, a lifestyle of giving, and service to humanity.

Compassion Reflects Love

Compassion is to feel what others feel. It is your association with the plight and difficulty of another. It was compassion for the poorest of the poor in India that led Mother Teresa to lay down her life and demonstrate God's love toward them. She left the comfort of the convent because of the compassion that came by the voice of the Lord that said, "Go to the poor. Leave the convent. Live with the poorest of the poor."[5]

It was compassion for African-Americans and the rest of humanity that moved Dr. Martin Luther King Jr. to sacrifice his life for the fight of equality and justice in a racially divided American society. It was God's great compassion for the world that caused Him to orchestrate the dying of His son on the cross for your forgiveness and salvation.

We now have a responsibility to unleash the power of this transforming love in our spheres of influence through acts of compassion. Look around. What makes your heart ache? What personal pain or societal ill bothers you to the point that you must do something? Whatever it is, don't remain silent, with your compassion locked up in the privacy and safety of your heart. Release it and let God's transforming power go to work. It will make a difference.

Giving Reflects Love

Philanthropy and giving are great ways of demonstrating God's love. You may find someone who says he is pursuing spiritual passion, then learn he is stingy and uncaring. I have trouble reconciling how such a person could claim real intimacy with God without ever modeling the very trait that sets God apart—His heart of generosity. God is a giver. The most famous verse of Scripture, John 3:16, proclaims this fact loud and clear: "For God so loved the world that he gave his one and only Son, that whoever believes in him shall not perish but have eternal life."

In journeying to the mountain of God, you should exhibit a marked difference in your giving to the work of the Lord. You should seriously consider the biblical idea of giving a tithe—10 percent of one's income—if you are not already doing this. Just imagine if every Christian decided against tithing. Where would Christianity be in the next twenty, thirty, or forty years? Christianity would cease to exist as we know it. Our faith is steeped in the ideology of generous self-sacrifice, deferred gratification, and giving. We live to give because of the example set forth by our Savior.

Serving Reflects Love

While some people give money rather than getting personally involved in serving people, we experience the true power of real love when we see changed lives through our direct involvement. Compassion and giving collide through serving others in a personal way.

Some Bible teachers say that unless we direct the powers we develop for the benefit of others, they will atrophy within us. A circuit has to be completed—from our souls to others and back to ourselves. Unless our hearts are open, we can easily become indifferent to the brutality of the world.

Imagine someone being indifferent toward the suffering of a starving child or a homeless person, or the spiritual desolation of a friend. This indifference in the world exists more than we would like to think. Many people cultivate their own little secret, private gardens. But we must realize that serving others is absolutely essential to our spiritual health. The virus of self-absorption is deadly and has only one cure . . . compassion.[6] And compassion is released in service to others.

Serving people can occur through a myriad of ways, from our vocational duties to our community involvement. The idea is that you must give back something to society and to humanity. Only selfish people hoard and hide their talents and resources. Selfless people give their skills away in service.

Hundreds of years ago, a man served you and me when he gave his educational talents and expertise to the work of God. As a consequence, selfish people who wanted to hide the truth of Scripture decided to kill John Wyclif because he had translated the Scriptures into English.

The prevailing sentiment of the hierarchy was given by Walsingham, chronicler of St. Albans, who characterized the Reformer in these words: "John de Wyclif, that instrument of the devil, that enemy of the Church, that author of confusion to the common people, that image of hypocrites, that idol of heretics, that author of schism, that sower of ha-tred, that coiner of lies . . ."

Writing to John XXIII, 1412, Archbishop Arundel took occasion to denounce [John Wyclif by writing,] "that pestilent wretch of damnable memory, yea, the forerunner and disciple of anti-christ who, as the complement of his wickedness, invented a new translation of the Scriptures into his mother-tongue."[7]

Those who authorized the martyrdom of Wyclif could not leave his corpse in peace. They decided to show more ill will: "The Council of Constance formally condemned his memory and ordered his bones dug up from their resting-place and 'cast at a distance from the sepulchre of the church.'" In fact, "they burnt his bones to ashes and cast them into Swift, a neighboring brook running hard by."[8]

As you see, Wyclif's service to humanity was misunderstood and he suffered violently for it. But even deadly opposition did not stop him from putting his life in the hands of God for the bet-terment of humanity.

It's your turn now. More than likely, your demonstration of love through service will not lead to your death. But when agape love is present, significant acts of service must follow.

Day 34: Steps to Rehearse

The power of love is the most dynamic resource available to the human race. God, in His genius, gave us the ability to love Him and one another. What a powerful gift! Let's use it.

1. Paul outlined fourteen dimensions of God's love that we are to strive to understand and practice.

2. When we release love, it will show in expressions of compassion, giving, and acts of service to humanity.

3. When compassion fills your heart, it will pour out in acts of love for people who are less fortunate than you. In so doing, you will show that your journey to the mountain of God infected you with the love of God.

The Power of Spiritual Warfare

We don't often mention *spiritual warfare* in the same sentence as intimacy with God. But the stark reality is that without victory through spiritual warfare, we cannot achieve or sustain intimacy with God. One of Satan's greatest desires is to pull you away from God, to render you a spiritual loser. God's blessings await those who prevail in battle against the forces of darkness.

My favorite Bible character next to Jesus is the apostle Paul. He was a brilliant scholar who pursued intimacy with God. Often believers excel in one area but fall short in the other. Some who have powerful intellect and knowledge regarding the Scriptures fail to develop a life of prayer and spiritual intimacy. These individuals have brains but lack spiritual passion for pursuing adventures in God.

On the flip side, some people can pray heaven down, but they know little and care to know little of the Scriptures. In this latter category, I am not referring to people who live in developing countries and may lack the educational skills to read a Bible. I am referring to people who can read but have no interest in gaining knowledge that comes from studying.

Fighting for God's Blessings

Paul was a worshiper and a warrior. He found no conflict in this duality. I believe that this is how we must see ourselves if we want to walk in the blessings of God gained through intimacy with Him. Intimacy with God is not as a stepping-stone to His blessings. The blessings of God are simply a by-product of a life of spiritual intimacy. At times these blessings flow without any action on our part. At other times we have to engage in spiritual warfare and use all of the weapons in the Christian's arsenal to secure the promises that God has already declared are ours.

The children of Israel had to engage in physical fights in order to obtain the promised land. Do you recall how God promised them the land of Canaan (Num. 13:2), yet they had to fight to dispossess the Canaanites from the land (Num. 14:5–9)? The promised land certainly proved to be a blessing from the Lord. Yet, the Israelites had to gain God's blessing through fighting, even though God had already decreed it. In the same manner, blessings await you, but you must fight for them. The fight may take on physical forms, but in every instance, you will have to use spiritual warfare.

Spiritual warfare becomes meaningful and effective when you understand your enemy, your protection, and your goal.

Understanding Your Enemy

When I became a Christian, I had never before heard the term *spiritual warfare*. I thought that praying the Sinner's Prayer assured me of heaven *and* of a problem-free life on earth. I soon found out that a dreaded enemy of God and of God's people existed named Satan. He does not want God's purposes to be satisfied in my life or in yours. Peter told the Jewish Christian community: "Be self-controlled and alert. Your enemy the devil prowls around like a roaring lion looking for someone to devour. Resist him, standing firm in the faith, because you know that your brothers throughout the world are undergoing the same kind of sufferings" (1 Pet. 5:8–9).

Peter identified Satan as our enemy. Forget the happy-go-lucky attitude that pursuing God is all about worship and praise. Pursuing God includes learning how to fight *and* win!

The Warrior's Perspective

Since you have a dreaded enemy who's on the prowl for you, you must adopt the mind set of a warrior. You must be ready for anything at any time. Peter said that you must be self-controlled, which speaks of the way you order your life. You must direct your life by an inward strength and not outward circumstances. In other words, *you* must pick your battles and not let others (namely, Satan and his cohorts—demons) pick them for you or goad you into a fight. Satan's trick is to get you all worked up over insignificant things so that you never have the time or strength to fight the real battles—the things that count in eternity. This is where sober thinking proves to be essential in the grand scheme of things.

Peter also warned you to be alert. Alertness refers to being cautious and sensitive to what's going on around you. You become spiritually cautious, circumspect, and alert through prayerfulness. As you are praying for your family, friends, ministry, God gives you a heightened sensitivity about the needs that are not apparent to the five senses. Through this watchfulness, you are able to stay alert so that you can discern and block any planned attacks of the enemy through prayer and fasting.

Since you are at war, you must *always* think of yourself as a warrior. Satan is not taking a vacation in Aruba. He is engaged, full-time, in his fight for the souls of men and women. Although we can rest in the Lord's grace and strength, we must also exercise alertness to impending spiritual assault. In our post 9-11 society, the United States of America understands what it means to live in a constant state of alertness. We are always ready for a terrorist attack to strike. This is how a warrior lives. Stay alert! Then you can thwart the attacks of Satan and stand your ground during the day of evil.

Understanding Your Protection

The apostle Paul informed the Ephesian Christians that God has provided a spiritual armor that they must wear at all times in order to fight spiritual warfare effectively. Prefacing the description of the armor is Paul's discourse about the spiritual fight that we're in. I want you to become familiar with the passage.

> *Finally, be strong in the Lord and in his mighty power. Put on the full armor of God so that you can take your stand against the devil's schemes. For our struggle is not against flesh and blood, but against the rulers, against the authorities, against the powers of this dark world and against the spiritual forces of evil in the heavenly realms. Therefore put on the full armor of God, so that when the day of evil comes, you may be able to stand your ground, and after you have done everything, to stand. Stand firm then, with the belt of truth buckled around your waist, with the breastplate of righteousness in place, and with your feet fitted with the readiness that comes from the gospel of peace. In addition to all this, take up the shield of faith, with which you can extinguish all the flaming arrows of the evil one. Take the helmet of salvation and the sword of the Spirit, which is the word of God. And pray in the Spirit on all occasions with all kinds of prayers and requests. With this in mind, be alert and always keep on praying for all the saints.*
>
> (Ephesians 6:10–18)

Paul encouraged us to be strong *in the* Lord. This strength is not in our own abilities, will, or accomplishments. The strength that we need to fight the enemy of our soul is *in the Lord*. Paul also told us that the fight is not natural, but spiritual. In fact, this spiritual fight is against Satan's hierarchal structure of evil: rulers, authorities, "powers of this dark world," and "the spiritual forces of evil in the heavenly realm." Spiritual warfare is no walk in the park. A deep trust and reliance in God's power *and* the armor we have been given will prove vitally important to standing our ground when the day of evil comes.

Notice, Paul did not say, "if the day of evil comes." He said, "when the day of evil comes." In other words, we will all face days of evil. This is guaranteed despite our level of intimacy with God.

Put on the Whole Armor of God

To help us understand how we are to put on our protective gear, Paul drew metaphors from the world of the Roman soldier. The apostle outlined six pieces that constitute the whole armor God has given us. Each piece protects a different part of the body.

We first learn of the soldier's belt. Roman soldiers wore wide, thick leather belts strapped around their waists. These had various pockets designed to hold their swords and other instruments of combat.

Paul titled this piece of the armor "the belt of truth." Thus, one of the ways you can protect yourself against the attacks of the enemy is to live a lifestyle of truthfulness. Truth is not only a moral virtue; it is also a protective device that can spare you unnecessary trials. The truth that the apostle spoke of referred to candor, sincerity, and truthfulness.

The second piece of our armor is the breastplate of righteousness. Again, Paul drew from the world of the Roman soldier to aid us in understanding how to prepare ourselves for spiritual warfare. The breastplate was a similar protective device for the front and back of the soldier, as a bulletproof jacket is for police officers. This breastplate protected the soldier's vital organs from being pierced by arrows, spears, or swords.

Paul was communicating that if we live lives of righteousness and purity before God, this moral stance will be protection against the fiery arrows of the evil one. We do not accomplish this kind of living through self-righteousness or through the righteousness imputed to us by the death of Christ on the cross. We accomplish it as we live exemplary lives, evidenced through our ethics, morals, and godly character.

The third piece of the soldier's armor is the shoes. According to Paul, we are to put on the shoes fitted with the gospel of peace. The Roman soldier's boots had spikes at the sole. These sharp nails were similar to our modern day cleats—shoes worn by athletes at their games. Paul was saying that we are able to protect ourselves against the day of evil and the assaults of the devil when we have the peace of God active in our lives.

As the soldier's boots firmly anchored him to the ground, he was able to engage in hand-to-hand combat with his enemy without slipping and falling. Likewise, when the peace of God is released in our lives, we will be anchored to God's comfort and strength when the turbulence of trials blows upon us. Paul said, "Therefore, since we have been justified through faith, we have peace with God through our Lord Jesus Christ" (Rom. 5:1). In another passage Paul said, "And the peace of God, which transcends all understanding, will guard your hearts and your minds in Christ Jesus" (Phil. 4:7). Consequently, not only do we have peace *with* God, we also have the peace *of* God.

The fourth piece of our armor is the shield of faith. The Roman soldier's shield was made of laminated wood covered by hardened leather. The shield of faith reflects our trust in God's abilities. As we apply faith in God, we will be able to appropriate all of His promises into our lives. In biblical days, some of the Roman soldiers did not want to carry their shields because they were too heavy. As a consequence, many solders died because they lacked protection.

It should be clear to you that without the shield of faith, you will be unable to block the fiery arrows of the evil one. Fiery arrows represent the temptations Satan uses to trip you up in your walk with the Lord. Wielding the shield in front of your body and head occurs when you walk in the power of what God's Word says about you. In so doing, you not only demonstrate your dependence in God's power and ability, you also extinguish Satan's fiery darts.

The fifth piece of the armor is our helmet. Roman soldiers' helmets were made of leather covered with metal. The helmet covered the soldier's head, face, and neck. There were openings for the soldier's eyes, nostrils, and mouth. Paul was communicating that we are assured of success in spiritual warfare when our thinking and reasoning faculties are anchored in the Word of

God. This worldview produces confidence within us that we can stand against all of the philosophies of this world.

The sixth and final piece of the Christian's armor is the sword of the Spirit. Paul explained that the sword of the Spirit is actually the Word of God. This means that if you use the Word of God to fight off Satan, you are assured a victory. To become comfortable with how to use the Scriptures in spiritual warfare, you should read, study, memorize, and meditate on the Word regularly.

Once the Word is planted deep in your heart, you will become quite skilled at wielding it when the time comes. Remember, Jesus used the Word of God when He fought Satan in the desert following His 40 days of fasting (Luke 4:1–13). The Bible declares: "For the word of God is living and active. Sharper than any double-edged sword, it penetrates even to dividing soul and spirit, joints and marrow; it judges the thoughts and attitudes of the heart" (Heb. 4:12). God has freely given you this protective power. Use it and walk in God's blessings.

The power of spiritual warfare is quite significant. Strive to grow in skill with these six protective pieces of the Christian's armor. It's one thing to grow in intimacy with God but quite another to walk in God's blessings. Go ahead! Enjoy God's promises for your life that you secure through spiritual warfare.

Day 35: Steps to Rehearse

Many Christians believe that you must choose the worship of God over the protection of God made available through spiritual warfare. Fortunately, we have been given both. You ought to become a growing worshiper and a growing warrior. You grow in spiritual warfare by:

1. Understanding your enemy, the devil.

2. Fighting for God's blessings. A position of neutrality is not an acknowledgment of the sovereignty of God. It merely represents your unwillingness to participate in the appropriation of God's promises.

3. Putting on the whole armor of God—all six pieces.

Step 8

A New Beginning

There are three kinds of people: those who have sought God and found him, and these are reasonable and happy; those who seek God and have not yet found him, and these are reasonable and unhappy; and those who neither seek God nor find him, and these are unreasonable and unhappy.
—Blaise Pascal

A New Perspective
on God

As the host and teaching pastor of the daily radio program *IM-PACT,* I had the privilege last year of taking several thousand people through a 40-day journey to the mountain of God. At the onset of the journey, I asked the participants to complete a prayer request card outlining their concerns or problems they wanted God to address during the trek toward spiritual intimacy. My commitment was to pray each day of the journey for God to work wonderful miracles in their lives.

At the end of the 40 days, we received scores of praise reports telling of the blessings people received along the way to a place of deeper intimacy with the Lord. Surprisingly, the praise reports fell into five categories, which will be the focus of this eighth and final step of our journey. The radio audience joyously described how the journey brought a new beginning in their lives by helping them form new perspectives of God, self, life, the world, and spiritual intimacy. Their experiences are worth passing on to you in a teaching format.

Meeting God, Again

Prior to embarking on the 40-day journey, some people had a casual relationship with the Lord, while others were just in a spiritual rut. Both categories of people had met Christ as Savior but had hit a lull in their spiritual pursuits. At the end of the 40 days, they unanimously testified of a brewing passion for the Lord and a transformed view of God. I suspect these things brought about this change of perspective toward the Lord: spiritual intimacy, spiritual strength, and God's view of their relationship with Him.

Spiritual Intimacy

One of the testimonies I repeatedly heard from journeyers was that they had discovered a new level of spiritual intimacy. It was like a dream come true for them. Prior to the journey most people had silently desired to have a more intimate relationship with the Lord, but they did not know how to achieve it. I have discovered that when left unaddressed, this unmet desire turns into disillusionment and condemnation. Once these perspectives set in, the discouraged believer turns away from spiritual pursuits to what he knows—natural things. As a consequence, church attendance and spiritual disciplines take a backseat to climbing the corporate ladder and pursuing the natural areas of success because they are familiar.

Fortunately, the journey offered some solid steps toward growth. Engaging in daily prayer, adopting a fresh commitment to live holy, and developing an attitude of humility began to turn around many lives spiritually. Turning away from natural living to spiritual living became an easy process for many. As this process unfolded, it continued to produce a greater sensitivity to the Lord's voice, promptings, and directives. Sensitivity created intimacy.

When you're sensitive to a person's needs and desires, you are intimate with that person. This principle works even in the spiritual realm. When you are sensitive to God, you will also be intimate with Him. This intimacy will cause you to join others in serving God's interests in the world around you.

Regular times of fellowship with God also produced spiritual intimacy. Prior to the journey, some people viewed God as a stern Father who wanted to discipline them into becoming good children. But the journey shattered that image. The travelers formulated a more biblically accurate perspective as they drew near to God in prayer, praise, and true devotion.

We tend to think that God is like us. But Isaiah prophesied:

> *"For my thoughts are not your thoughts,*
> *neither are your ways my ways,"*
> *declares the LORD.*
> *"As the heavens are higher than the earth,*
> *so are my ways higher than your ways*
> *and my thoughts than your thoughts."*
> (Isaiah 55:8–9)

God is not like us, but we need to become like Him. Spending time in regular prayer, worship, and submission to God's Word helps us to form not only a more accurate image of God, but a better relationship with Him. These practices produce an image of God that shows Him as a benevolent Father who wants His children to approach Him with boldness and love.

As the writer of Hebrews put it: "Let us then approach the throne of grace with confidence, so that we may receive mercy and find grace to help us in our time of need" (4:16). This is the image of God that we ought to have. It's accurate. It's biblical. It's redemptive. God conveys that He knows our human frailty and, in wisdom, He has provided a way for us to confidently access His help. When we blow it, we can approach Him. We need not run from Him cowering in fear or guilt, because God is a forgiving God and a Healer. This is the perspective the radio audience took away from the 40-day journey to the mountain of God. This new perspective of God was a breath of fresh air.

Spiritual Strength

Remarkably, with spiritual intimacy comes spiritual strength. They are opposite sides of the same coin. In the way that vitamins make you nutritionally strong, daily prayer makes you spiritually strong. The practice of praying daily also helps you to grow in dependence on the Lord. If you take time to pray and worship regularly, you communicate that God is an integral part of your life and you value that relationship.

As you deal with personal issues through prayer and become encouraged by the answers that God releases, you will become spiritually stronger over time and increase your service to others. As God witnesses your bearing the burdens of others (Gal. 6:2), He will also see evidence of your deep commitment to His plans.

Your willingness to help others demonstrates the new spiritual strength and godly compassion you have gained. This journey not only has resulted in a heightening of sensitivity to God, but also toward people. This is why Paul said to the Galatian church: "Brothers, if someone is caught in a sin, you who are spiritual should restore him gently" (6:1). Compassion is a sign of spiritual strength.

Paul took it one step farther and encouraged strong people to help in the restoring process of those who have fallen. This is commendable because, prior to their dealings with God through the journey, many people could not see themselves bearing someone else's burdens. Previously, they were the ones being carried. Now, the tables have turned and the ones who were weak are now carrying others due to their newfound strength in God.

God's View of Your Relationship with Him

I'm always curious to know what God thinks about me. I want to measure up to His expectations. Some people have expectations you can never meet. It is as if the direction of the wind determines how they are going to view us from one day to the next. The target keeps moving! Thankfully, God is not like capricious humanity. He is constant. What He expects from us is also constant.

As a result of journeying to the mountain of God, you have assented to God's ability to meet your needs and accomplish great things in your life. But the question remains: how does *He* view *you*?

By now, I'm sure that you recognize that God has opened the door of intimacy to you. Imagine that! You are so important to God that He allowed you, through your prayers, repentance, and efforts toward personal consecration, to get to know Him better. If God opened the door to intimacy with you, this must mean that His view of you is positive and affirming.

We can obtain a true glimpse of God's view of us from the Bible. As we've seen, the writer of Hebrews said, "Without faith it is impossible to please God, because anyone who comes to him must believe that he exists and that he rewards those who earnestly seek him" (11:6). The usage of faith is quite important as a relational barometer. Faith pleases God. If you are employing faith through prayer, God is pleased with you. If you are earnestly seeking God, He promises to reward you. No one rewards people he despises or with whom he is dissatisfied. Journeying to the mountain of God is an intentional method of earnestly seeking the Lord. Rewards are to be expected!

Although the rewards were not our primary focus, they are not to be negated. Our primary focus was for you to attain a greater level of spiritual intimacy with God. But a secondary benefit comes in gaining God's rewards for your life, including His promises.

We've mentioned that we learn God's view of us in the Bible: "Thou art worthy, O Lord, to receive glory and honour and power: for thou hast created all things, and for thy pleasure they are and were created" (Rev. 4:11 KJV). When God created you, it was for His pleasure. Nothing you can do or say will change His mind on that reality. Now that you are growing in your love and passion for spiritual intimacy with God, how much more will He show His favor toward you and find pleasure in you!

Day 36: Steps to Rehearse

Taking a journey, especially a 40-day spiritual journey, can be a life changer. After I took several thousand people on the journey to the mountain of God, a number of them indicated that their perspective of God changed. The shift was as a result of these changes:

1. A heightened sense of spiritual intimacy with God.

2. A realization that they had grown in spiritual strength.

3. A renewed understanding of how God viewed them: as created for His pleasure.

Day 37

A New Perspective
on Self

We began our journey by looking at Moses and how he skill-fully prepared the children of Israel to journey to the mountain of God. This journey followed specific steps that God had outlined to him, which Moses was to convey to the million-plus former slaves. The Hebrews, though freed from the bondage and brutality of their Egyptian slave masters, had not been freed emotionally from the baggage of 430 years of severe mistreat-ment. The journey to the mountain of God would definitely re-sult in a heightening of spiritual intimacy. For the Hebrews, this had to occur given that they were going to meet the God who had heard their cry for deliverance and who responded by power-fully liberating them. You always show thankfulness and apprecia-tion for your deliverer. And if your deliverer wants a strong relationship with you, you should feel honored to facilitate that desire. Intimacy with God should be a true delight.

Since God's ways are higher than our ways, He not only al-lowed the process of spiritual intimacy to occur, He prepared the Israelites to develop a new perspective of themselves. God first initiated this when He said to the children of Israel *prior* to their coming to His mountain: "Now, if you obey me fully and keep my covenant, then out of all the nations you will be my treasured possession. Although the whole earth is mine, you will be for me a kingdom of priests and a holy nation" (Exod. 19:5–6).

When God used such phrases as "treasured possession," "king-dom of priests," and "a holy nation," He was replacing an old, destructive image of self with a new, constructive image of self. This transformed view was not germane just to the Israelites; the scores of people I took on this journey also testified of it. The recurring points I heard about their new identities were: I can receive love from others, and I can give love to others.

I Can Receive Love

People who face oppressive situations first experience damage to their self-esteem. Obviously God knows this and used His words to erase certain images that had colored the Israelites' perspectives of themselves. Once you erase certain perspectives, you have to replace them with others that are positive and life-giving.

Many people, after undergoing a family or relational trauma, develop an inability to receive love. When someone who has pledged his devotion to you tells you horrible things about yourself, you may decide you are simply not worth loving.

One woman who wanted to join our church several years back stopped me in passing and said: "Pastor, I just want to be straight with you. I have just come out of a horrible marriage where my husband—a fellow Christian—told me that everything was wrong with me. He said I was too hard. I was demon possessed. I was selfish. Everything you can think of that is bad, described me, according to him."

My heart went out to this dear lady because she carried such deep emotional scars. This woman had begun to believe that she was unlovable. This destructive thought had actually become so entrenched in her mind that she stopped me to find out if I would have her as a member of my congregation. Can you imagine how low her self-esteem must have fallen to think that she had better forewarn the pastor of how repulsive she was before joining his church?

Now the problem is not one-sided, where men are the bad guys and women are the innocent parties. Both can be innocent and both can be guilty. My focus is not casting blame but highlighting the devastating blow to self-esteem a person feels after receiving abuse from someone he or she loves. Although I shared only this one case with you, I suspect that lots of people feel the way this woman felt, but they are too afraid to say anything. They suffer in silence, often steering clear of small groups and friendship-building opportunities because they feel unlovable. They are almost like modern day lepers. In biblical days, lepers had to yell at the top of their voices when walking into a public place, "Unclean! Unclean!" They told everyone to stay clear of them. Nowadays, these low self-esteem people don't audibly yell, "Unclean!" but they scream it on the inside.

In journeying to the mountain of God, we realize that God has to heal our emotional and psychological scars to help us become healthy worshipers. A healthy worshiper is someone who freely proclaims her love for the Lord without the past weighing her down and impeding her worshipful expression. The healthy worshiper can convey an accurate image of Christ to others through her worship experience. Robert Webber defines worship in a broad sense as a "meeting between God and His people." In a more particular sense, Webber says, "In this meeting God becomes present to His people, who respond with praise and thanksgiving. Thus, the worshiper is brought into personal contact with the one who gives meaning and purpose to life; from this encounter the worshiper receives strength and courage to live with hope in a fallen world."[1]

Since worship provides a forum where personal contact with God occurs, it's in this environment that deep and lasting healing can come to the emotional and psychological parts of who you are. The very act of opening your heart to the Lord in worship is therapeutic and provides strength to combat the forces of evil.

On a practical level, the healing of our wounds also has to occur by our learning to embrace the perspective God wants us to have of ourselves. The writer of the book of Hebrews exhorts, "Therefore, since we are surrounded by such a great cloud of witnesses, let us throw off everything that hinders and the sin that so easily entangles, and let us run with perseverance the race marked out for us" (12:1). This verse clearly tells us to take off everything that hinders. This includes the perspective that we are unlovable. Intimacy with God strips off that damaging self-image so that you begin thinking, *If God can love me, human beings can love me too.* When this shift in perspective occurs, it validates again the journey to the mountain of God.

I Can Give Love

The ability to receive love from God and others is great. But the ability to give love is even greater. Jesus proclaimed, "It is more blessed to give than to receive" (Acts 20:35). This principle applies not only to material things, but to giving love to others. Just as some travelers on the road to the mountain of God struggle to see themselves as lovable, other journeyers struggle in demonstrating love to others. Whichever category you may find yourself in, the passage in Hebrews 12 still applies: "Throw off everything that hinders and the sin that so easily entangles, and let us run with perseverance the race marked out for us."

In order for God to empower you to love others, your heart must be sensitized toward people in need. Another way of saying this is: you must throw off condemnation and put on compassion. Compassion is the deep idea of the awareness of another person's plight and the desire to relieve it. In his book on illustrations, Brian Larson gave this moving example of compassion:

> *The boy entered the store and asked the owner how much the puppies cost. "From $30 to $50," the owner replied. Reaching into his pocket, the boy pulled out several coins. "I have $2.37," he said. "Can I please see them?" The proprietor smiled and whistled. Out of a kennel came Lady, followed by five tiny, adorable puppies. One puppy, however, was lagging considerably behind. Immediately, the boy's attention was on the slower, limping puppy. "What's wrong with that one?" he asked.*
>
> *The owner explained that his veterinarian had discovered the puppy was missing a hip socket. "It will always be lame and walk with a limp," he added. The little boy became very excited and said, "I'll take that one." "Naw," the owner argued. "I couldn't sell you*

that one. *He's flawed. If you really want him, I'll just give him to
you.*"The little boy became angry, looked the owner in the eye,
pointed his finger at him and said, "*I don't want you to give him to
me. This puppy is worth just as much as these other puppies. And I
will pay full price. I'll give you $2.37 now and 50 cents a month
until I have paid for him.*"

"*But young man,*" the owner persisted, "*you really don't want this
puppy. He won't be able to run and jump and play with you like the
others could.*"The young boy reached down and rolled up his pant
leg, revealing a badly twisted, crippled left leg supported by a metal
brace. He looked up at the store owner and softly said, "*Well, I don't
run so well myself, and this little puppy will need someone who understands.*"[2]

Compassion for others occurs when you put yourself in other
people's places. This is why intercessory prayer is so critical to the
process of sensitizing Christians to the world around them. As
you recall, the word *intercession* means to take the place of someone else. In essence, you are praying for others who are unable to
pray for themselves or see the problems they must avoid. This
prayerful position produces compassion for others and facilitates
the answers to their predicament.

As you journey to the mountain of God, you will find yourself praying for others. Whenever you really pray for other people and their discomforting situations, you will find your heart
flooded with a desire to ease their pain. This process is one of
God's ways of endearing you to other people. You cannot become evangelistic—share your faith with lost people—unless you
love them.

If you really want to grow in your ability to share your love
with others, start praying for them. Not only will you feel more
compassionate toward them, you will also discover creative ways
to demonstrate love to them. Journeying to the mountain of God
draws you closer to the Lord and changes your concept of self.
You become someone worth loving, and you become someone
who can radically love others.

Day 37: Steps to Rehearse

The concept of self is a very important aspect of spiritual development. This is why God deals with you about how you see yourself, how you see others, and the values that flow from that dynamic. If you are to continue growing in your relationship with Christ, you must keep growing in your concept of self. Here are a few things to consider.

1. If you live with a sense of worthlessness and shame, you will not worship God because you will continuously feel unworthy.

2. God made you lovable, despite your need to be forgiven of sin.

3. God wants you to grow in your ability to show love and compassion to others. One surefire way is to pray for others. In so doing, you will be drawn to show them acts of kindness in an effort to ease their pain.

Day 38

A New Perspective
on Life

Drawing closer to God is like flying in an airplane. The higher you go, the smaller everything else appears. Similarly, when you soar in the Lord, earthly things—conflicts and problems—seem so irrelevant. The most popular praise report I received from those who journeyed to the mountain of God reflects a paradigm shift about what is really important. Prior to the journey, little things got people bent out of shape, but by the time the journey ended, people's perspectives took a 180-degree turn. Walking closely with the Lord will produce a healthy outlook on this life because the life that is to come far overshadows this one.

The word *perspective* captures the idea of "a way of looking at things; a view; a vista." God has His view of things, and we have ours. Often these views don't match. But the view that must remain is the Lord's. If we can get God's perspective on the things that we wrestle with in our lives, we will experience less stress and anxiety.

While we need to hear God's heart on our personal matters, we're usually too busy to hear from Him. Fortunately, the journey to the mountain of God is helping to correct us in this area so that our outlook can harmonize with the Lord's as closely as possible.

Getting God's Perspective

Mentoring is an interesting way of being groomed to handle life and trying situations. When I train church leaders, particularly candidates for eldership, I take them through an in-depth, one-year program. The candidates' year with me is like a boot camp. I teach them things they cannot learn in Bible school or seminary, such as how to seek God for answers for the challenges facing a congregation, how to fast with other people for breakthroughs, and how to solve problems in the local church.

We also cover problem solving, which deals with the candidates' perspectives. I call into question the way they see things. It's frightening to think that we can go through five or ten years of post-high school educational training and never have anyone challenge our perspectives. What I do is create case studies that depict real-life problems and ask the candidates to solve them. The guidelines stipulate that they must use the Bible as the basis for their decisions, and they must keep in mind the welfare of the local church and the testimony of Jesus Christ in a society that is often antagonistic toward clergy and the Christian church.

I'm often amazed that so many people can see only as far as one foot in front of them. Once I give feedback on the candidates' stated solutions, I always ask: "Have you protected the church and its reputation in the answer you are recommending?" It's not that I see myself as the guru of solving church dilemmas. But I feel that my role is to help potential church leaders to stretch their perspectives to think governmentally, not just as an individual or someone representing a small family.

Likewise, God is interested in stretching your perspective so that you will not be flustered when you confront situations in this life that have no impact on eternity. This perspective can be stretched through a formal mentoring relationship that you prayerfully initiate with someone who is more advanced than you are in the area of interest. If you are not involved in a mentoring relationship regarding the improvement of your marriage, career, parental practices, and so on, I highly recommend that you seek out such an opportunity that will result in your gaining more wisdom. In an attempt to broaden his own perspective, Moses prayed: "Teach us to number our days aright, /

that we may gain a heart of wisdom" (Ps. 90:12). Moses understood that prioritizing life's situations is necessary for accomplishing God's purpose.

The cliché is correct: time flies. If you had not cleared your schedule over the past 38 days, you could not have come this far in this 40-day journey to the mountain of God. Before you cleared your schedule, didn't it look impossible? Some people never seem to have any time to do the things that are purpose-oriented because they are bogged down with other time-consuming activities.

In drawing closer to the Lord, you gain an appreciation for the more important things in life. The apostle Paul offered a practical guideline in helping us to discern the priorities and perspectives that we should adopt as our own: "So watch your step. Use your head. Make the most of every chance you get. These are desperate times! Don't live carelessly, unthinkingly. Make sure you understand what the Master wants" (Eph. 5:15–16, *The Message*).

Paul urged us to discover what the Master wants. This is another way of saying: pray before you do or commit to doing something significant. If you don't have God's mind on the matter, you may waste resources or time. Prior to journeying to the mountain of God, some journeyers have testified that they did not pay much attention to this issue. But after having sought God in a protracted way, they have learned that they must be stewards of their time, talent, and treasure.

Your life is a gift of God and how you prioritize or spend it matters to God. It is not an insignificant point. God allowed His Son, His only Son, to die for you. Based on that level of sacrificial giving, you have all the reason in the world to make your life really count.

God's Purpose for Your Life

When Moses and the children of Israel journeyed to the mountain of God, God told them His purpose for their lives: they would be a kingdom of priests and a holy nation (Exod. 19:6). Moses received the Ten Commandments, which became a moral code that the Israelites used to govern themselves (Exod. 20). The Ten Commandments also became a moral code for humanity down through the ages. God gave significance to both the emerging nation and its leader, Moses. My point is that whenever people draw near to God in search of spiritual intimacy, they will find the intimacy they are looking for as well as a life purpose. Jeremiah confirmed this very point when he said: "Then you will call upon me and come and pray to me, and I will listen to you. You will seek me and find me when you seek me with all your heart" (Jer. 29:12–13).

If you seek God with a true devotion, you will find Him. God wants to disclose Himself to you. He also wants to satisfy the longing of your heart by making your life sing with fulfillment and purpose. As you are journeying to the mountain of God, ask God this question in prayer: "Lord, what is the purpose for which You have created me?" I spent much time in my book *Perfecting Your Purpose* outlining ways to discover God's purpose for your life.[1] Asking God direct questions is one method for discovering His purpose for your life.

The journey to the mountain of God should result in a new perspective on life. You should see the world around you through the lenses of God's purposes. God gave your life to you as a gift. He also has a plan that includes using you. The best thing you can do is to surrender to His order for your life. Let Him use you!

After completing the journey to the mountain of God, some people inadvertently go back to what they used to do without guarding the precious things they received from God. Don't fall into that trap! Embrace the new perspective the journey has brought to your life. Your new life identity is one that makes you value God's purpose, efficient use of your time, and the proper management of relationships.

Meaningful Relationships

As a minister, I have never buried anyone with money in the coffin or with the person's car lowered into the grave. I have stopped people from climbing into the casket alongside the corpse a few times. When this happened it was due to guilt, unresolved conflicts, or the premature death of a loved one. On these rare occasions, I always wonder why the living person did not proclaim his or her love for the deceased *before* he or she died. The sad fact is that the person will never regain that opportunity on this side of heaven.

Crisis has a way of sobering us about our need for meaningful relationships. But if you are sensitive to the promptings of the Holy Spirit, you don't need a crisis to move you along the right path. You simply have to yield to the Holy Spirit's desires and you'll be on your way to engaging in healthier relationships.

If God has been dealing with your heart regarding the significant relationships in your life, please do not ignore this. Take a few minutes and get alone with God. Ask the Lord to give you a specific strategy that will guide you in heightening the meaningfulness of your relationships. I believe that He will give you what you need.

Day 38: Steps to Rehearse

Looking at life from God's perspective will always cause you to reevaluate your priorities. A journey to the mountain of God is also a journey into the heart of God. You will see and understand the things that God cherishes more perfectly. In so doing, a few vital lessons will be honed in your mind.

1. If you look at life from God's perspective, you will view small issues appropriately and begin to see eternal matters as more significant.

2. God wants to stretch your perspective through mentoring relationships and a heightened sensitivity to the management of your time.

3. Drawing closer to God is a way of learning God's purpose for your life.

A New Perspective
on the World

One conversation with God can change your whole outlook on the world around you. After such an encounter, not only will you look at your life differently, you will look at everyone else's life differently as well. When the Israelites were summoned to the mountain of God, they knew that whatever was to occur would be memorable and life changing. They were right. The mere fact that they had to prepare themselves by way of consecration suggests that meeting with God was different from meeting with human beings. They knew they should not take interfacing with Him lightly or treat it irreverently.

As the Israelites stood at the base of God's mountain, they drew this conclusion unanimously:

> *When the people saw the thunder and lightning and heard the trumpet and saw the mountain in smoke, they trembled with fear. They stayed at a distance and said to Moses, "Speak to us yourself and we will listen. But do not have God speak to us or we will die."*
>
> *Moses said to the people, "Do not be afraid. God has come to test you, so that the fear of God will be with you to keep you from sinning."*
>
> (Exodus 20:18–20)

All of the Israelites understood that God was not to be toyed with, although He loved them beyond their imagination. They all recognized this fact: either you are for God or against Him.

Vacillation was unacceptable. That day God reinforced a healthy fear of the Lord in their hearts and minds.

God wanted people who could worship Him devotedly without compromise. These Hebrew worshipers were to be distinctly different from the people of the world. They would know how to show their appreciation to Him for delivering them from the slavery of Egypt and pointing them to their own promised land.

Several facts shaped the Israelites' perspective of the world based on their journey to the mountain of God: God was in charge, they were to be a heavenly community on the earth, and they were to be God's representatives in the earth. These realities were also evident in the new perspective that my radio audience members articulated following their 40-day journey to the mountain of God. The way they saw the world was different.

God Is in Charge

To say that God is in charge and to live that way are two entirely different things. God specifically communicated how He saw the Israelites. His perspective had to become their reality. As we've seen, the Lord said to them: "Although the whole earth is mine, you will be for me a kingdom of priests and a holy nation" (Exod. 19:6). In this brief statement God declared His expectations. He announced the fact that He was in charge of the entire earth. He was not boasting but simply sharing the truth. God's supervisory role communicated that there was nowhere the Israelites could have gone where His power and presence were not also.

Further, the statement conveys that although God has everything, He also desired to have a people who would serve Him in a unique way. They were to function as priests and as a holy nation.

The job of priests is to offer sacrifice to God on behalf of the people of the land. The priests are also to represent the people's needs before God *and* represent God's concerns before the people. In the New Testament, the word *minister,* rather than *priest,* is the term with which you may be more familiar. Although the modern day church has created a distinction between clergy and laity, the Bible makes no such distinction. We are *all* called to be clergy—priests before the Lord (Rev. 1:6).

God's idea of having an entire nation of priests is that He wants to dispatch us into the entire world. Imagine what would happen if every believer in Jesus Christ took the message of God's love to the broader society. The world would be permanently changed. In the New Testament, Jesus repeated God's original intention when He said to His disciples: "You are the light of the world. A city on a hill cannot be hidden. Neither do people light a lamp and put it under a bowl. Instead they put it on its stand, and it gives light to everyone in the house. In the same way, let your light shine before men, that they may see your good deeds and praise your Father in heaven" (Matt. 5:14–16).

As you strive to apply this passage of Scripture to your life, recognize Jesus' instruction that you make a difference in the world. Intimacy with God must ultimately translate into righteous actions that can change an unrighteous world. A priest is to be an ambassador of heaven. This means that *you* are to represent God in the earth. Whether you are an accountant, architect, or a counselor to troubled children, you are to represent God's interests in the earth. The world needs people like you to take your post—your stand in the troubled areas of life—and make a difference.

You may say, "David, you really don't understand my world and my life. It's very hectic and complicated. I don't have time to do such things." My response would be: we all have a responsibility to fulfill God's stated expectation of being priests. And that translates into your need to make this stated expectation work in your life. You know your life better than anyone else. If you travel constantly for business, then you need to look at yourself as God's missionary to the business world.

In other words, if God is in charge, you need to carry out His intentions in your life. You cannot enjoy intimacy with God and walk away without a deep commitment to carry out God's intentions in the world around you. The world needs what you have. You must reprioritize your life and how you manage your time in order to let your priestly light shine before the world.

A Heavenly Community on Earth

Imagine seeing a whole community of people living morally upright lives that stem from a clear devotion to God. This is what the Christian community is to be like, since we are all called to be priests. In the days of the early church, Christians were martyred in the coliseums, but not because they were worshipers of Jesus. They were made sport before the Romans because

> *they worshiped Jesus as God and they worshiped the infinite-personal God only. The Caesars would not tolerate this worshiping of the one God only. It was counted as treason. Thus, their worship became a special threat to the unity of the state during the third century and during the reign of Diocletian (284–305), when the people of the higher classes began to become Christians in larger numbers.*[1]

In those days when people became Christians, they knew that their lives were no longer their own. In fact, they understood that at any time they could be martyred because of their devotion to Christ. With that severe threat hanging over their heads, they took their calling of being priests very seriously.

In our modern day society, Jesus is still calling for your complete devotion as a priest. The people of the world still need a representative to go before God on their behalf. God still needs more priests to represent Him before the people. Though we are no longer martyred as a form of entertainment before huge crowds, the idea should remain the same: your life is not your own. You are to model complete loyalty to Christ.

Imagine that you were living in the first three centuries in the Roman world. Why would someone become a Christian if Christians were being martyred regularly? The only answer I have discovered is that their lives were so attractive—in the way they lived before God and with one another—that people were willing to become a part of their community. Certainly history shows that some people secretively accepted Christ's forgiveness but steered clear of making their decisions known publicly. They were afraid. I'm not knocking them because I'm not sure how I would have handled my relationship with God had I lived back then. The fact of the matter is that the Christian community was so appealing that many people joined its ranks by accepting Christ as Savior. They also were willing to lay down their lives for this new life and new community. The new converts must have seen a glimpse of heaven while on earth.

I am not suggesting that the early church was perfect. To dispel such a notion, read Paul's first letter to the Corinthian church and you'll learn of the people's struggles with sin—all types of sin. What I am suggesting is that in comparison to the world around them, the new converts were able to experience a clear distinction in terms of values, human dignity, and the way members of the community treated each other socially.

During my college days, when I was contemplating becoming a Christian, I started hanging out with a few Christians. They brought me into their social circles, although I was still a scientific atheist. And while I did not share their faith or worldview, I was still pleasantly intrigued by how they lived with one another. They were not cursing each other or sharing vile jokes. Neither were the guys talking about what girls they hoped to sleep with. That atmosphere felt like heaven on earth. And after months of it, I wanted what they had. I wanted their community experience to become my community experience. And I wanted their God, who was the source of such experience and manner of social interaction.

How committed are you to modeling a true Christian community in your sphere of influence? People are watching and admiring from afar the way you love and treat other believers, and they are being drawn to heaven or not based on what you do. Keep drawing them!

You Are God's Representative on Earth

Being God's representative is a big hat to wear. Not many people want that responsibility. But when you became born-again, the responsibility accompanied the salvation experience. Being a representative is synonymous with being an ambassador. In fact, Paul used that exact language to outline our function in the world: "We are therefore Christ's ambassadors, as though God were making his appeal through us. We implore you on Christ's behalf: Be reconciled to God" (2 Cor. 5:20). This verse makes clear that God expects us to represent Him in our deeds, doctrine, pursuits, and example before the whole world. Talk about expectations!

Once you have made a deep commitment to following Christ, your ambassadorial function is an easy fit. The problem is you have to remember that all the time and everywhere, you must speak for God and not for yourself. You must remind yourself of this until it sinks down deep into your heart to affect your values and behavior.

Last year I had the opportunity to speak at a conference in New Zealand. The deputy ambassador from the United States to New Zealand was a member of the church that hosted the conference. He and his wife were strong Christians who enjoyed their faith. After the service I was introduced to him in the hospitality room. He mentioned that he was going home—back to the States—the following October for a few weeks of vacation. We exchanged addresses in the hopes that we would connect stateside.

What caught my attention, aside from the possibility of a future reconnection, was that an ambassador needs to go home on furlough periodically to recharge. Just as a missionary needs to go home, away from the mission field, in order to recharge, ambassadors need the same opportunity to refresh themselves and receive new directives from the nations they represent.

The journey to the mountain of God is intended to refresh your soul and your relationship with the Lord. It also provides a great environment to hear a fresh word from the Lord, which may offer a new directive for your life. To represent God well, you always need to know your spiritual assignment. There are times God may change aspects of your assignment or change the emphasis in a previous assignment. This kind of spiritual furlough, namely, journey to the mountain of God, gives you the needed downtime to get refreshed for your ambassadorial calling.

You cannot carry out your function as God's representative if you are exhausted, depleted, or disillusioned due to broken focus. Spiritual vacations back home—or back in the presence of God—are vital to your ongoing effectiveness as an ambassador. Get renewed in your journey to the mountain of God; it is important for your spiritual survival as God's representative on the earth.

Day 39: Steps to Rehearse

Formulating a new perspective of the world may not have been your intention when you embarked on this 40-day journey. Yet it may have been a clear part of God's plans. God wants to use you to effect change in the world around you. In order for this to occur, your perspective has to change. A new perspective of the world offers you:

1. A fresh understanding that God is in charge of the world. He says, "The whole earth is mine."

2. A revelation that you are to build a heavenly community on the earth. Christians are to model Christlikeness so beautifully that it will attract unbelievers to Christ.

3. A new job assignment. You are to be God's ambassador to the world. You represent all of God's concerns, character, and dealings in your sphere of influence. Let the people know that heaven has assigned you to them as an ambassador.

A New Perspective on Spiritual Intimacy

Congratulations! You've made it to the end of the journey. You have spent the last 40 days pursuing intimacy with God. I would love to hear your testimony about what you learned, experienced, or now know to be true about spiritual intimacy. Others who have completed the journey commented that their perspective on spiritual intimacy with God has been totally revamped. Their prejourney perspective was far too narrow and limited. Now they have a richer view as to what it means to draw closer to the Lord.

The way I designed this 40-day journey is so that you can repeat it at any juncture in your life. In fact, I have taken my congregation through the journey a number of times. Each time you trek toward intimacy with God, He shows you a new dimension of Himself that may not have been apparent on the previous journey. This doesn't mean that God is hiding aspects of Himself from you. The fact is that you may now be in a different place emotionally, spiritually, or even physically. Being in a different place causes you to have a different set of expectations and a different level of openness to the Lord. It is exciting to walk with the Lord!

I Want More of God

God is forever captivating us with His beauty. One of the effects of achieving spiritual intimacy is that it makes you long for more of the presence of God in your life. Getting a glimpse of the beauty of the

Lord makes you want to see more of it. God takes full advantage of your captivated state by allowing you to become even more enchanted by His love. To do this, He shows you yet another dimension of His person as you continue to draw closer to Him. This is one of the fun things about God: He is unsearchable. The psalmist declared: "Every day will I bless thee; and I will praise thy name for ever and ever. Great is the LORD, and greatly to be praised; and his greatness is unsearchable" (Ps. 145:2–3 KJV).

God is not only unsearchable in His beauty and His praiseworthy nature, He is unsearchable in His wisdom and judgment. The prophet Jeremiah shared: "This is what the LORD says, he who made the earth, the LORD who formed it and established it—the LORD is his name: 'Call to me and I will answer you and tell you great and unsearchable things you do not know'" (Jer. 33:2–3). In other words, God's wisdom runs so deep that no matter what predicament you find yourself in, you can simply ask God for a nugget of His wisdom.

The apostle Paul knew this to be true, and that's why he included the following expression of praise in his letter to the Roman church:

> *Oh, the depth of the riches of the wisdom and knowledge of God!*
> *How unsearchable his judgments,*
> *and his paths beyond tracing out!*
> *"Who has known the mind of the Lord?*
> *Or who has been his counselor?"*
> *"Who has ever given to God,*
> *that God should repay him?"*
> *For from him and through him*
> *and to him are all things.*
> *To him be the glory forever! Amen.*
>
> (11:33–36)

God's judgments are also unsearchable. He knows how to bring about a conclusion of a matter that may appear extremely gnarled to the ordinary human mind. This uniqueness of God also extends to our relationship with Jesus Christ. Paul, in his letter to the Ephesians, noted: "Although I am less than the least of all God's people, this grace was given me: to preach to the Gentiles the unsearchable riches of Christ, and to make plain to everyone the administration of this mystery, which for ages past was kept hidden in God, who created all things" (Eph. 3:8–9). Imagine that: Paul said that you can never tire of walking with Jesus. We don't have to look for some other faith or religion to feel a rush of excitement. Paul tells us that there are "unsearchable riches in Christ."

In this world you often hear about husbands and wives divorcing because they claim that their relationship is stagnant. Just yesterday I heard a woman seeking counseling from a radio host who happens to be a licensed family therapist. The caller had engaged in an affair and did not know how to get free from the guilt and pain it had caused her and her boyfriend. When asked why she did it, she replied, "I succumbed to the temptation regarding the excitement of committing an affair." How sad!

There is no such need for the Christian. I have known Christians who became disillusioned in their relationships with Christ and decided either to put their walk with the Lord on hold or to abandon the Christian faith for something more convenient. Each time I have witnessed this, I was pained in the fact that I could do nothing to help other than pray. I have also seen people walk away from the Lord because the Lord would not condone their sin. Others fell away from the faith because they could not distinguish between Christ and His church. When a local church fails in its dealings with an individual, the misguided believer often walks away from Christ—rather than simply seeking out a more balanced New Testament church.

These things deeply trouble me as a pastor, but the stark reality is that these immature saints made choices that had nothing to do with God or the Bible. If they had chosen to stay with Christ, they would have discovered all of the excitement their hearts could hold, along with the strength to overcome any adversity that came their way. My overarching point is that you can never get tired of walking with the Lord *if* you are truly walking with the Lord. With the unsearchable beauty, wisdom, judgment, and riches in Christ, what else can you turn to that offers you such an inexhaustible, adventurous experience? The answer is: nothing.

True Spiritual Intimacy

Communing with God is an ongoing experience. It never ends because your relationship with God is not static but dynamic. Consider Enoch. The Bible states, "By faith Enoch was taken from this life, so that he did not experience death; he could not be found, because God had taken him away. For before he was taken, he was commended as one who pleased God" (Heb. 11:5). I would love to have met Enoch—a man who had an ongoing encounter with God. He did not only journey to the mountain of God; He lived on the mountain of God. This testimony regarding this friend of God was: "Enoch walked with God; then he was no more, because God took him away" (Gen. 5:24). This is a wonderful picture of spiritual intimacy.

Had I known Enoch, I would have learned firsthand that there are various levels of intimacy with the Lord. Just as there are different levels of intimacy in marriage, there are ever-changing levels of intimacy in your relationship with Christ. You don't just get there overnight or after one week of fasting and praying—just as you cannot achieve a mature and satisfying marriage after one week's vacation in Hawaii. Enoch demonstrated to us that God enjoys human companionship, especially if you do the things that please Him. Enoch did. Enoch attained such an exemplary height of spiritual intimacy that God just said to Him one day: "Don't even go back home. Stay at My house."

My youngest daughter, Jessica, has a really good friend also named Jessica. When the Jessicas get together, watch out—lots of fun, excitement, and busyness. Since they are too young to drive, Marlinda and I have to chauffer them around. If truth be told, I would rather read a book than run all over the place with the Jessicas for hours and hours.

Sometimes during the summer months they'll go back and forth to each other's homes for days on end. My Jessica will spend two or three days at the other Jessica's house. And at the end of the stay, the other Jessica will come home with my Jessica for another couple of days. Apparently, Enoch and God were like that. Enoch was always hanging out with God. And God loved the fellowship.

You may ask: how does a person hang out with God? It's simple. You worship, praise, pray, and fast regularly before the Lord. You get actively involved in God's plan of redemption and restoration in your sphere of influence. In other words, you cultivate an atmosphere where you delight yourself in the Lord and in His work. As this increases over time, you find new ways of becoming more involved with God. This is a sign of spiritual intimacy.

Upon hearing that you've just spent 40 days pursuing intimacy with God, some people would say: "It doesn't take that long." They are speaking out of their ignorance and spiritual coldness. Yet, there are others who would say to you: "I am so happy for you. Continue to press into the heart of God so that you can learn more about Him and become more passionate for Jesus." The latter people are confessing that there is more to spiritual intimacy than a onetime 40-day journey. They are so right.

Let me encourage you. You have done extremely well in journeying these 40 days with the Lord. But don't let it end here. Plan to take this kind of spiritual journey at least once each year. Now that you have received a glimpse of what spiritual intimacy with the Lord is, you know now, more than ever, that greater levels of intimacy await you. Use Enoch as a role model and continue to walk with God as His friend.

Day 40: Steps to Rehearse

Congratulations! You did it! You have just completed your 40-day journey to the mountain of God. As you now know, spiritual intimacy is an ongoing pursuit. The more you attain, the more you desire. This is why you must commit to:

1. Creating a personal desire to have an insatiable appetite for relationship and fellowship with the Lord.

2. Realizing that the beauty, wisdom, judgment, and riches of Christ are unsearchable.

3. Pursuing new levels of spiritual intimacy with the Lord. Make journeying to the mountain of God an annual activity in your life. This way you will reinforce the reality that serving Christ is not boring. It is exciting!

Notes

Day 1: The Search for Spiritual Intimacy

1. Jess Stein, ed., *The Random House College Dictionary,* rev. ed. (New York: Random House, Inc., 1980).

Day 3: Learning to Trust

1. Philip Yancey, *Where Is God When It Hurts?* (Grand Rapids, MI: Zondervan, 1990), 53.
2. Frank E. Gaebelein, ed., *The Expositor's Bible Commentary,* vol. 5, *Psalms-Song of Songs* (Grand Rapids, MI: Zondervan, 1991), 917.

Day 4: The Treasured Possession

1. C. F. Keil, F. Delitzsch. *Commentary on the Old Testament,* vol.1, *The Pentateuch-Exodus* (Peabody, MA.: Hendrickson Publishers, 1989), 96.

Day 5: A Glimpse of the Future

1. Gary R. Collins., ed., *Counseling and Self-Esteem* (Dallas, TX: Word Publishing, 1988), 46.

Day 6: Spiritual Cardio

1. M. G. Easton, MA, DD, *Easton's Bible Dictionary* (CD-ROM) (Oak Harbor, WA: Logos Research Systems, Inc., 1996).
2. Kenneth H. Cooper, *Faith-Based Fitness* (Nashville, TN: Thomas Nelson Publishers, 1995), 202.

Day 7: The Heart's Soil

1. Cecil B. Murphy, *The Dictionary of Biblical Literacy* (Nashville, TN: Thomas Nelson Publishers, 1989), 563.

2. Eta Linnemann, *Parables of Jesus: Introduction and Exposition* (London, UK: S.P.C.K., 1980), 19.

Day 8: A Pure Heart

1. James Strong, *Strong's Exhaustive Concordance of the Bible* (McLean, VA: Macdonald Publishing Group, 1990), 133.
2. Warren Baker, *The Complete Word Study—Old Testament* (Chattanooga, TN: AMG Publishers, 1994), 2356.
3. Derek Kidner, *Tyndale Old Testament Commentary: Psalms 1–72* (Downers Grove, IL: InterVarsity Press, 1973), 190.
4. Baker, *Complete Word Study,* 2325.
5. J. J. Stewart Perowne, *Commentary on the Psalms* (Grand Rapids, MI: Kregel Publications, 1989), 414.
6. H. C. Leupold, *Exposition of Psalms* (Grand Rapids, MI: Baker Book House, 1994), 401.

Day 10: Getting Rid of the Excess Weight

1. William Douglas Chamberlain, *The Meaning of Repentance* (Philadelphia, PA: The Westminster Press, 1943), 22.
2. Frank Gaebelein, ed., *The Expositor's Bible Commentary,* vol. 12, *Hebrews* (Grand Rapids, MI: Zondervan Publishing House, 1981), 134.

Day 12: Learning the Fear of the Lord

1. Charles H. Spurgeon, *The Treasury of David,* vol.1, *Psalm 34* (Peabody, MA: Hendrickson Publishers, 1988), 133.
2. Gaebelein, *Psalms-Song of Songs,* 284.

Day 13: Wisdom and the Fear of the Lord

1. D. J. Wiseman, ed., *Tyndale Old Testament Commentaries—Proverbs* (Downers Grove: IL: InterVarsity Press, 1964), 117.
2. G. L. McIntosh and S. D. Rima, *Overcoming the Dark Side of Leadership* (Grand Rapids, MI: Baker Books, 1997), 143.

Day 14: Living with the Fear of the Lord

1. Wiseman, *Proverbs,* 110.
2. Warren Baker, ed., *The Complete Word Study—Old Testament* (Chattanooga, TN: AMG Publishers, 1994), 2315.

Day 15: God's Treasure

1. "Leaf from Gutenberg Bible sold for $48,400," http://archives.cnn.com/2000/STYLE/arts/12/22/bible.sale/index.html. Accessed August 5, 2005.
2. Strong, *Strong's Exhaustive Concordance*, 9.
3. Milton Rokeach, *Beliefs, Attitudes, and Values: A Theory of Organization and Change* (San Francisco, CA: Jossey-Bass, 1968).
4. H. C. Leupold, *Exposition of Isaiah* (Grand Rapids, MI: Baker Book House, 1971), 513–514.

Day 16: Moses Discovers a Holy God

1. Frank E. Gaebelein, ed., *The Expositor's Bible Commentary,* vol. 2, *Exodus* (Grand Rapids, MI: Zondervan Publishing House, 1990), 316.
2. H. D. M. Spence and Joseph S. Excell, *The Pulpit Commentary,* vol. 1, *Genesis and Exodus* (Peabody, MA: Hendrickson Publishers, 1990), 56.
3. George Arthur Buttrick, *The Interpreter's Bible,* vol. 1 (Nashville, TN: Abingdon-Cokesbury Press, 1952), 872.

Day 17: The Call to Holiness

1. Strong, *Strong's Exhaustive Concordance,* 53.

Day 18: Making Sense of Holiness

1. R. C. Sproul, *Loved by God* (Nashville, TN: Word Publishing, 2001), 35.
2. Eugene Peterson, *A Long Obedience in the Same Direction*

Day 19: Flirting with Temptation

1. Strong, *Strong's Exhaustive Concordance,* 35.
2. Brian Whitlow, *Hurdles to Heaven* (New York: Harper & Row, 1963), 15.
3. David D. Ireland, *Secrets of a Satisfying Life* (Grand Rapids, MI: Baker Publishing Group, 2006).
4. Kerby Anderson, "Baby Boomerangs," http://www.leaderu.com/orgs/probe/docs/boomer.html. Accessed December 13, 2005.

Day 20: The Beauty of Holiness

1. Strong, *Strong's Exhaustive Concordance,* 54.

Day 21: Obedience: The Breakfast of Champions

1. Frank E. Gaebelein, ed., *The Expositor's Bible Commentary,* vol. 3, *Deuteronomy-2 Samuel* (Grand Rapids, MI: Zondervan Publishing House, 1992), 677.

2. Jim Bakker, *I Was Wrong* (Nashville, TN: Thomas Nelson Publishers, 1996), 19–20.

Day 22: Faith: The Fuel of Champions

1. David D. Ireland, *Why Drown When You Can Walk on Water?* (Grand Rapids, MI: Baker Publishing Group, 2004).

2. E. F. Adcock, *Charles H. Spurgeon—Prince of Preachers* (Gospel Trumpet Company: Anderson, IN, 1925), 96.

3. L. Samovar and R. Porter, *Intercultural Communication* (Belmont, CA: Wadsworth Publishing, 1982), 67.

4. Spiros Zodhiates, *The Complete Word Study Dictionary—New Testament* (Chattanooga, TN: AMG Publishers, 1992), 671.

5. Kenneth S. Wuest, *Wuest's Word Studies,* vol. 2, *Hebrews* (Grand Rapids, MI: Wm. B. Eerdmans Publishing Company, 1947), 198.

6. http://www.sermonnotes.com/members/deluxe/illus/ndxillus.htm. Accessed August 19, 2005. Topic: Discouragement.

Day 23: Sensitivity: The Touch of Champions

1. Zodhiates, *Complete Word Study,* 1010.

2. Dr. and Mrs. Howard Taylor, *Hudson Taylor's Spiritual Secret* (Chicago, IL: Moody Press, 1989), 22.

Day 24: Humility: The Attitude of Champions

1. (From *Reader's Digest* April 2002): http://www.sermonnotes.com/members/illus/ndxillus.htm. Accessed: August 17, 2005. Topic: Humility.

2. Frank E. Gaebelein. *The Expositor's Bible Commentary,* vol 12,: *Hebrews-Revelation.* (Grand Rapids, MI: Zondervan, 1981), 194.

3. http://www.sermonnotes.com/members/illus/ndxillus.htm. Accessed: August 17, 2005. Topic: Humility.

4. Bakker, *I Was Wrong,* 45.

5. Billy Graham, *Just As I Am: The Autobiography of Billy Graham* (New York: HarperCollins, 1997), 257.

Day 25: Learning: The Commitment of Champions

1. Robert L. Sumner, *The Wonders of the Word of God* (Raleigh, NC: Biblical Evangelism Press, 1969).

2. C. H. Spurgeon, *Lectures to My Students* (Grand Rapids, MI: Zondervan Publishing House, 1954), 206.

Day 26: The Fire of Worship

1. Zodhiates, *Complete Word Study,* 2311.
2. Robert E. Webber, *Worship Is a Verb* (Peabody, MA: Hendrickson Publishers, 1992), 1.
3. Terry Wardle, *Exalt Him* (Camp Hill, PA: Christian Publications, 1988), 8.

Day 27: The Power of Prayer

1. E. M. Bounds, *Purpose in Prayer* (Grand Rapids, MI: Baker Book House, 1920), 48.
2. Zodhiates, *Complete Word Study,* 1415.
3. Charles G. Finney, *Revivals of Religion* (Grand Rapids, MI: Fleming H. Revell Company, 1993), 264
4. Bounds, *Purpose in Prayer,* 53.

Day 28: The Need for Relationships

1. George Arthur Buttrick, ed., *The Interpreter's Bible,* vol. 12 (New York: Abingdon Press, 1957), 220.
2. Henry Cloud and John Townsend, *How People Grow* (Grand Rapids, MI: Zondervan Publishing, 2001), 128.
3. M. Scott Peck, *The Different Drum* (New York: Touchstone, 1987).
4. F. Hesslebein, et.al., eds., *The Community of the Future* (New York: The Peter Drucker Foundation, 1998).
5. Cloud & Townsend, *How People Grow,* 128.

Day 30: Total Surrender

1. Zodhiates, *Complete Word Study,* 483.
2. J. Bordwine, *A Guide to the Westminster Standard* (Jefferson, MD: The Trinity Foundation, 1991).
3. Paul Lee Tan, *Encyclopedia of 7,700 Illustrations* (Garland, TX: Bible Communications, Inc., 1996).

Day 31: The Power of Faith

1. Taylor, *Hudson Taylor's Spiritual Secret,* 32.
2. John Owen, *Communion with God* (Carlisle, PA: The Banner of Truth Trust, 1991), 104.

3. J. D. Douglas, Philip W. Comfort, and Donald Mitchell, eds., *Who's Who in Christian History* (Wheaton, IL: Tyndale House Publishers, 1992).

Day 32: The Power of Persistence

1. Desmond Tutu, *God Has a Dream* (New York: Doubleday, 2004), 2.
2. http://www.bibleplace.com/works/sgiveup.htm. Accessed August 26, 2005.
3. Kenneth S. Wuest, *Wuest's Word Studies from the Greek New Testament,* vol. 1, *Romans* (Grand Rapids, MI: Wm. B. Eerdmans Publishing Company, 1973), 181.

Day 33: The Power of Agreement

1. J. Kouzes and B. Z. Posner, *Credibility* (San Francisco, CA: Jossey-Bass, 1933), 15.

Day 34: The Power of Love

1. Kenneth S. Wuest, *Wuest's Word Studies from the Greek New Testament*, vol 3, *Golden Nuggets* (Grand Rapids, MI: Wm. B. Eerdmans Publishing Company, 1973), 60–61.
2. *Ibid.*, 325.
3. G.W. Bromiley, gen. ed., *The International Standard Bible Encyclopedia*, vol. 3 (K–P) (Grand Rapids, MI: Wm. B. Eerdmans Publishing Company, 1986), 174.
4. James S. Hewett, ed., *Illustrations Unlimited* (Wheaton, IL: Tyndale House Publishers, 1988), 324–325.
5. Sam Wellman, *Mother Teresa—Missionary of Charity* (Uhrichsville, OH: Barbour Publishing, 1997), 76.
6. Source: http://www.sermonnotes.com/members/illus/ndxillus.htm. Accessed: August 26, 2005.
7. Philip Schaff, *History of the Christian Church*, vol. vi. *The Middle Ages* (Grand Rapids, MI: Wm. B. Eerdmans Publishing Company, 1973), 324, 344.
8. *Ibid.*, 325.

Day 37: A New Perspective on Self

1. Robert E. Webber, *Worship Old and New* (Grand Rapids, MI: Zondervan, 1982), 11–12.
2. Craig Brian Larson, *Contemporary Illustrations for Preachers, Teachers and Writers* (Grand Rapids, MI: Baker Books, 1996), 110.

Day 38: A New Perspective on Life

1. David D. Ireland, *Perfecting Your Purpose: 40 Days to a More Meaningful Life* (New York: Warner Faith, 2005).

Day 39: A New Perspective on the World

1. Francis A. Schaeffer, *How Should We Then Live?* (Wheaton, IL: Crossway Books, 1976), 24–25.

Dear Friend:

I am honored that you are willing to take the 40-day *Journey to the Mountain of God* with me. The Lord placed this burden upon my heart for you as I penned this book. Your willingness to join me is an affirmation of the Holy Spirit's leadership in both our lives.

I believe this spiritual journey is important because every one of us gets spiritually depleted at one time or another. And the road to recovery oftentimes seems so long. Yet, when God calls you and me to come away with Him for a sacred time of spiritual renewal, it is one of the most significant invitations we will ever receive.

From this journey you can expect to receive a brand new identity in God—one replete with deeper passion and heightened spiritual intimacy. You can also expect to see a greater degree of godly influence in your relationships with the people around you. This journey is designed to serve as the catalyst to a new beginning in your walk with the Lord.

Drawing from the rich experience Moses and the children of Israel gained when they approached the mountain of God (Mount Sinai—Exod. 19), I anticipate an equally rich encounter with you as we draw near to God.

Our King cometh!

David D. Ireland

David D. Ireland, PhD

What are the eight steps to take on the journey to the mountain of God?

Step 1:   Invitation to God's Mountain

Step 2:   Preparing My Heart for the Climb

Step 3:   Valuing the Fear of the Lord

Step 4:   A Heart of Holiness

Step 5:   Disciplines for Mountaintop Living

Step 6:   Ingredients for Spiritual Health

Step 7:   Unleashing God's Blessings

Step 8:   A New Beginning

What should you expect after completing the 40-day journey to the mountain of God?

- Expect God to personally renew you in your faith and life.

- Expect a new anointing upon your life.

- Expect God to answer your prayer requests.

- Expect God to give you a greater revelation of His purpose for your life.

- Expect to grow closer to the Lord and arrive at new heights in your spiritual development.

What will you do over the 40 days as you journey to the mountain of God?

You will establish a thirty-minute daily prayer time; fast two or three days per week, read two chapters each day from the Bible, and journal.

1. **Prayer Time**—Set aside a thirty-minute block of time each day for the express purpose of prayer.

2. **Fasting**—Fasting means *to cease from eating for spiritual purposes.* We recommend choosing one of these options:

- On three days each week, eat only one meal, or

- On two days each week, eat no food and only drink beverages.

NOTE: Consult with your physician first to determine whether fasting is recommended given your physical condition.

3. **Scripture Reading**—Follow the daily Scripture reading chart provided on the last page of this guide. It lists one Old Testament chapter and one New Testament chapter for each of the 40 days.

4. **Journal Writing**—There are many benefits to journal writing. Write down your various spiritual experiences during the 40 days in a notebook or journal. If you have never done this before, here are some suggestions:

- Write down your prayer concerns for your life and the lives of your family members, for your finances, for your career, and for your ministry work.

- Detail how God has answered your prayers in the journal.

- Summarize your daily activities and personal experiences so you can review your progress throughout the journey.

How should I pray for myself and the world around me?

To establish a prayer shield around you and your loved ones, pray on behalf of yourself and others in five areas of life: problems, passions, people, possessions, and purpose. This helps to bring a clear focus to spending a minimum of thirty minutes each day in prayer.

1. **Problems**—Pray that God's wisdom will combat every problem in your life and in the lives of your loved ones.

2. **Passions**—Pray that the cravings in your life and in the lives of your family and friends will come under the lordship of Christ.

3. **People**—Pray that God will bring people into your life, and into the lives of those you are praying for, who can be a source of good, not evil.

4. **Possessions**—Pray that you and your loved ones increase in wealth and resources, but that your possessions do not take your focus away from God.

5. **Purpose**—Pray that you and those around you discover and serve the purpose of God.

How can I stay committed in this 40-day journey to the mountain of God?

- Sit down with your calendar and purposely eliminate nonessential activities for the next 40 days. Physical exhaustion is a great deterrent to spiritual growth and the pursuit of God.

- Establish prayer partners who will pray with you over the course of the journey. You can even pray over the telephone at a time that is mutually convenient to your schedules.

- Review your journal notes and be sure that you understand each of the eight steps we are taking during the journey to the mountain of God.

Then Moses led the people out of the camp to meet with God,
and they stood at the foot of the mountain.
(Exodus 19:17)

PROBLEMS

Pray that God's wisdom
will combat every problem
in your life.

PASSIONS

Pray that your passions,
cravings, and desires come
under the lordship of Christ.

**30 MINUTES
OF PRAYER**

PURPOSE

Pray that you
will discover and serve
the purpose of God.

PEOPLE

Pray for God to bring people into
your life who are a source of
blessing and not a bad influence.

POSSESSIONS

Pray that possessions will
not own you, but you will
increase in wealth and resources.

DAILY SCRIPTURE READING CHART

Day	Old Testament	New Testament	Done	Day	Old Testament	New Testament	Done
1	Exodus 1	Acts 1	☐	21	Exodus 21	Acts 21	☐
2	Exodus 2	Acts 2	☐	22	Exodus 22	Acts 22	☐
3	Exodus 3	Acts 3	☐	23	Exodus 23	Acts 23	☐
4	Exodus 4	Acts 4	☐	24	Exodus 24	Acts 24	☐
5	Exodus 5	Acts 5	☐	25	Exodus 25	Acts 25	☐
6	Exodus 6	Acts 6	☐	26	Exodus 26	Acts 26	☐
7	Exodus 7	Acts 7	☐	27	Exodus 27	Acts 27	☐
8	Exodus 8	Acts 8	☐	28	Exodus 28	Acts 28	☐
9	Exodus 9	Acts 9	☐	29	Exodus 29	James 1	☐
10	Exodus 10	Acts 10	☐	30	Exodus 30	James 2	☐
11	Exodus 11	Acts 11	☐	31	Exodus 31	James 3	☐
12	Exodus 12	Acts 12	☐	32	Exodus 32	James 4	☐
13	Exodus 13	Acts 13	☐	33	Exodus 33	James 5	☐
14	Exodus 14	Acts 14	☐	34	Exodus 34	1 Peter 1	☐
15	Exodus 15	Acts 15	☐	35	Exodus 35	1 Peter 2	☐
16	Exodus 16	Acts 16	☐	36	Exodus 36	1 Peter 3	☐
17	Exodus 17	Acts 17	☐	37	Exodus 37	1 Peter 4	☐
18	Exodus 18	Acts 18	☐	38	Exodus 38	1 Peter 5	☐
19	Exodus 19	Acts 19	☐	39	Exodus 39	2 Peter 1	☐
20	Exodus 20	Acts 20	☐	40	Exodus 40	2 Peter 2 & 3	☐